TURN AROUND AND RUN LIKE HELL
amazing stories of unconventional
military strategies that worked

URGENT TELEGRA

ONMEROM, No. OF WORDS AND CHECK

Order from High Command

TURN AROUND AND RUN LIKE HELL
amazing stories of unconventional military strategies THAT WORKED

Joseph Cummins

PIER 9

For Peter Bayard Cummins
and Mark David Cummins,
my partners in stealth during
the epic wars between
the Raiders and the Indians

CONTENTS

PART THREE: IF AT FIRST YOU DON'T SUCCEED
Persistence, Resistance and the Art of Siegecraft

PART FOUR: SMOKE AND MIRRORS
Intelligence, Deception and Subterfuge

INTRODUCTION

Accursed be he that first invented war.

Sixteenth-century English playwright Christopher Marlowe wrote these words in his play *Tamburlaine the Great* (about the adventures of the terrible Temur the Lame, of whom you'll read more in these pages), showing that, five hundred years ago, as now, people understood that while fighting tooth-and-nail is probably innate to the human condition, war isn't. War is a human invention—something to be imagined, concocted and refined.

Turn Around and Run Like Hell is a tour of the extraordinary ways in which inspired military leaders have invented and reinvented the black arts of war for the last several thousand years. We're not talking about your run-of-the-mill, by-the-book, plodding military men here (although history abounds in those). No, this is a history of *unorthodox* military strategies, unprecedented ideas from leaders who thought outside the box—who, in fact, wouldn't even know a box if they saw one—and whose unconventional, even heretical, tactics not only changed the course of battles, but sometimes, in turn, became part of the military canon. Hannibal Barca's carefully wrought trap at Cannae in southern Italy in 216 BC killed fifty thousand Romans in a single day and has been emulated (mostly unsuccessfully) ever since. Admiral Togo's sudden U-turn in the face of an onrushing Russian fleet off the coast of Korea won for the Japanese the epic battle of Tsushima in 1905. Alexander the Great's besiegement of Tyre in 332 BC—in which he built a causeway across a harbour to tear down a supposedly impregnable fortress—ranks as one of the most mulish and stubborn-minded sieges of all time. And in 'Operation Fortitude', Allied leaders, through the most elaborate intelligence ruse in history, fooled the German high command into thinking the D-Day landings would take place anywhere else *but* Normandy.

Turn Around and Run Like Hell isn't just about the strategies of well-known generals, however. The title refers to the tactic of feigned retreat, which the Mongols perfected but which has been employed by nameless thousands throughout history. In the mid-nineteenth century, the Maori of New Zealand stalemated a great modern power, the British, through the use of ingenious trench systems and near-bulletproof palisades. During the Civil War, an alcoholic Confederate general with a lisp managed to hold off an entire Union army in fighting in Virginia in 1862. Since war is a desperate enterprise, desperate tactics—often devised on the spur of the moment—have a chance of completely turning the tide of battle. During the siege of the town of Caffa on the Black Sea in 1346, the besieging Tartars, decimated by bubonic plague, hurled the corpses of their dead over the walls of the Christian city, proving that misery loves company. Richard Meinertzhagen, a legendary British intelligence officer, helped win a World War I battle against the Turks by dint of getting them high. And an unsung French peasant named Ralph the Snubnose precipitated the capture of an English castle for his king by climbing up a latrine chute—well beyond what most of us would consider the call of duty.

A true tactician in war is not only concerned with troop deployment and concentration of weaponry, but also with psychology. Thus, General Daniel Morgan, forming his lines the night before the battle of Cowpens in 1781, during the War of American Independence, *knew* that his opponent, the aggressive Major Banastre Tarleton, would certainly attack. Shaka of the Zulus understood that his people would more readily adapt to formal military training if he shaped their formations like their most valued possession: a bull. And Francisco Pizarro shrewdly perceived that the best way to get out of a situation in which he was surrounded by tens of thousands of Inca troops was to snatch their ruler from right under their noses.

Courage, cunning, ingenuity, honed instincts and the ability to manufacture one's own luck—had all these traits been devoted to the more benevolent and enlightened aspects of the human condition, we might have had electricity, hip-hop and a cure for smallpox by, say, AD 1000. But instead we invented war. *C'est la guerre*—and good reading!

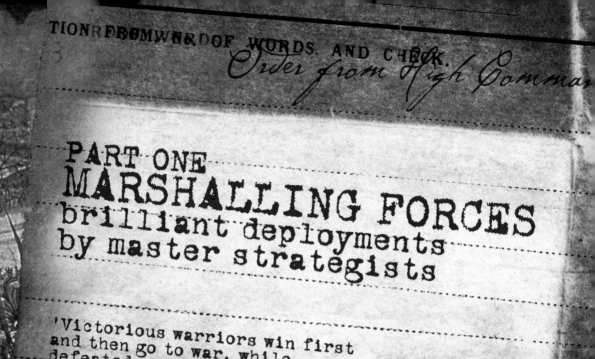

PART ONE
MARSHALLING FORCES
brilliant deployments
by master strategists

'Victorious warriors win first
and then go to war, while
defeated warriors go to war
first and then seek to win.'

Sun Tzu, The Art of War, c.512 BC

SURROUND AND KILL: HANNIBAL'S DOUBLE ENVELOPMENT AT CANNAE, 216 BC

THE ANNALS OF THE ANCIENT WORLD ARE FILLED WITH STIRRING TALES OF GREAT military leaders who achieved stunning success using unorthodox tactics: Cyrus the Great, Alexander the Great, Julius Caesar, to name but a few. But none of these heroes, great though they were, was a cooler battlefield strategist than a general named Hannibal Barca, from Carthage, in modern-day Tunisia. (Barca, which meant 'lightning' in Punic, the language spoken in Carthage, was not a surname but a description.) Hannibal's brilliantly unorthodox tactics achieved many remarkable victories, none greater than his triumph near the Italian town of Cannae, on a hot, dusty summer's day in 216 BC, which haunted the nightmares of Romans for generations and has influenced military thinking right up to the present day.

THE PUNIC WARS

During the course of two long wars in the third century BC, Carthage fought Rome for dominance over the Mediterranean. The wars were known as the Punic Wars, from the Latin word *Punicus*, meaning 'Phoenician', for Carthage had begun in the sixth or seventh century BC as a Phoenician mercantile colony, but eventually outstripped its origins. By the middle of the third century BC, it was the pre-eminent power of the western Mediterranean, holding territory extending from southeastern Spain along the North African coast all the way to present-day Israel, including the islands of Corsica and Sardinia and the western half of the island of Sicily. It was almost inevitable that Carthage would come into conflict with Rome, the great imperial power of the day, which by 264 BC, the date of the commencement of the First Punic War, had conquered most of the Italian peninsula.

Sicily was the battleground of the First Punic War, which lasted twenty-three years—the longest conflict in ancient history. By 241 BC, the Romans had the upper hand, and a peace treaty ensued, with Carthage handing over Sicily and being forced to pay an indemnity to cover Roman war costs. Trying to make up for what they had lost to Rome, the Carthaginians decided to expand their possessions in Spain. In the eyes of the Romans, Carthage posed a threat to Rome's western flank.

By 221 BC, Hannibal, the twenty-five-year-old son of a prominent Carthaginian commander, was the head of the Carthaginian armed forces. Hannibal besieged a Roman-sympathising city in Spain. When Rome protested and demanded that Carthage send Hannibal to Italy to face justice, the Carthaginian government replied by declaring war and thus the Second Punic War began.

Little is known about Hannibal. He left no verifiable likenesses on coins or busts. His only intimates appear to have been his two brothers, Mago and Hasdrubal, who also served as his closest commanders. What we know for certain, however, is that Hannibal was devoted to Carthage and to the notion of defeating the Romans.

INTO THE LION'S DEN

As the Second Punic War began, Hannibal devised a plan that was both simple and daring. He would take his force of up to thirty thousand infantry, nine thousand cavalry and forty war elephants over the Pyrenees, through the part of Gaul that is now southern France, and across the Alps into northern Italy—something that had never been done before.

Hannibal moved north from Spain in the summer of 218. His was a polyglot army—Carthaginians, Italians and Greeks, as well as more exotic soldiers: Numidian horsemen (Berbers from North Africa) who could ride without reins while they wielded both sword and spear; primitive Spanish clansmen who wore wolf and lion heads as helmets; Celtiberians from northern Spain and Portugal, who carried short, heavy spears with terrible piercing power.

Hannibal made his epic crossing of the Alps in fifteen days, losing some twelve thousand men along the way and almost

This Roman bust of Hannibal was found at Capua in Italy and may have been made during the Carthaginian leader's lifetime. It is now in the Museo Nazionale, Naples.

all his elephants. No one is quite sure which pass he took, but in November he appeared among the Gauls of northern Italy, a tribe only recently subjugated by the Romans. A Roman army commanded by Consul Publius Cornelius Scipio met Hannibal near the Ticino River, where their forces skirmished and Hannibal forced the Romans to withdraw. This was a small battle but a large victory for the Carthaginian commander, because it impressed the Gauls, who joined his command as allies when he promised them freedom and Roman spoils. Hannibal's forces swelled and he headed south, towards Rome.

On the face of it, Hannibal's journey through Italy was sheer madness. He was operating in enemy territory, with the only supplies available to him those he took from the land, and with an army that was miniscule compared to what the Romans could muster. Yet in his year-and-a-half-long expedition down the length of the Italian peninsula, Hannibal outwitted the Romans time and time again. At the battle of the Trebia River, which took place in northern Italy in late December 218 or early January 217 BC, Hannibal hid his forces in the misty half-light of early morning, on one side of the river, and lured the Romans into attacking by sending out his Numidian cavalry as bait. When the Romans charged across the river, Hannibal sprang his trap. Only ten thousand out of forty thousand Roman troops managed to fight their way out.

Hysteria mounted in Rome as Hannibal crossed the Apennines into central Italy. Somewhere during this arduous journey over rough country that included swamps and mountains almost as challenging as those of the Alps, Hannibal developed ophthalmia, an inflammation of the eye, which caused him to lose sight in one eye (although some sources claim this was a battle injury). Undeterred, the Carthaginian leader defeated another Roman army on the shores of Lake Trasimene (now Trasimeno), early in May.

When news of this second disastrous battle reached Rome, the Senate appointed a new commander in chief, the elderly but wise Quintus Fabius Maximus. He tried to shadow Hannibal without doing battle, to cut off his supply lines and deny his army sustenance, but Hannibal simply moved south through modern-day Apulia and Campania and took his army to winter quarters on the Adriatic coast to rest his troops and replenish his supplies. By 216, the Roman people had grown tired of Fabius's approach and replaced him with two consuls, Lucius Aemilius Paullus and Gaius Terentius Varro, who were given command of a massive army numbering perhaps eighty thousand men, although many of them were raw and inexperienced recruits. As this army was gathering, Hannibal and his forces moved about one hundred kilometres south, to the small town of Cannae, which was uninhabited and half in ruins, but which contained important grain deposits. Then he prepared to wage the battle of his life.

ARRAYED FOR BATTLE

The exact site of the battle of Cannae has not been definitively located, but was probably on a plain east of the present-day town of Monte di Canne, on the banks of the Ofanto River (the modern name for the ancient Aufidus River, which flowed east into the Adriatic Sea, about five kilometres away). The fight probably took place in early July—although some sources suggest August—when the heat would have been sweltering. Both the Romans and the Carthaginians made their camps on the north side of the river, but the ground was better on the south side, and Hannibal's forces arrayed themselves there, offering to do battle.

On the first day, the Romans did not accept this offer. But on the second morning they crossed the river and presented themselves on the plains of Cannae. More than twice the size of Hannibal's force, the Roman army was a fearsome sight, the most brutal fighting machine in the world. The infantry were arrayed in maniples (meaning, literally, 'handfuls'), the basic tactical unit of the Roman army. There were thirty maniples per legion, each consisting of one hundred and twenty men. The *hastati* were the first line of the infantry, the *triari* the last, each composed of the most experienced soldiers. In between were the *principes*, usually the greenest soldiers, those who needed to be pushed forwards from behind and protected in front. Each heavy infantryman was equipped with his *gladius*, a short sword used mainly for stabbing; his *pilum*, the heavy Roman throwing spear; and his *scutum*, an oval, metre-long shield.

Hannibal, in fights down the peninsula against the Romans, had noticed that Roman legions operated best in phalanxes—large bodies of infantry, armed with spears and swords

- -

AN ELEPHANT'S TALE

Even more than for his crushing victory at Cannae, Hannibal is known in the popular imagination for crossing the Alps with his war elephants. Actually, it was this arduous journey that rendered his elephants almost useless in his campaign of 218–216 BC against Rome, since all but three of the creatures (out of about forty) died along the way. However, war elephants were a force to be reckoned with in the ancient world.

The use of elephants in combat probably began around 4000 BC, in the Indus Valley. They were used by almost all major combatants, from Alexander the Great to the Romans and from the Carthaginians to various sultans of India. Elephants were the ancient world's tanks. A herd of elephants heading right at infantry at high speed was awe-inspiring and unstoppable.

The downside to elephants was that they were expensive to feed and maintain, and also highly volatile creatures that could be easily stampeded. They were panicked hopelessly by guns and gunpowder, and made ideal targets for artillery. By the time guns were widespread, from about the sixteenth century, riding elephants had been relegated to the circus.

that moved straight ahead in an armoured wedge in almost unstoppable fashion. He had also noticed that the commanders of these phalanxes were not trained to think independently: once the maniples moved forwards, they were committed to action and they found it hard to adapt to changing circumstances.

The Roman right flank, almost flush against the river, consisted of cavalry led by Consul Paullus. Facing it, Hannibal placed his Spanish and Gallic heavy cavalry under the command of his brother Hasdrubal. On his far-right flank, facing more Roman cavalry, Hannibal positioned his brilliant Numidian cavalry under an aggressive and daring commander named Maharbal. The battle lines stretched across four kilometres.

In the centre of his line, Hannibal did something that was so at odds with conventional military wisdom that even the rawest lieutenant might have felt justified in looking askance at the Carthaginian leader. Instead of anchoring the centre of his front line with his most trusted heavy African infantry as usual, he replaced them with his lightly armed Gauls and Celtiberians, deliberately creating a weak centre. To make it all the more prominent, he bulged the front line forwards, so that it formed a crescent with its outer edge facing the enemy. On the left and right of this soft core he placed his most trustworthy infantry.

To the Romans, Hannibal's formation would have looked like a classic ancient battle array, which in fact matched their own: cavalry on the flanks, infantry in the centre. Playing into Hannibal's hands, Consul Varro, the overall Roman commander that day, decided to take advantage of his superior strength in numbers by massing his maniples in extra depth (rather than width) so that they could punch through Hannibal's central lines more easily. Unlike other battles with Hannibal, there was no place on the battlefield where additional Carthaginian troops could be hidden to surprise the Romans, so Varro was sure the extra depth and force of his legions would carry the day.

THE TRAP CLOSES

After both lines skirmished with light infantry, the two armies advanced on one another. As they did so, Hannibal extended his centre forwards even more, presenting an enticing target for the veteran Roman troops, who could sense weakness behind the bulge. In the meantime, cavalry from both sides met on the flanks in fierce fighting.

The centre of the armies then crashed together with a clash of arms and a clamour of war cries, the Romans throwing their spears from about twenty metres out, then attacking with their short swords, the Carthaginian forces replying with their own spears before swinging their curved, slashing swords. Dust swirled and the din was enormous as thousands of separate duels to the death took place. Almost immediately, the Carthaginian lines began to give

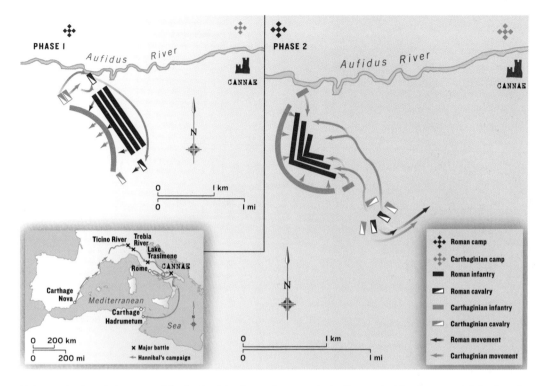

Main map: In phase I, the centre of the Carthaginian line pushes towards the Romans, inviting them to attack. In phase 2, the centre withdraws and the flanks envelop the Roman army. Inset: Hannibal's campaigns of the Second Punic War.

way as the lightly armed and armoured Gauls and Celtiberians fell back against the sheer physical weight of the Roman maniples—combat in the ancient world depended as much on weight and mass as individual fighting skill.

But then, on the Carthaginians' left flank, Hasdrubal's cavalry routed the Romans and swung around behind the legions to attack the rear of the cavalry on the Romans' other flank, which was engaged in a fierce battle with Maharbal's Numidians. When Hasdrubal hit them from behind, they disintegrated.

By now, the Roman formation in the centre resembled a V, with its pointed tip pushing deeper and deeper into the Carthaginian lines. In the wild chaos of battle, the soldiers would not, immediately, have noticed that they were about to be surrounded. Hannibal, who was most likely positioned behind the centre of the Carthaginian lines along with his brother Mago, waited till just the right moment—then sprang his trap.

Probably using prearranged smoke signals, he sent the Carthaginian cavalry to attack the rear of the main Roman lines just as the heavy Carthaginian infantry came in from both

A sixteenth-century fresco of Hannibal fighting his way through Italy. Most of the Carthaginian leader's elephants had died crossing the Alps, but he did have several left as he marched south, though none made it to Cannae.

flanks. The Romans were now completely encircled. The inexperienced troops of the second ranks, the *principes*, were hit with a shower of javelins from the side, which probably appeared suddenly, with horrifying effect, out of a cloud of dust. The survivors turned to do battle, but were slaughtered by the far more experienced Carthaginians. The legionaries at the front of the battle, who had thought they were winning, now began to realise they were being attacked from all sides.

When the encirclement was complete, the slaughter began. It probably took most of the day. The Romans, crowded together, exhausted and terrified, possibly blinded by dust, were killed by the thousands. There were so many of them to be butchered that the Carthaginians took to slashing their hamstrings to cripple them, so they could be finished off the next day. Among those who died was the Roman consul Paullus. Consul Varro escaped, with perhaps fifteen thousand Roman troops, most of whom had formed fighting wedges and slashed their way out of the trap.

By best estimates, fifty thousand Romans lay dead on the field when the battle was over. This killing count for a one-day battle would remain unmatched until the first day of the battle of the Somme in World War I; and that, of course, was a battle fought over a huge front with modern weapons including machine guns and artillery. Cannae remains one of the single bloodiest days in recorded human history.

HANNIBAL'S LEGACY

Hannibal was to wage war against Rome for another thirteen years. The Romans, having learned their lesson, avoided pitched battles as much as possible. Finally, in 202 BC, they managed to defeat Hannibal at the battle of Zama in North Africa. The Carthaginian general went into exile, wandering the Mediterranean for some years. The Romans tracked him down on the shores of the Black Sea, in 182; the sixty-four-year-old general took poison rather than be brought back to Rome.

But Hannibal's legacy, and in particular the legacy of his innovative and unprecedented strategy at Cannae, has endured for centuries. As historian Will Durant has written, Cannae 'was a supreme example of generalship never bettered in history … and [it] set the lines of military tactics for two thousand years'. Indeed, it has proved an inspiration to generations of military thinkers, from Frederick the Great to U.S. General Dwight Eisenhower. Most notably, Germany's Chief of Staff prior to World War I, Count Alfred von Schlieffen, based his plan for an invasion of France and Belgium—an invasion that went ahead in 1914 (see p. 114)—on Hannibal's strategy at Cannae. American commander Norman Schwarzkopf also used a Cannae-style strategy during the First Gulf War, when in February of 1991 he enveloped the Iraqi army with two sweeping armoured wings from the south and west. But almost no one has succeeded like the Carthaginian, Hannibal Barca.

THE ROMANS' REVENGE

In 203 BC, Publius Cornelius Scipio—son of the general Hannibal had defeated on the Ticino River after crossing the Alps—commanded a Roman army that invaded Africa and threatened Carthage, causing Hannibal's recall from Italy to defend his nation. On 19 October 202 BC, the forces of Scipio and Hannibal met on a large plain in what is now western Tunisia, near the village of Zama.

For once, the Carthaginians outnumbered the Romans—Hannibal had a mixed force of infantry and cavalry estimated at about forty-five thousand, while Scipio's troops numbered about thirty-six thousand. Hannibal sent his eighty war elephants charging into the Roman lines, but Scipio had prepared his men well: when the elephants approached, the troops opened up lanes in their ranks, funnelling the animals between lines of screaming Romans. The great beasts panicked and stampeded, some turning and racing back into the Carthaginians' own lines.

Having gained the upper hand, Scipio's army then destroyed the Carthaginians. Twenty thousand of Hannibal's men were killed; almost an equal number were taken prisoner and enslaved. Hannibal escaped to Carthage, where he and the government sued for peace. Scipio became known as Scipio Africanus for his great victory over the Romans' most hated enemy.

'GOD BELONGING': MONGOL SUICIDE SQUADS AT THE BATTLE OF LIEGNITZ, 1241

ON A SPRING DAY IN 1241, DUKE HENRY II OF SILESIA, ALSO KNOWN AS HENRY the Silent, passed through his home city of Liegnitz at the head of a long procession of soldiers. He was on his way to do battle with a terrifying threat not only to Poland but also to all of Europe: the 'Tartar' hordes who had poured in from the east, seeking plunder and blood. They had already defeated—destroyed may be a better word—two armies. Duke Henry's force was the last in Poland that stood in their way.

Crowds watched his progression, praying. But as the duke passed the venerable church of St Mary's, a stone fell off the roof, nearly striking and killing him. He proceeded, but both he and others saw this as an evil omen. As it was. By the end of the day, Henry would be dead and his army in tatters after a display of Mongol ferocity and battle tactics such as these Christian knights had never seen before.

The battle of Liegnitz was a clash, not just between two armies, but between two continents and two utterly alien cultures. The knights believed in the complete superiority of their civilisation and their Christian faith, to the exclusion of all other religions; they considered most races aside from Europeans to be inferior, if not subhuman. The Mongols, on the other hand, while they could be stone-cold killers, allowed religions in conquered countries to flourish and even adopted customs of foreign peoples as their own, when this proved useful.

This flexibility was also the key difference when it came to strategy. Generally, the proud Christian knights, usually wearing full armour and waving banners and standards, knew only how to charge straight ahead and kill. In contrast, the Mongols had learned from their long campaigns over varied territories how to adapt to every new situation. When the lightly armed Mongol troops charged, it was always with a specific purpose. And at Leignitz that purpose was to deceive.

A portrait of Genghis Khan (1162–1227), the great warrior leader who established the Mongol Empire.

THE STUFF OF NIGHTMARES

There are some historians who believe that the Mongol invasion of Europe in the winter and spring of 1241 haunted an entire continent for centuries to come. It wasn't just the immediate physical scars—the thousands who died or were wounded in battle, and the thousands of others who died of starvation from the ensuing famines in a huge swath of land from the Baltic to the Danube—but the psychological ones. 'Against the wrath of the Tartars, O Lord, deliver us' was a prayer used well into the twentieth century by churches in Hungary, Poland and Russia. There is the sense that after 1241, people in Europe always felt themselves vulnerable, open to terrifying, inexplicable and savage attack.

'Tartars' was just one of many names the Europeans gave the Mongol forces under the dual command of the late Genghis Khan's grandson, Batu, and the illustrious Mongol general Subotai. The word 'Tartar' comes from the Latin *Tartarus*, meaning 'hell', which the European clergy felt these horsemen had sprung from. Some commentators attached 'dog-faced' as an adjective when describing the invaders, as in 'dog-faced Tartars', possibly because the hats of rank-and-file Mongol soldiers were made of dog skin.

In Germany, it was rumoured that the Mongols were a lost tribe of Israel, their invasion secretly aided by European Jews, which led to numerous travelling Jewish merchants being murdered. It was also said that the Tartar soldiers ate the bodies of the dead and especially enjoyed feasting on breasts ripped from young women. The reality was, of course, somewhat different, though the Europeans had good reason to be afraid.

Before Genghis Khan was born in 1162 (his real name was Temujin; Genghis Khan means 'Great Lord'), the nomads on the steppes of eastern Asia lived a feudal existence, each tribe led by its khan and divided into patriarchal clans. The ambitious and energetic Temujin changed all this. By 1206, with a loyal band of followers, he had conquered and united the tribes of Central Asia, and acquired the name by which he has since been known. He went on to triumph over China, Afghanistan and Persia, after which his forces (led by his two generals, or *orloks*, Subotai and Jebe) attacked Georgia in 1221—giving Christian Europe a foretaste of Mongol violence—and swept back through Russia, winning every battle they fought.

Europe was spared for the next twenty years; Genghis Khan died in 1227 and the Mongols, under his son Ögödei, were kept busy consolidating their gains in Asia. The society they set up in conquered territories was, in some ways, a fair one. They allowed subjugated communities freedom of worship, and instituted improved legal, postal and transportation systems. At the same time, the Mongols remained essentially a warrior people, whose main raison d'être was conquest—and not so much, it seemed, for the sake of plunder and territory as for the sheer exhilaration of combat.

The Mongol army was, without question, the best fighting force of the thirteenth century. Any man over twenty in the Mongol Empire, with a few highly specific exceptions (such as those whose profession was to wash the bodies of the dead), had to be in the army. Divided into organisational units of multiples of ten, from the *arban* (ten men) to the *touman* (ten thousand men), the army was highly trained and extremely loyal. Mongol forces were made up almost entirely of cavalry and Mongols were the best riders in the world, able to stay on their horses literally all day, if necessary, eating yoghurt and dried meat stored in their saddle-bags. In combat, these men were ferocious, shooting arrows from small but powerful bows. They gave no quarter and asked for none, killing pitilessly and remorselessly, often tracking their enemies over great distances, like wolves.

And they looked the part: beneath their hats of dog and monkey skin, the older soldiers in particular, their faces a welter of scars from the gashes they inflicted on themselves to keep their beards from growing, were terrifying to their enemies.

FEIGNING RETREAT

It wasn't just the ferocity of the soldiers that set the Mongols apart, however; it was also their battlefield tactics. One of the most innovative and effective tactics they developed was to

STRAIGHT SHOOTERS

The Mongols' chief offensive weapon was the bow, and they were without peer in its use until the appearance of the English longbowmen in the fourteenth century, who turned the tide in battles against the French, such as Crécy and Agincourt. Though equally effective, Mongol and English archers operated in quite different ways.

The Mongol bow was made of layers of horn and sinew, waterproofed with lacquer, and had a pull of up to 72 kilograms and a range of 320 metres. The English longbow, made from yew or ash, pulled only 34 kilograms, and shot a hundred metres less. The English fired their arrows from a stationary position, feet firmly planted on the ground. The Mongol warrior was very often on horseback; despite this, he was normally able to shoot either in front of himself or behind, timing the firing of his arrow to the moment when all four of the horse's hooves would be off the ground, so that the arrow would not be jolted.

The Mongol warrior carried a wide variety of arrows—metre-long armour-piercing arrows tipped with tiny explosive grenades, arrows cut so that they would whistle, thus providing a means by which to signal friends. Mongol arrows flew extremely fast and therefore penetrated deeply, as European armies found to their sorrow. In part, this was due to an ingenious method of firing, known as the Mongolian thumb lock, whereby the archer used a stone ring worn on his right thumb to release the arrows more smoothly, thus increasing their velocity.

Mongol horsemen fighting a battle in a mountain pass. The Mongols were the best mounted troops in the world at the time, riding hardy ponies and armed with their peerless horn-and-sinew bows.

pretend to retreat in the face of an approaching enemy—to turn around and run like hell, in other words—and, when the enemy gave chase, to lead them deeper and deeper into a trap, where the main Mongol forces would leap from cover and annihilate them.

Not an easy job. For one thing, turning your back to an advancing foe is a good way to get ridden down and killed, despite the fact that Mongols were known for their ability to twist around in their saddles and shoot arrows behind them with great accuracy. For another, in order to tempt opponents into chasing you, you have to be few in number (so that they are not too intimidated) and also get very close to their lines (so that you are a tempting target).

This dangerous job was given to the Mongol light infantry, who were called the *mangudai*. The word literally means 'God belonging', and could be rendered as 'already with God'. That is, 'already dead', a convenient way to think of yourself when acting as mouse before a very large and nasty cat. *Mangudai* were volunteers—in fact, in a society with such a fierce warrior ethic, this chance to prove your bravery was highly coveted. (Some historians believe that these men came only from two specific Mongol tribes, the Uru'ut and Maghut, known for their utter fearlessness.) Essentially, the *mangudai* were suicide troops.

When an enemy force had been located, the *mangudai*, armed only with bows and arrows and light shields, would ride ahead of the main Mongol army and attack their foe recklessly. When their opponents saw how few they were, they almost always attacked in force, at which point the Mongol horsemen would gallop back the way they had come, enticing the enemy to follow them, further and further and further—until the main Mongol forces sprung their trap. Developed and refined through decades of conflict in Asia, the strategy would be used to devastating and terrifying effect at the battle of Leignitz.

THE MONGOL INVASION OF EUROPE

It is common for conquerors to seek a pretext for actions that are essentially founded on greed. The Mongols were no exception. Having consolidated their eastern territories, they turned with hunger to the west. Their excuse for attacking Europe was that King Béla IV of Hungary was harbouring their sworn enemies, the Cumans, a nomadic people the Mongols had driven out of the steppes.

Batu wrote a note to Béla in December of 1240, which, almost eight centuries later, is notable for its blunt cruelty: 'Word has come to me that you have taken the Cumans, our servants, under your protection. Cease harbouring them or you will make me an enemy because of them. They who have no houses and dwell in tents will find it easy to escape. But you who dwell in houses within towns—how can you escape me?'

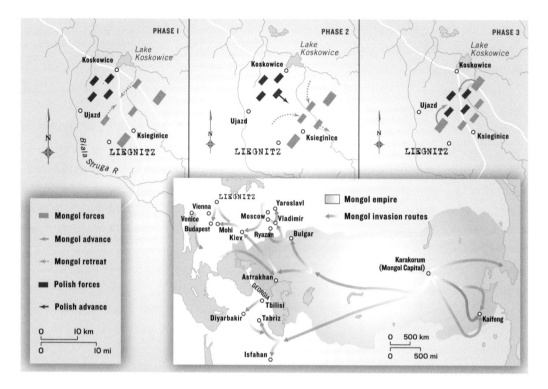

Top: In phase I of the battle of Liegnitz, the *mangudai* attack the Christians. In phase 2, Henry launches an all-out attack on the Mongols, who feign retreat. In phase 3, Mongol forces hidden on the flanks ambush the Christians, while the Mongol cavalry turns to join the counterattack. Inset: The Mongol advance across Asia and into Eastern Europe.

Béla rejected this ultimatum, and the Mongols prepared for war. The attack on Europe was planned and led by Subotai, the great Mongol general. While his main force of perhaps 120,000 men headed for King Béla and Hungary, he sent a much smaller force, perhaps 20,000 strong, north into Poland under the command of Ögödei's son Kadan and nephew Baidar. This army was essentially a diversionary force; Subotai hoped that the presence of Baidar and Kadan in Silesia and Poland would keep the armies there occupied and render them unable to help in the defence of Hungary.

February 1241 saw harsh winter weather, the kind of conditions in which no European army would generally campaign. But to the Mongols weather was almost meaningless. Baidar and Kadan burned the cities of Lublin and Zawichost and numerous small villages in between, killing men, women and children alike, and stealing any livestock or stored grain they could get their hands on. The Vistula River froze and the Mongols crossed it to burn the town of Sandomierz. Yet, no army came out to meet them.

Since their goal was not conquest but to draw forces away from Hungary, Baidar and Kadan divided their army and swept through Poland and Bohemia, laying waste to these regions. Then word came that Henry the Silent had assembled an army, so Baidar and Kadan rejoined forces and marched hurriedly to Liegnitz, the present-day Polish city of Legnica, to meet him.

SETTING THE TRAP AT LIEGNITZ

Going into the battle of Liegnitz, the forces assembled under the banner of Henry the Silent totalled perhaps twenty-five thousand men, slightly more than faced him on the Mongol side. But although Henry's own army was made up of trained knights and his forces included contingents of Knights Templar and Teutonic Knights, who were superb fighters, the majority of his men were poorly trained conscripts and volunteers, mainly peasants and gold miners. The Mongol fighters, veterans of long-lasting and wide-ranging Asian campaigns, possessed far more combat experience.

The two forces met on a plain not far from the city, today known as Walstadt ('the chosen place'). Henry carefully arrayed his forces: his own Silesian knights and the Knights Templar and Teutonic Knights in the centre of his lines, his less experienced peasants and miners on the outer edges. Henry did not know that King Wenceslas was only a day's march away with an army of fifty thousand men, or he might not have chosen to do battle. In contrast, Baidar and Kadan, as a result of their superior intelligence system, were aware of the approach of Wenceslas. Therefore, they decided to do battle immediately, before the two Christian armies could join forces.

Baidar and Kadan sent out a skirmishing force of *mangudai*, which rode straight across Henry's front, shooting arrows with deadly accuracy from a range of less than one hundred metres. There were at most several hundred of them. Henry saw that the force was small, and committed knights and the Teutonic fighters to the battle. The *mangudai* took heavy losses and retreated, but then wheeled, stood their ground and began firing arrows again.

Now Henry made a fatal mistake: he charged with everything he had—all his cavalry, the Knights Templar and Teutonic Knights and his Silesian knights. The *mangudai* broke and ran, and the Christian knights, praising heaven, chased them ferociously.

This pursuit is what a knight of the Middle Ages lived for—heavily armoured on his stout and valiant warhorse, chasing down a more lightly armed enemy, prepared to hack him to pieces with axe or broadsword in the name of Christ and country. As the Christians gained speed, their momentum became almost unstoppable. The Mongol horsemen remained, tantalisingly, just a little ahead, occasionally turning and firing arrows, but for the most part seeming to run on in panic, their pony's eyes rolling. Certain that a magnificent victory would be theirs, the knights bore down harder, waving their swords, preparing to come in for the kill.

Then the trap was sprung. Mongol archers who had been hidden on the flanks suddenly appeared and shot arrows into the knights from the side. Other Mongol warriors let off smoke bombs to the rear of Henry's knights—the use of smoke and explosives was something the Mongols had picked up from the Chinese—screening them from the rest of their army. Reeling in shock and surprise, the knights reined in the horses, but were quickly surrounded by five or ten warriors at a time, who shot arrows into the Christian steeds, causing them to collapse to the ground.

Then the Mongol heavy cavalry rode in for the kill, with sharp lances and curved swords, wreaking havoc among the confused knights, who only a few moments before had thought that they were winning the battle. Fighting on foot, with their horses dead around them, the knights were easily run down. The Knights Templar fought bravely but were killed to the last man, as were the Teutonic Knights and five hundred others. In the meantime, Henry's infantry were easily routed and slaughtered. Henry tried to flee, but was chased down by

- -

HUNTER-KILLER SQUADS

One reason why the Mongols' enemies were so terrified of them was that the Mongols turned killing into a very personal business. Anyone who took on the Mongols could expect no mercy if he lost. Prisoners were seldom held captive, let alone for ransom. If caught alive on the battlefield, an enemy soldier was usually either killed on the spot or tortured to death later.

Even worse, Mongols would not let a retreating enemy, especially one of royal blood, get away. Before they went into battle, special squads were assigned to seek out and kill enemy commanders. These assassination squads did not stop their work at the battle's end, as King Béla IV of Hungary found out in 1241. After the Christian forces were routed at the battle of Mohi, Béla was forced to flee for his life. Initially, he managed to outrun his Mongol pursuers by switching

to a fresh horse (readily available in his own realm) every time the horse he was riding tired. But the Mongol assassins did not give up and continued to chase him relentlessly. Béla made his way across the Carpathian Mountains to Croatia, and was joined along the way by his wife and family. Still the Mongols came after him, continually picking up his trail thanks to intelligence gleaned from a network of spies that probably included Venetian merchants.

The terrified and exhausted King Béla finally made his way to the island of Trogir, in the Adriatic Sea. Even there, he was followed by a *touman* of Mongols—ten thousand men led by their commander, Kadan. Just as they prepared to lay siege to the island, they received the news of Ögödei's death. Like the rest of Europe, Béla was saved by the death of the khan.

determined Mongol riders, who killed him, cut off his head and mounted it on a spear. This horrible trophy they paraded outside the walls of Liegnitz, where most of the citizens of the region were now cowering. They then cut off the right ears of the Christian dead to send to Batu, as evidence of their great victory. It was said that they filled nine bags full.

TURNING DEFEAT INTO VICTORY

As the army of King Wencelas approached, Baidar and Kadan realised that they didn't have enough strength to face him in a head-on battle. Therefore, they decided to keep him pinned down in Poland for a while; they feinted to the west, drawing him in that direction. Then, when he committed his forces, the Mongols broke up into small groups and headed south towards Hungary, burning and pillaging as they went. In the meantime, on 11 April, Subotai's main army engaged King Béla's Hungarians at the battle of Mohi and utterly destroyed them. Soon, the Mongols closed in on Vienna, getting close enough to view its church spires. They also forged south—a reconnaissance force appeared one hundred kilometres north of Venice, striking terror into the hearts of the Italians.

But then the Tartars disappeared. As all of Europe prayed, this mysterious foe turned around and left. The religious thought that God had answered their supplications. Perhaps he had. The Mongols, however, were returning to Central Asia for a very specific reason: Ögödei had died and a new khan needed to be elected. Europe, which had lain open for the taking, was saved, but permanently affected. Areas of Poland were so depopulated by the Mongols that they had to be resettled with German immigrants.

The average Polish person at the time did not know who the Mongols were or why they had attacked Poland and destroyed its finest knights at Liegnitz. The smoke screen used in the battle by the Mongols, and possibly also the strong incense they often burned around their camps, gave rise to a myth that Henry's forces had been killed, not in fair combat, but by a mysterious gas attack. The Polish people began to believe that Henry's sacrifice at Liegnitz was in fact a pyrrhic victory, one that heroically delayed the Mongols. Indeed, for centuries afterwards, the families of certain nobles who had participated in the battle wore the Mongol cap as a sign of honour.

In retrospective accounts, the number of Mongols arrayed on the field at Leignitz was inflated, sometimes as much as fivefold. This was probably because the Mongols' tactics made it seem like they were everywhere at once. In fact, the Polish forces had been completely outmanoeuvred and utterly destroyed by the Mongols' superior military expertise and, in particular, by the fearlessness and cunning of the *mangudai*, who rode out and enticed the Christian knights into a foolish battle.

TIMUR THE LAME AND THE ROARING CAMELS OF FIRE: THE BATTLE OF DELHI, 1398

HE WAS BORN TIMUR, WHICH MEANS 'IRON' IN HIS TURKIC LANGUAGE, AND IN his youth, after receiving a wound that crippled him, he became known as *Timur Lenk*, which means 'Timur the Lame'. Hence the name by which the West knows this infamous Tartar leader: Tamerlane, or, sometimes, Tamburlaine. But if you were trembling in his august presence, you would be far better off referring to him as Lord of the Fortunate Conjunction, or Conqueror of the World, or—the name he personally preferred—Scourge of God.

Timur, who in thirty-five years of campaigning created an empire that stretched from the eastern Mediterranean to China and from Moscow to the Persian Gulf (he did not bother with Europe proper, which he considered poor pickings), was a master of the use of terror. After each of his victories, huge pyramids of the skulls of the vanquished were erected on the battle-field and specially trained teams of torturers would meet with the wealthy inhabitants of conquered cities to discover the location of hidden treasure caches, eliciting screams that haunted the dreams of anyone who heard them. As Timur was destroying the Christian port city of Smyrna in 1400, a fleet of galleys arrived, filled with knights coming to the rescue. Timur, to greet them, had his men catapult the severed heads of their dead comrades out over the water, these dreadful projectiles smashing into the wooden decks of the ships and crashing against the shields of the horrified knights. The Christian fleet turned around and went home.

As terrible as Timur was, however, he was also a brilliantly innovative tactician and wily campaigner. For example, in a huge battle at Kunduzcha in 1391 against Tokhtamysh, khan of the Golden Horde (or Kipchak Khanate)—a battle of almost World War II-like proportions,

Opposite: In this Persian print, Timur the Lame, Scourge of God, receives the heads of his vanquished foes from his faithful retainers to add to his trademark pile of skulls—in this case, after the capture of Baghdad in 1401.

involving hundreds of thousands of men fighting along a sixteen-kilometre-wide front on the Russian steppes—he bribed Tokhtamysh's standard bearer to pretend to throw down his banner, which fooled the soldiers of the Golden Horde into thinking their leader was dead and sent them into flight. But it was during his invasion of Delhi in India—an invasion undertaken when he was past sixty and for no other reason than booty and blood—that Timur employed perhaps his most audacious and outlandish tactic. It became known as the Roaring Camels of Fire. Sounds a bit like an exotic flambé dessert or a nightclub joke, doesn't it? Except the joke, at least from Timur's point of view, was on the Indians: fifty thousand of them were to die, and it would take Delhi one hundred years to regain its former glory.

CONQUERING THE WORLD

The ancient chronicles have the Scourge of God born, in the town of Kesh, in what is today Uzbekistan, in April of 1336 (although some historians claim that Timur was at least five years older than this and, like an ageing film star, later retro-engineered his curriculum vitae). Kesh was then part of a region called Transoxania, a large swath of land bounded by the Caspian Sea to the west, the southern Russian steppes to the north, China to the east and Afghanistan to the south. A hundred years earlier, Genghis Khan had blown through the region, and at the time of Timur's birth Kesh remained a Mongol fiefdom. Timur was later to establish a genealogy that traced his roots back to Genghis Khan, but this was fictitious. It was true that his family had arrived with the Mongols, but it was not of Mongol royal lineage, and by the mid-fourteenth century, had intermarried with people of Turkic stock and converted to Islam.

Timur grew up the son of a minor chief of the Barlas clan, learning much about the art of war from the intermittent skirmishing that went on between the local tribes. By the time he was in his twenties, he had offended powerful leaders and was as a result operating as a solitary highwayman, plundering caravans and stealing sheep. It was on one such livestock-pilfering expedition that he was knocked off his horse by ambushers and sustained the injuries to his right arm and leg that crippled him for life and earned him his nickname.

But Timur had ambitions beyond thievery. He was charismatic—tall, with unusual pale skin and reddish-coloured hair and beard—and as courageous and generous with his friends as he was ruthless with his enemies. Gradually, he gathered an army around him, and, with the help of his brother-in-law Husayn, seized control of Samarkand, the central town of Transoxania, in 1366. Four years later, after he and Husayn had a falling out, he defeated Husayn, had him executed and married his widow, Saray. Saray *was* a descendant of Genghis Khan, so Timur began styling himself as the legendary ruler's son-in-law.

From 1370, Timur began an extraordinary career of conquest. His motives for this appear to have been mixed. Like Alexander the Great, he was driven by a desire for personal glory and wealth. Like Genghis Khan, he was nomadic at heart and loved roaming the world and fighting, although unlike Genghis he left little in the way of government behind him in his conquered territories—in fact, much of Timur's thirty-five years of campaigning was devoted to reconquering countries that had rebelled after he had moved on.

But Timur did learn an important lesson from Genghis. A ruler needs a strong army; but, left with little to do, an army of traditionally nomadic men will degenerate into tribal factions and eventually turn against its commander. In order to keep nomadic clans occupied, let alone paid, you needed war. Timur managed to give his tribes war, which meant booty. For those who needed a higher purpose to justify conquest, Timur could provide that, too, being a religious man, of sorts. He practised a highly idiosyncratic and opportunistic brand of Islam, one that allowed him to pretend that his invasions constituted a jihad, even when many of his opponents were Muslims themselves.

Timur began his conquests by moving against the Mongols of Khwarezm and Moghulistan, near the shores of the Aral Sea. He then moved further west, around the base of the Caspian Sea, to conquer Mazandaran and Khorasan. By 1382, he had moved on to Persia, sweeping away all opposition and securing the trade routes to this rich and important area. After that he turned north, waging a ferocious campaign against Tokhtamysh, khan of the Golden Horde, which culminated in Timur's great victory at Kunduzcha.

- -

DYING FOR WATER

After Timur conquered Georgia in 1396, he came into conflict with his new neighbour, the Ottoman Empire, headed by Sultan Bayazid I. Following years of exchanged insults and slights, the two enemies met on the plains near Ankara on 20 July 1402. The temperature was in the mid-thirties Celsius, but Sultan Bayazid I was not concerned: his men and horses were aligned along Cubuk Creek, a major source of fresh water.

Unbeknownst to him, however, Timur's engineers had dammed Cubuk Creek upstream of the Ottoman forces and created a reservoir into which they could divert the water. When Bayazid I arrived, the water was still flowing, probably through a gap deliberately left in the dam by Timur's men. But as combat began, the dam was closed and water stopped pouring downstream to the Ottoman forces. In the blistering heat of a daylong battle, the exhausted and thirsty men of the sultan were no match for Timur's well-hydrated soldiers.

The battle of Ankara was a major defeat for the Ottoman Empire. Sultan Bayazid was captured and carried off in a cage, and Ankara was sacked. And the usual huge pyramid of skulls was erected outside the city.

In 1396, Timur reached as far south as Egypt, at whose borders he stopped, and as far west as Georgia, the Christian country he pillaged and destroyed several times. With each victory Timur's net worth increased—in terms of wives (he eventually had eight), concubines, gold, silver and precious jewels, palaces, and soldiers to add to his armies. Also increased was his reputation for ferocity. When one Khwarezm city put up a fight, Timur bound two thousand of its people hand and foot, and placed them alive in the walls of a tower he had built, literally sandwiching human beings between bricks and mortar. The Syrian city of Sivas also resisted him, so Timur buried three thousand of its inhabitants alive, and tied the heads of numerous others to their own thighs and then tossed them into a moat. And when Timur's horde overran Damascus, according to a local chronicler, the inhabitants were 'subjected to all sorts of torture: they were bastinadoed, crushed in presses, scorched in flames and suspended head down … When near death, a man would be given a respite to recover, then the tortures of all kinds would be repeated'.

A NEW JIHAD

By late 1396, Timur had been campaigning almost without ceasing for twenty-six years and he decided to return home to his capital city of Samarkand. He was then sixty years old. He remained in Samarkand for two years, embarking on urban renewal projects including parks, gardens, mosques and palaces, helping to turn his capital into a fabled city known as the 'Pearl of Islam and Centre of the Universe'.

But Timur could not sit still for long. When he heard that the Kingdom of Delhi, which lay sixteen hundred kilometres to the southeast, was undergoing a civil war, he sensed an opportunity. Not only was Delhi reputed to be enormously rich, but neither Alexander the Great nor Genghis Khan had been able to make much headway in India. Timur's advisers thought he was crazy—to get to Delhi he would have to cross deserts, fast-moving rivers and some of the highest mountains in the world. But he would not be dissuaded. In March of 1398, declaring that India was 'inhabited by idolaters', he announced a jihad against the Kingdom of Delhi.

As well as cloaking his opportunism in the white robes of a holy war, declaring the campaign a jihad was a way to reassure his Muslim warriors that anyone killed in battle would go straight to paradise. This was just as well, as the soldiers in Timur's army knew what they were up against. Aside from facing warlike tribes in what is now Afghanistan and crossing the six-thousand-metre peaks of the Hindu Kush, they would have to pit themselves against the

Opposite: A sixteenth-century Persian depiction of Timur's Tartar forces in action. The inhabitants of conquered towns could expect little mercy from Timur. In one case, he bricked up two thousand citizens alive in a tower.

most terrifying war machine in the world: the Indian battle elephant. Dressed in a full coat of armour, with curving tusks that could gut a man, and carrying Indian archers atop their backs in wooden towers, the elephants belonging to the Sultan of Delhi constituted a fearsome weapon that could change the course of a battle with a single charge.

PASSAGE TO INDIA

Although it is far less known than some of the fabled military marches of the world, such as Hannibal's journey over the Alps or Alexander's crossing of the Hellespont, Timur's advance into India was an extraordinary feat. When he and his forces arrived at the Hindu Kush, Timur left his main army behind and took with him a smaller body of men to cross the mountains and deal with the ferocious Kafir tribes who stood in their way. Following a route through a pass with an elevation of 3,800 metres, Timur and his men travelled only at night, when the ice had frozen solid under their feet and was less treacherous. Still, men and animals slipped and fell into bottomless chasms with alarming regularity. At one point, the sixty-two-year-old Timur had to be lowered three hundred metres on a litter. All the horses were lost, but still the Tartars proceeded. When they finally reached the other side, they attacked the Kafirs. After a terrible fight, they wiped out the tribesmen. Timur's main army then rejoined him.

By September, Timur had reached the Indus River. His engineers constructed a bridge and his entire army crossed it in two days. On his way to Delhi, Timur made his presence known by burning any town or village in his path and killing or making captive those inhabitants who had not fled before him. By the time his army reached Delhi, it had swelled by one hundred thousand prisoners. Indian cavalry made a lightning strike against Timur's advance forces, which the Tartars were easily able to beat off. But Timur became concerned because his Indian prisoners had cheered as the Delhi horsemen attacked. Fearing that there might be an uprising among the prisoners, he ordered every one of the one hundred thousand captives to be slaughtered.

The massacre of so many thousands even before the battle began was a horrible portent for the Indians, but Timur's soldiers were nervous, as well. Not only had they heard that the Indian forces possessed more than one hundred battle elephants, but also the Indian prisoners had told them that the great creatures had giant scimitars attached to their tusks, and that each scimitar was dipped in a special poison before battle, so that even a scratch from the blade would mean certain and agonising death. Even the Tartar officers were afraid. The great sixteenth-century Persian historian Ghiyas ad-Din Muhammad Khwandamir wrote that: 'The rows of mighty elephants, clad in complete steel, emptied the brains of the chieftains of their ardour ... they entertained great fears and regarded the overcoming of the elephants as an impossibility.'

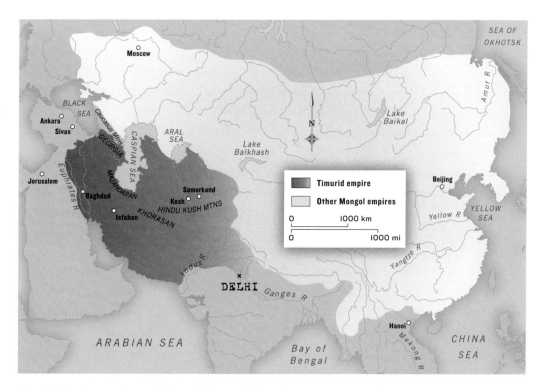

Timur the Lame's control extended into what is now India and north as far as Lake Baikal and the Russian steppes, but the heartland of his empire (shown in red) was Central Asia, centred on his glorious capital of Samarkand.

Timur responded to these fears not by downplaying them or by going into a rage and executing anyone showing the slightest amount of cowardice, but by coming up with an ingenious plan. First he ordered his men to dig deep trenches around their positions and protect them with ramparts. Then he ordered his armourers to make hundreds of the four-pronged iron spikes known as caltrops. Looking a little like large and very sharp versions of the objects used in the game of jacks, caltrops had been used for thousands of years to break up horse, elephant and chariot attacks by puncturing the animals' hooves. Timur's men, however, built their caltrops larger and sharper than normal, and then went out on the plain the night before the battle and placed them in the path the Indian elephants would likely take.

So far, these were fairly common precautions that any commander might take in order to protect against elephant attack, and it's unlikely that they would have reassured Timur's soldiers. But then the men saw that Timur had ordered that camels be brought to the front lines and tethered there. The animals' backs were piled high with wood and straw. There was much curiosity among the men when they saw these creatures, but only a very few knew what Timur had planned.

CLASH OF BEASTS

On 17 December 1398, the army of the Sultan Mahmud Khan poured out of Delhi to do battle with the waiting Tartar army. The Indian commanders arrayed their troops for battle in the usual fashion, with cavalry on the wings and, in the centre, their unassailable force of about 120 elephants. Behind the great beasts, much like soldiers following a tank attack in World War II, were hordes of infantry, ready to take advantage of the gaping hole the elephants would surely punch in the Tartar lines.

The armies came together with a terrible noise that those on the city walls later described as the sound of furious thunder. On both flanks, Tartars and Indians locked in desperate battle, while the Sultan's elephants prepared to charge and Temur's troops grimly awaited them. For each side, it was a fight without quarter: the Tartars were sixteen hundred kilometres away from home, the Indians defending their city against a pitiless intruder.

Just as it seemed that the Tartars were gaining the advantage, Sultan Mahmud ordered his war elephants to charge. Gathering force from about a kilometre in front of the Tartar lines, the elephants came roaring at their enemy, lifting up huge clouds of dust and making trumpeting noises that sounded like a horrible scream. According to one ancient historian, 'there were great brass kettle drums … beat on the back of the elephants as they charged', so Timur's men, waiting in their trenches, would have been faced with a fearful cacophony.

As the elephants came within sight, they were revealed to be even more fearsome than the Tartars had imagined. They were clad in chain-mail armour so that their head and body were completely impregnable. On their tusks gleamed the gigantic scimitars. Atop them were the Indian archers who were already unleashing arrows at the Tartar lines.

Timur could see his men starting to mill around and break to the rear. So he had the camels driven in front of his lines and then ordered their drivers to set afire the piles of wood and straw on their backs. Then, prodding them with iron sticks, the drivers sent the beasts towards the elephants. Maddened by their own burning flesh and by the smoke that choked them, the camels charged at the elephants, howling with pain.

Timur had understood that elephants were easy creatures to panic. Faced with the strange spectre of the burning camels flying straight at them with flames leaping from their backs and emitting their fearful wails, the elephants turned and stampeded back towards their own lines. The Indian infantry, which had been confidently charging behind the great beasts, was suddenly confronted by elephants that had gone berserk. Deaf to the panicked shouts of their mahouds, the creatures tore huge swathes in the infantry, trampling some, causing some to be impaled on the caltrops and tossing still others in the air like so many toys. 'The heads of the Indians were reduced to atoms; they were like coconuts dropped from trees', wrote the historian Khwandamir.

RAZING DELHI

Very shortly, the Indian army was in full rout. The Tartars pursued the Indians into their city and the slaughter began. Although some historians claim that Timur did not know what was happening (unlikely, given his iron control), the Tartar soldiers unleashed an orgy of rape, looting and killing. During the course of three days, fifty thousand men, women and children were murdered, and Delhi was put to the torch. The Tartars stayed two weeks, consolidating their fabulous captured treasures of gold, silver, jewels and slaves, and then left the once-glorious metropolis a smoking, reeking ruin. There was no food. The city was struck by a fearsome pestilence, probably bubonic plague, and, as one contemporary writer put it, 'not a bird moved wing' for two months. It would take Delhi more than a century to recover fully.

Taking the elephants with him (he would use them in his defeat of Sultan Bayazid I at Ankara, a few years later), Timur left, never to return. Though he continued to roam the world seeking to plunder and destroy, he would soon be an elderly man so infirm that he had to be carried on a litter to battle, and in 1405 he would die of disease in China.

But in the aftermath of his great victory at Delhi, all glory was Timur's. Thousands of mere human beings had paid obeisance to him, and now even war elephants, the mightiest creatures in the world, were forced to bow down to him, too. Soon after the battle, in a scene that strikes the modern eye as unimaginably grand and savage, Timur had the elephants brought before his tent, where they were forced to kneel to him, one by one, to show their submission to the Scourge of God and Conqueror of the World.

- -

THE CURSE OF TIMUR

After his death in 1405, Timur was buried in a fabulous mausoleum in Samarkand, known as the Gur-e Amir, meaning 'tomb of the king' in Persian. It was surmounted by a blue, grooved dome rising almost forty metres high, and it still stands today.

There Timur lay, for six hundred years, until 1941, when Soviet archaeologists decided to open the tomb. They did so despite the fact that there was a strong local belief that if anyone tampered with the tomb of Timur, a curse would befall the land.

Inside the tomb, the Russian scientists found the skeleton of a man who was about 172 centimetres tall— large for his day—and who, indeed, had an injury to his right leg, just above the knee, that would have caused him to limp, and a wound in the bones of his right arm, as well. There were traces of a red moustache and beard.

The Soviets learned much about Timur's body that corroborated the truth of the ancient chronicles, but hours after they opened up the tomb, Hitler unleashed his invasion of Russia. The curse of Timur? Many people thought so.

TURNING WEAKNESS INTO STRENGTH: THE AMERICAN VICTORY AT COWPENS, 1781

IT LASTED PERHAPS FORTY MINUTES, ABOUT THE TIME IT MIGHT TAKE YOU OR me to make a quick shopping trip or grab a sandwich with a friend. But in that forty minutes the course of the War of American Independence was changed.

The battle of Cowpens took place on 17 January 1781, in common pasturing ground in rural South Carolina, and led directly to the epochal surrender of Lord Cornwallis's forces at Yorktown, Virginia, some ten months later, and, in turn, the beginning of the American nation. But Cowpens is also important because it was won by a homegrown American commander, Brigadier General Daniel Morgan, whose alignment of his Continental forces on the battlefield was brilliant, and harked back, albeit on a smaller scale, to Hannibal's double envelopment at Cannae (see p. 12). Morgan was a commander who stood common military wisdom on its head. He turned his enemy's strength against it, and turned his own troops' weakness to his advantage. As a result, as historian John Buchanan put it, he became 'the only general in the American Revolution, on either side, to produce a significant original tactical thought'.

REVOLUTION IN THE SOUTH

Most of the early part of the War of American Independence, which began in 1775, was fought in the northern states, especially Massachusetts—the tinderbox that had sparked American discontent with British rule—New York and New Jersey. After initial defeats, American armies under Generals George Washington and Horatio Gates defeated the British at Trenton, New Jersey, and Saratoga, New York, in 1777. In 1778, General Sir Henry Clinton, the British commander, withdrew his forces to New York in order to preserve the army and protect the city against French naval power, France having just entered the war on the side of the Americans. Washington followed with his army, and a stalemate in the North ensued.

In the South, however, it was a different story. The British hoped to take advantage of the fact that the American regular army was much weaker there, and that a greater proportion of American civilians were Loyalists—or Tories, as they were called—and could be counted on to rally around the Crown. Clinton sent an expeditionary force from New York to Georgia in late 1778, which captured the city of Savannah with relative ease. After this success, Clinton himself, along with Major General Charles Cornwallis, set sail from New York with a large force of British regular army troops and captured Charleston, the region's biggest port. Cornwallis then shattered the forces of General Horatio Gates, sent south to do battle, at Camden, South Carolina, in August of 1780.

By December of 1780, the Continentals had been driven out of South Carolina and were regrouping in Charlotte, North Carolina, under Gates's replacement, the very capable General Nathanael Greene, who had been sent by George Washington to try to salvage the depressing situation. Greene's ragtag army of perhaps two thousand regular soldiers had little to eat, clothing inadequate for winter weather and little hope left after a series of bloody setbacks.

Prefiguring the conflict that would take place in the South eighty years later, the fighting in South Carolina had the vicious, psychotically violent, extremely personal nature of a civil war. While the professional armies might clash on the battlefield, militias belonging to the Loyalists and the Patriots fought impromptu skirmishes, after which prisoners could expect to be hung or hacked to death with sabres. Women and children were murdered in midnight raids, homes burned to the ground, politics used as a means to settle old scores.

Into this terrifying mix came the dashing figure of twenty-six-year-old Major Banastre Tarleton, commander of the British Legion, which was made up primarily of British Loyalists recruited in the North and trained exactingly by Tarleton and a small core of British army officers. Brave, impulsive and

Aggressive and uncompromising, Major Banastre Tarleton (1754-1833) became a symbol of British oppression to Americans fighting the war in the South.

quite brutal, Tarleton was Cornwallis's right-hand commander, responsible for clearing American armies from South Carolina in a series of forceful fights at places like Monck's Corner, Lenud's Ferry and Fishing Creek, whose names give a sense of their isolation, deep in rural valleys. An incident during which Tarleton's men slaughtered a defeated and helpless American force at Waxhaws, North Carolina, led to the British commander becoming known among the Patriots as 'Butcher' Tarleton, or 'Bloody Ban'. The phrase 'Tarleton's Quarter!' became a sneering and ironic reference to the mercy Americans intended to offer the British when next they met. They would soon have their opportunity, at Cowpens.

'TO SPIRIT UP THE PEOPLE'

Nathanael Greene knew that if he kept his forces in the same place for too long, the superior British army could simply throw a noose around them and gradually tighten it. So he decided to take action first, and in mid-December divided his troops. He himself, with the bulk of his force, would threaten the British in eastern South Carolina. Sent west into the countryside with a force of eight hundred men was Brigadier General Daniel Morgan, whose orders were to 'take command in that quarter, to act offensively or defensively, to protect the country, spirit up the people, annoy the enemy [and] collect provisions and forage'. To 'spirit up the people' meant to show the flag, so that patriotic Americans would join forces to drive out the British; and, indeed, as Morgan went, more and more militia joined his forces.

Just as Banastre Tarleton was the face of the British forces in the South, so Daniel Morgan came to typify the Americans. Not a great deal is known about Morgan's early life except that he was born in New Jersey in

Brigadier Daniel Morgan was worshipped by the troops who fought with him at Cowpens and Saratoga.

1736 and as a teenager moved to Virginia. There he got a job driving a wagon—hence his own self-applied nickname, 'The Old Waggoner'. His first experience with the British was at the age of twenty, when he was a driver for the British army during the French and Indian War, the North American component of the Seven Years' War (1754–63) between Britain and France. A year later, he and two soldiers were attacked by Indians. The soldiers were killed and Morgan shot in the back of the neck, the bullet smashing his teeth and exiting just above his left lip, leaving a livid scar. The incident showed that Morgan—a solidly built, stocky, plainspoken and rough-humoured man—could survive almost any hardship. After the War of American Independence began, he became famous for leading a group of backwoods riflemen in fighting in Canada and at Saratoga. By 1781, after a leave of absence for health reasons, Morgan was a brigadier general in charge of Greene's 'light troops'—a strike contingent comprised of regular soldiers, militia, dragoons (mounted infantry) and cavalry.

IN HOT PURSUIT

As far as Cornwallis was concerned, Greene had made the cardinal military mistake of dividing his army in the face of a superior force; now he could be cut up, piecemeal. Accordingly, Cornwallis decided to send Tarleton after Morgan. Given two regular infantry companies in addition to his infamous British Legion (about eleven hundred men in all),

- -

THE WAXHAWS MASSACRE

Central to the image of Banastre Tarleton as a butcher—and therefore to the rage of the Americans fighting at Cowpens—was the skirmish that took place on 29 May 1780, in the rural Waxhaws District of South Carolina. On that day, Tarleton, leading a force of several hundred British regulars, caught up with two regiments of Virginia Continentals led by Colonel Abraham Buford. Tarleton sent a note to Buford, greatly exaggerating the size of British forces, and demanding surrender. Buford replied by saying, 'I shall defend myself to the last extremity', but made two crucial errors: he kept on marching, rather than align his troops for battle, and, when Tarleton's dragoons charged on horseback, he waited until they were ten metres away before ordering his men to fire. The Continentals were thus unable to stop the massed horsemen from breaking through their lines. What happened next was sheer horror: British dragoons hacking down Americans who held up white flags of surrender or knelt and begged for their lives.

Tarleton said this happened only because his horse had been shot out from under him and his men, thinking him dead, 'engaged in a vindictive asperity not easily restrained'. Buford managed to escape, but more than one hundred Americans died. However, it was a pyrrhic victory for Tarleton, for it caused more and more Americans to join the Continental forces.

Tarleton began to trail Morgan through the countryside in typically Southern winter weather—almost freezing, and raining much of the time.

Each time Tarleton came near Morgan, however, Morgan withdrew, and Tarleton was forced to follow further and more aggressively. On the evening of 15 January, learning that Morgan was encamped nearby, Tarleton drove his men in an all-night march, which brought them so close to Morgan's forces on 16 January that the Americans were forced to abandon their breakfast and run for their lives. Sure now of an easy victory, the British marched all that day and camped that night. Very early the next morning, Tarleton's advance scouts came out of a pine forest to discover an American skirmish line arrayed at a place called Cowpens.

A COUNTERINTUITIVE PLAN

On the afternoon of 16 January, Daniel Morgan, with the help of local scouts, had finally arrived at the battleground of his choosing. Cowpens ('the cow pens') was a grazing area in the high-pasture country of South Carolina, which was used in common by the settlers in the area. About five hundred metres across and five hundred long, the land here was almost park-like: an open, sloping area dotted with trees where the underbrush had been eaten away by livestock or cleared by farmers. The ground rose up in a gentle swell, and near the top of the slope there was a swale, or fold, in the land, just deep enough to hide a man on horseback.

Now Morgan began to do things that were brilliantly counterintuitive. Beyond the woods behind him, about ten kilometres away, was the Broad River, which effectively cut off the Americans' means of escape (an army attempting to cross a river under fire is an army inviting massacre). Setting up here therefore violated a cardinal military rule—always give yourself an avenue of retreat. But Morgan did not want to provide his militia, which made up fully a quarter of his force, with a chance to retreat. For militia were notorious in the War of American Independence for *always* running away in the face of well-trained, regular army troops, particularly if the latter employed bayonets. George Washington himself had gone on record to say that they were worse than useless.

Morgan planned to turn this 'uselessness' to his advantage. Understanding that these men would likely run, he arrayed them as his first and second lines of defence: his skirmishers and his initial battle line. *And then he gave them permission to run.* Indeed, an eyewitness described how, the night before the battle, Morgan went among the militia, telling them that they were going to whip 'Benny' [Tarleton] handily the next day and that all he needed them to do was, 'just hold up your heads, boys; three fires and you are home free, and then when you return to your homes, how the folks will bless you, and the girls kiss you, for your gallant conduct'.

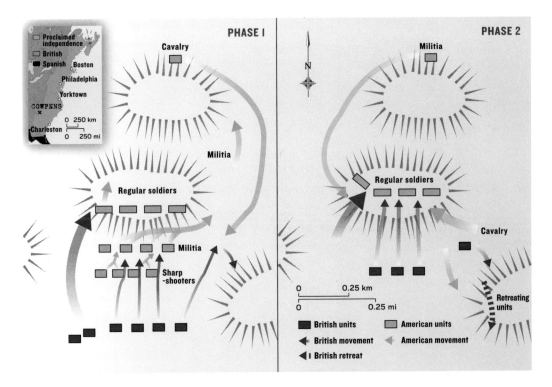

In phase I of the battle of Cowpens, the British advanced on the American lines, unaware of the troops hidden in the swale. In phase 2, the Continental envelopment sent the British reeling. Inset: The military situation in 1781.

The next part of Morgan's ingenious plan was to place his regular army soldiers—his third and last line of defence—in the swale at the top of the slope. Conventionally, a commander would have placed them on the brow of the swale, looking down at the enemy, but Morgan wanted to keep these men hidden, to make the British think that the militia retreating before them represented the main force they faced. Morgan also understood something vital about the mechanics of firing muskets and rifles in battle: men who fire downhill tend to fire too high, whereas men aiming uphill fire low and hit their targets more often. This was particularly true, the Americans had noted, of the British, whose muskets may have contained too much powder, which caused the bullet to fly higher than it ought to.

Morgan's flanks were protected on the right by a ravine and a small creek, and on the left by a swamp. In the woods directly behind his forces, he hid his cavalry and light dragoons commanded by Colonel William Washington.

There was one other factor on which his plan hinged, and on which he knew he could depend: Banastre Tarleton's aggressiveness.

Colonel William Washington rallies the American troops at Cowpens. Washington's dragoons ensured victory for the Continentals by charging into the British right flank and completing a decisive double envelopment.

MORGAN'S TRIUMPH

When Tarleton rode out of the misty woods on the morning of 17 January, he saw what he expected to see—a skirmish line of American scouts, and, further up the hill, what he assumed was the main body of the American forces. Without waiting to reconnoitre further, he formed his men into their usual attack formation: his Legions and artillery (in this case, only two small field pieces which played little part in the battle) in the middle, and his dragoons on the flanks. A command was given and the men headed up the slope.

Almost immediately, Morgan's skirmishers began firing. These men, sharpshooters mainly from the backwoods of the Carolinas and Georgia, armed with long rifles rather than the shorter-ranged, less accurate, smooth-bore muskets carried by most militia and Continentals, fired from about 150 metres in front of Morgan's initial battle line. Their job was to pick off British officers, and they may have killed about fifteen of the dragoons. When they were done firing their two (or three) shots, the skirmishers retired to the initial line, which opened to let them through.

At this point, the battle was proceeding just as Tarleton had expected—a typical display from the skirmishers, then a retreat to the main line. He now sent his infantry forwards in a broad charge along the whole front of the Cowpens pasture, heading straight at the militia.

On the American side, officers roamed behind their nervous men, encouraging them to hold their fire. Morgan himself was on the militia line, telling jokes and admonishing the men to 'squinney [aim] well and don't touch a trigger until you see the whites of their eyes'. When the British forces, moving at quick step, got within forty or fifty metres, Morgan screamed the order to fire, and the entire militia line erupted in smoke and yellow flame. The British line faltered, taking serious casualties, about forty per cent of which were officers, but the well-trained men continued their attack. The militia fired again. Then they turned and ran as fast as they could up the slope.

The enraged British chased them, determined to wreak revenge for their dead and wounded. Most of the militia made it back to the protection of the back line (which had been ordered to open up to let them through), but one group of militia on the left of the Continental line were caught in the open by Tarleton's dragoons, who began to exact a fearful toll on the panicked men, cutting them down with flashing sabres. Witnessing this, William Washington's cavalry raced out of the woods and drove off the dragoons.

Meanwhile, the main body of British troops, in three lines, fifes playing and drums beating, continued to advance on the last line of American defence, which was now apparent in the distance. Continental veterans of the battle later remembered Daniel Morgan everywhere among them, crying: 'Form, form, my brave fellows! Old Morgan was never beaten!'

The British crested the swale and aimed down at the American soldiers. Volley after volley of musket fire was unleashed by both sides—soldiers fired by company, rather than individually—at a range now of about fifty metres; the bullets, said one participant, 'produced much slaughter'. Yet much of the British fire went high, as Morgan had predicted, while the Americans were able to aim up at British forces silhouetted against the skyline.

Instead of coming up against a line of Americans that cracked like the other two, the British now found themselves facing their strongest opposition of the day. They began to wither under the intense pressure. Seeing this, Tarleton threw in his reserves, the Seventy-First Highlanders, who entered the battle to the unnerving shriek of bagpipes. Americans on the right flank misunderstood an order from their commander and began to retreat, with the British chasing them, but just as quickly Morgan rode up, turned the retreating Continentals around and had them fire a devastating volley into the pursing enemy at a range of ten metres.

Although this retreat and about-face was unplanned, it broke the British will. A moment later, Washington's mounted men swept in on the British right flank while the re-formed militia came in from the left. This double envelopment proved too much for the British, who began running or surrendering. Tarleton took a group of some forty Legion dragoons and made a charge to try to save the day, but it was too little, too late. Yelling 'Tarleton's Quarter!' the Americans swarmed over the British; it was only by the exercise of firm control on the part of Morgan's officers that a slaughter did not ensue.

A TURNING POINT

Tarleton and his battered forces made their way back to rejoin Cornwallis. They had lost one hundred dead, more than two hundred wounded and six hundred prisoners. Morgan reported his total casualties as twelve dead and seventy-three wounded, though the real number of dead was probably closer to seventy. Morgan did not count the militia casualties since they were, technically, outside his command—not unnaturally, he wanted to make his victory seem even more impressive than it was. He needn't have feared. His victory was one of the most impressive of the war.

Not only that, despite being a relatively small battle, involving just three thousand or so combatants in all, Cowpens turned the tide of a stalemated war in the direction of the Americans and was a major psychological victory for the Patriots. In the next ten months, Greene carried on a campaign of attrition against Cornwallis, facing him on numerous battle-grounds after Cowpens and always, technically, losing—but in the end the British victories were hollow ones which cost them thousands of dead. Cornwallis was finally cornered at Yorktown, Virginia, and forced to surrender in October 1781, bringing the war to an end.

Old Dan Morgan had retired by then—sciatica from a herniated disc made it nearly impossible for him to mount his horse—but he took great glee in his victory. As he wrote a friend shortly after Cowpens: 'I was desirous to have a stroke at Tarleton … & I have Given him a devil of a whiping [sic]'.

A DISPUTED DUEL

A powerful part of the American lore and legend surrounding Cowpens is a *mano a mano* combat encounter that supposedly took place at the end of the battle between Colonel William Washington and Major Banastre Tarleton. Realising all was lost, Tarleton and two of his staff officers galloped away from the battlefield, with Washington in hot pursuit. According to the way Americans told the story, Washington got out in front of his men and rapidly closed in on Tarleton and his two aides. Seeing this, the British turned and attacked Washington, with Tarleton personally shooting the American commander's horse out from under him. Only the timely intervention of Washington's young bugler, who shot at an Englishman who had his sword raised over Washington, saved Washington's life (as shown above). Another American version has Washington and

Tarleton engaged in a clash of sabres, which ended with Washington cutting off two of Tarleton's fingers with his sabre (Tarleton, in fact, did lose two fingers of his right hand, but not at Cowpens: a bullet severed them during a later skirmish with Americans).

British sources, however, claim that a party of retreating British cavalry (not including Tarleton) fought with a group of Washington's men, and one of the British was killed as he was about to sabre Washington.

Lawrence E. Babits, author of *A Devil of a Whipping*, a definitive modern history of the battle, points out that the American sources actually say the 'duel' took place between Washington and 'an officer believed to be Tarleton'—in other words, no one there really knew for sure.

Neither William Washington nor Tarleton mentioned the incident in any later writing about the war.

HORNS OF THE ZULUS: THE BATTLE OF ISANDHLWANA, 1879

THE GREAT SHAKA, FOUNDER OF THE ZULU EMPIRE OF THE EARLY NINETEENTH century, was, quite probably, a psychopath. He thought of killing human beings the way you or I might think of swatting flies on a summer's day. Once he became the ruler of the Zulus, he walked everywhere with executioners who, at a flick of his finger, would club or stab someone to death—for sneezing, not bowing low enough or simply looking the wrong way at the wrong time. When Shaka's mother, Nandi, died, he declared a year of mourning and summoned twenty thousand of his Zulu citizens to his kraal, or village. He ordered that no crops be grown or children conceived for an entire year. Then a week of enforced grieving ensued. If someone was found without tears, he or she was executed. According to a European present, seven thousand people were thus massacred within a few days.

There are some who feel that these incidents are greatly exaggerated or invented by Europeans who must find a way to turn Africans into savages, but evidence indicating Shaka's brutality, even allowing for the culture in which he was brought up, seems overwhelming. But proof also exists for another, incontrovertible fact: that Shaka was an original military genius whose innovations changed the face of warfare in Africa. Growing into manhood in the late eighteenth and early nineteenth centuries, without ever having met a white man or studied military science, he came up with an original way of fighting which perfectly suited his army, made Zululand a powerful nation and gave it the tools, long after his own death, with which to inflict an epic defeat on Great Britain, at the battle of Isandhlwana in 1879. Shortly thereafter, the massed firepower of the 'civilised' world finally brought the Zulus to a halt, dead on the ground beneath their coloured shields; but had Shaka still been around, who knows what would have happened?

A nineteenth-century British depiction of Shaka. The rendition is somewhat inaccurate in that Shaka lacks his short assegai spear, but it does capture the fabled chief's imposing presence.

THE RISE OF THE ZULUS

The Zulu homeland, now encompassed by the South African province of KwaZulu-Natal, borders on the Indian Ocean in southeastern Africa. Zulus are members of the Bantu nation, a nomadic, cattle-driving race who probably arrived in Central Africa from the Middle East over ten thousand years ago. Eventually, after perhaps a thousand years of wandering, the Bantu spread south and west and finally down into the southeastern part of the continent, pushing the original inhabitants of the region, the Bushmen, before them. The first European settlers of South Africa, the Dutch settlers known as Boers (Dutch for 'farmers'), also pushed the Bushmen out as they moved northeast over the course of a hundred years, beginning in the mid-seventeenth century.

Neither Boers nor Bantu were aware of each other until they collided in the valley of the Great Fish River, in the late 1700s, each on their own separate migration. As the races collided, vicious fights and border skirmishes took place, a series of conflicts known as the Cape Frontier Wars. While this was going on, the British seized South Africa from the Dutch in 1794, inheriting a rich land and, eventually, a lot of trouble.

In the meantime, five hundred kilometres to the northeast, the Zulu tribe developed. The Zulus were part of a splinter group of Bantus, the Nguni, who had headed all the way into present-day KwaZulu-Natal and settled in the fertile area near the White Mfolozi River. The first chief, whose name was Zulu, which means 'the heavens', was followed by three brothers. The third brother, Senzangakona, fathered a child out of wedlock with a neighbouring chief's daughter, Nandi. Since she did not have the status of bride, Nandi tried to claim that her pregnancy was really an illness caused by a *shaka*, an intestinal beetle, and thus,

----

THE WASHING OF THE SPEARS

One of the reasons that Zulu warriors were so feared by their enemies, particularly Europeans, is because of a practice known as 'the washing of the spears'—the ritual disembowelment of the dead on the battlefield.

When a Zulu warrior killed an enemy, it was essential to him that he gut his fallen foe. This was to protect him from any malign spirits within the dead man that might infect him and eventually drive him to madness. After 'washing his spear' (although often a knife was used rather than a spear) in the blood of the dead, the warrior then had to have sex with a woman who was not his wife. This was in order to leave any possible trace of evil with another woman, and not bring it home.

Because of this need for further cleansing, Zulu campaigns were often short, with the warriors leaving almost immediately after the battle to begin the cleansing as soon as possible.

when her son was born in about 1787, this was the name he was given. As an illegitimate and barely acknowledged son of a king, Shaka was subjected to ridicule as a youth—ridicule for which he later took ferocious revenge. By the age of twenty-four, he had become a much-feared warrior working for a neighbouring chieftain to whom the Zulus paid tribute. Much of Bantu warfare at this point consisted not of pitched battles, but of relatively bloodless skirmishes in which insults were exchanged and spears thrown from a distance. But the tactics of the chieftain, whose name was Dingiswayo, were more brutal: Shaka was now involved in deadly battles in which Dingiswayo sought to capture slaves and take territory.

Young Shaka did not invent this kind of warfare among indigenous Africans, as is often claimed, but, as a commander appointed by Dingiswayo, he perfected it. To begin with, he changed himself. Deciding that he did not need sandals, he toughened his feet by going barefoot everywhere, no matter what the terrain. (Ultimately, Shaka ensured his soldiers could run barefoot as much as eighty kilometres a day and he made them practise on ground littered with thorns; those who winced or complained were executed.) He then modified the basic Zulu weapon of war: the spear. Prior to Shaka, the spear was used like a javelin, for throwing from a distance, which Shaka found absurd: once it was gone, you could not get it back and it was often turned against you. Shaka developed a shorter, flat-bladed stabbing spear, with a heavier handle, called the assegai by Europeans (but known far more descriptively in the Zulu language as the *ikwa*, for the sound the blade made as it was pulled out of a human body). Zulus carried several of these, which could be thrown if necessary at short range, but they always kept the last one for thrusting.

Shaka also refined the Zulus' wood and cowhide shield, cutting it down in size so that it could be carried more easily in battle. Shaka showed his men how, in a fight, they could hook the shield under their opponent's larger shield, knock it out of the way and at the same time sweep in for the kill with the assegai. (At which point, Shaka always shouted 'I have eaten!', a phrase taken up by all Zulu warriors after blooding their spears.)

Shaka was allowed to train an *impi*, or regiment, this way and it proved highly effective. What's more, a few years later he developed the brilliant innovation that would become his most powerful and influential strategy: the *impondo zankomo*, or 'horns of the bull'.

A SHAPE IN THE SAND

The Zulus were a people in love with their cattle. Everything revolved around these animals. Wives were bought with cattle, wealth measured by cattle, almost every need of the Zulus, from clothing to the milk curds that were a staple of their diet, was provided by cattle. So it was Shaka's genius to design a military manoeuvre based on the very form

Zulu warriors practising the 'horns of the bull' formation, as shown in a nineteenth-century British illustration. In battle, the formation was used on a larger scale to overcome all enemies, except, ultimately, the British.

of these animals—a strategy that could be represented by a picture of a bull drawn in the sand and would easily be understood and appreciated by any Zulu.

Although it hadn't been his innovation, the Zulu regiment, or *impi*, was central to his plans. *Impis* could vary in size, having no precise number; in the beginning, Shaka's *impis* probably included no more than a hundred men each and possibly far fewer. In Shaka's plan, the main and strongest *impi* became the 'chest' of the bull, the main line facing the enemy. Behind it was a reserve force, which formed the bull's 'flanks' and was ready to be called into action if needed. On either side of the chest was Shaka's most important innovation, 'the horns'. The left and right horns, each consisting of one *impi*, raced out as the chest was moving forwards, flanking the opposing army and meeting behind it. If all worked according to plan, horns and chest met, surrounding the enemy and crushing it.

After endless training, Shaka put his strategy into effect one day around 1817. Fighting against a tribe that had persecuted him and his mother—and which was led by his half-brother—Shaka aligned his forces and attacked. The fast-moving horns of the bull swept behind the enemy, while Shaka and the main body of his men made short work of opponents in front of them. Shaka killed his half-brother and ruthlessly executed every member of the enemy clan, including women and children.

SHAKA IS DEAD. LONG LIVE SHAKA.

By about 1819, Dingiswayo having been murdered by a rival chief, Shaka took control of the Zulus and led them to victory after victory, using the 'horns of the bull' tactic repeatedly. His force grew to as many as twenty thousand warriors—after every victory, the enemy soldiers who remained were trained by Shaka's commanders and absorbed into the Zulus.

By 1824, Shaka had conquered all the various tribes and clans within a territory that stretched from the Indian Ocean west to the Kalahari Desert, north to Lake Malawi and south to the Cape. He ruled brutally, but as effectively as any Ottoman or Mongol king; he was unimpeachable and seemingly unassailable.

Around 1824, he discovered a small British settlement at Port Natal and, out of curiosity, invited a party of Britons to visit him at his royal hearth, a kraal with the welcoming name of *kwaBulawayo*, or 'the place of him who kills'. While these visitors were in attendance, there was an attempt on Shaka's life by members of a neighbouring tribe. Shaka survived, in part because one of the Britons nursed him back to health. Because of this, he became well disposed to the white men and signed an agreement leasing them a large amount of territory around Port Natal (present-day Durban).

This one instance of benevolence from a brutal ruler turned out to be a great mistake from the Zulu point of view. In 1828, there was another assassination attempt on Shaka's life, by his two half-brothers, Dingane and Mhlangana, and this one succeeded. Bleeding from numerous wounds, Shaka pleaded with his killers to spare him, but they ruthlessly eviscerated him with the very assegais he had invented.

ZULUS AND BRITISH: FRIENDS, THEN FOES

Dingane immediately murdered his brother Mhlangana and assumed the Zulu throne, instituting a pogrom against pro-Shaka family and chiefs that lasted several years; even so, his reign was far less bloody than that of Shaka. His main battles were with the Voortrekkers, those Boer farmers who had decided to escape British rule and trek into the interior of South Africa and Natal. Dingane double-crossed and massacred a great many of them, but the Voortrekkers beat off a major Zulu attack at Blood River, mainly through the use of modern firepower which included at least one cannon. Dingane was murdered and another half-brother, Mpande, ascended the throne just as the British moved in and took over Natal from the Boers in 1840.

Mpande and the British managed to co-exist peacefully for a time, although there was internal dissension—as always—within the Zulu nation. However, in 1856, Mpande's two sons fought one of the most brutal conflicts in South African history, involving more than fifty thousand Zulu warriors. Prince Cetshwayo won and slaughtered his brother's supporters by the thousands. Old King Mpande subsequently ruled as a figurehead, but Cetshwayo was the true power of Zululand and ascended the throne in 1872.

He was careful to cultivate good relations with the British, even going so far as to make sure his position as King of the Zulus was recognised by Queen Victoria. But the peace did not last long. Cetshwayo was continually skirmishing with the Boers who had settled in Transvaal, bordering Zululand in the north. At first, the British encouraged Cetshwayo, but once they took over Transvaal from the bankrupt Boers, they saw things very differently. A commission led by Sir Henry Bartle Frere sided with the Boers on boundary issues and provoked the Zulus into certain minor infringements. After the British issued a deliberately unreasonable ultimatum to Cetshwayo (telling him he must disband his army, among other things), they declared war and invaded Zululand in early 1879.

THE GHOST OF SHAKA

The British entered Zululand in three separate columns on 11 January 1879. All told, British forces numbered 5,700 white troops and 8,000 Africans. Their plan was to converge in three directions on the Zulu capital of Ulundi. Facing them were forty thousand Zulu warriors. The British, under Lieutenant General Frederic Augustus Thesiger, Lord Chelmsford, thought that superior British firepower, which included artillery and Gatling guns (forerunners of the modern machine gun), would easily win the day.

They had not bargained on the ghost of Shaka. Although some Zulu tactics and strict Zulu army discipline had been abandoned by the rulers who had succeeded Shaka, Cetshwayo had resurrected the king's militant ways. Every male over the age of sixteen was trained as a soldier. The Zulu army had been structured around twelve corps, with each corps made up of regiments segregated according to marital status and age—men as old as sixty still fought. The Zulus had acquired some ancient muskets, though they still relied mainly on the assegai and were generally suspicious of firearms (some Zulus thought that bursting artillery shells contained British soldiers who leaped out of the explosion, and so could be seen spearing at the ground after shells burst among them). They also retained the 'horns of the bull', and the tactic was now worked on an even larger scale than in Shaka's day, creating a massive encircling movement that would take place over kilometres of ground and end up with the enemy caught in a bloody trap. As the British were about to find out.

On 21 January 1879, a portion of the central British column pitched its camp near the small mountain of Isandhlwana, just past the Buffalo River. The British were about seventeen hundred strong, including about four hundred African auxiliaries, and were supported by artillery and rockets. Under the command of Lieutenant Colonel Henry

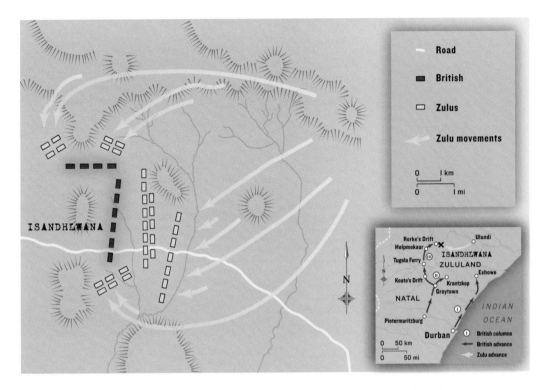

Main map: The Zulu 'horns of the bull' spread out around the doomed British defences at Isandhlwana.
Inset: In 1879, three British columns entered the land of the Zulus, intending to converge on the capital, Ulundi.

Pulleine, the men made did not entrench, perhaps owing to an overestimate of their strength, but they did pick what appeared to be an ideal spot from a conventional military viewpoint: they had their backs to the sheer rock face of Isandhlwana and in front of them was a broad and extensive plain, seemingly empty.

In the early afternoon of 22 January, however, British scouts on horseback reconnoitring a few kilometres in front of the British positions, found a large ravine hidden from sight on the plain. Peering over the edge of the chasm, they saw an astonishing thing: sitting in perfect silence, as far as the eye could see, were twenty thousand Zulu warriors. Seeing the British, the Zulus arose as one. The scouts rode in a frenzy back to their camp as the Zulus began to come up over the edge of the ravine and across the plain.

Alerted, the British troops, which included two battalions of the veteran Twenty-fourth Warwickshire Regiment, formed an extended line to face the challenge of the onrushing Zulus. At first, they were relatively unconcerned; in fact, some of them were even laughing and chatting, happy in the knowledge that, finally, they were about to have their chance to

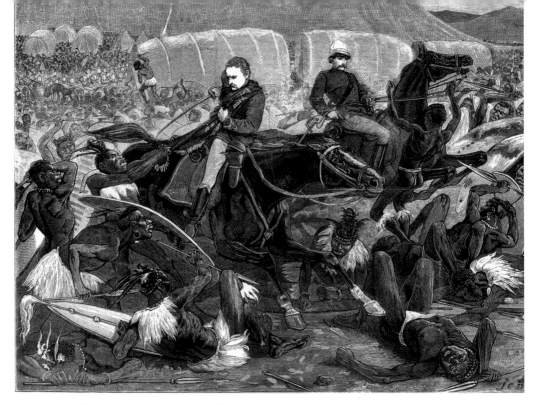

This magazine illustration of the battle of Isandhlwana captures some of the chaos and desperation of the fight. In the background loom the walls of the mountain of Isandhlwana, which the British had thought would protect them.

bag some of the enemy. They might not have been so sanguine if they had known of the extensive plans the Zulus had made for their destruction.

Interestingly enough, King Cetshwayo had decided the British could not be defeated in the traditional way and wanted to besiege them, but his generals had ignored him. They decided to use the age-old method of Shaka, but in a far grander way. At Isandhlwana, the 'chest' of the bull extended an incredible eight kilometres. As these main troops began to run at the British positions at a slow speed, the younger and faster men who made up the horns began their encirclement. Here, too, there was a refinement: the Zulu commanders sent out their left horn in plain sight of the British defenders, but kept the right horn hidden in the distance. It slipped behind the mountain of Isandhlwana, and the defenders knew nothing of its existence until the Zulus fell upon the wagon trains at their rear, slaughtering everyone in sight.

The British, who were familiar with the 'horns of the bull' tactic, but had not thought that it could be employed on such a vast scale, fought valiantly, beating off wave after wave of Zulus until their overextended line was simply overwhelmed. After two hours, almost the entire British contingent—1,300 officers and men—had died, along with hundreds of black auxiliaries. About fifty-five British troops managed to escape, most of them wearing blue coats, since, for some reason, King Cetshwayo had told his men to concentrate on killing British soldiers wearing red coats. Up to three thousand Zulu warriors lay dead among them.

BRITAIN FINDS AN ANSWER

The Anglo–Zulu War lasted six months but was as savage as it was brief. Immediately after Isandhlwana, the Zulus attacked British forces camped nearby at Rorke's Drift (a shallow river crossing) but these soldiers, forewarned, had barricaded themselves and were able to slaughter the Zulus, who advanced in wave after wave, with superior firepower. Finally, at the battle of Ulundi that July, the British army formed a hollow square, supported by artillery and Gatling guns, and sent twelve thousand Zulus reeling back, having finally discovered a way to defeat the 'horns of the bull': by firing a vast amount of ammunition—in this case, an estimated thirty-five thousand rounds.

The war cost the Zulus their nation and ten thousand lives. Afterwards, under British administration, they endured misery and chaos: civil war, famine and disease. There was just one small consolation: the Zulus could take pride in the fact that they had handed the British their worst defeat in Africa and one of their worst defeats of the colonial era.

THE AMMUNITION BOXES

The British defeat at Isandhlwana was almost certainly due to the Zulus' brilliant use of their 'horns of the bull' strategy, but for over a century, some British historians, unwilling to admit that British units could be devastated in such a fashion by an indigenous army, have sought to find another explanation.

One reason cited is the Mark V ammunition box. Cartridges for the British Martini-Henry rifle came in a long, sturdy, wooden box lined with tin and bound on each side with two copper straps, each held in place by nine screws. For reasons to do with bureaucratic bean-counting, only one screwdriver was supplied to each battalion. At Isandhlwana, this meant that the bulky ammunition boxes had to be slowly and laboriously unscrewed, while Zulu bullets and spears rained all around. Because of this, British forces ran out of ammunition and the Zulus were able to overwhelm them. Evidence of desperate attempts to pry open ammunition boxes with bayonets was found after the battle.

Other writers suggest that there was no shortage of ammunition at Isandhlwana. For one thing, they claim, the new, improved Mark VI box was in use, which could be much more easily opened by sliding a wooden tongue. Still other writers say that there had to be plenty of ammunition present: the Zulu victors themselves spoke of the British firing until they were overwhelmed. The damage to the ammunition boxes may have occurred when Zulus attempted to break them open after the battle, having armed themselves with captured British rifles.

GHOSTLY RETREAT: THE JAPANESE WITHDRAWAL FROM KISKA, 1943

DURING THE PACIFIC ISLAND FIGHTING OF WORLD WAR II, THE JAPANESE GAINED A well-deserved reputation for never retreating without a fight to the death. Even when completely surrounded on some desperate battle-torn atoll, with no chance whatsoever of finding their way out, Japanese troops routinely killed themselves before withdrawing or giving up. This is why it is all the more surprising to learn that in 1943 the Japanese initiated one of the most brilliant tactical withdrawals of the entire war: six thousand soldiers of the Japanese Imperial Army stole away so quietly from the island of Kiska, in the Aleutian chain off Alaska, that American forces subsequently bombed the uninhabited island for two whole weeks, mounted a full-scale invasion with thirty-five thousand troops and fought a pitched battle—against each other—that resulted in hundreds of casualties.

As with many successful unconventional tactical manoeuvres, the Japanese took their enemy's expectations and turned them on their head. And, since the episode occurred in the Aleutians, they also had a little help from the weather.

NO PLACE TO FIGHT A WAR

Even for those who love wilderness, salt air and mountains, the Aleutian archipelago can seem a godforsaken place. The islands stretch in a semicircle for 1,600 kilometres across the Bering Sea from the southwestern tip of Alaska all the way to within fifty kilometres of Siberia's Kamchatka Peninsula. Closest to Alaska are the bigger islands of Unimak and Unalaska (with its port at Dutch Harbor); furthest into the ocean are the tiny islands of Attu and Kiska.

The Aleutians—the name comes probably from the Aleut Indian word *aliat*, or island— may have formed the land-bridge by which some of the earliest peoples occupied North America. The first European to come across the islands was Alexei Chirikov, a Russian captain temporarily separated from Vitus Bering's 1741 expedition to Alaska. Bering himself landed on several of the islands in the sea that would later bear his name, before finally becoming marooned in the Commander Islands off the Kamchatka Peninsula and dying there.

For the next hundred years or so, the Aleutians were populated mainly by Siberian seal hunters and Aleut natives. Even after the United States bought Alaska from Russia in 1867, they were visited by few people. Hardy travellers who did venture there found rocky and treeless expanses towered over by dead volcanoes (fifty-seven in the archipelago in all) and drenched by almost constant rain—the Aleutians receive the greatest amount of rain-fall in the United States, with Unalaska, for example, having 250 days of rain a year. A low-pressure system is almost permanently in place over the islands, covering them with dense fogs that hug ground and ocean. And when it isn't foggy or rainy, the wind howls, hard—160 kilometres per hour is fairly commonplace.

By any standards, the Aleutians are a tough place to fight a war, but by the late 1930s, with both the Japanese and American military sure that conflict was imminent, it looked like they would soon become a battleground. From the Japanese perspective, they were the closest bit

of America to Japan. The Japanese had been spying on the Aleutians for years in the 1930s, using 'fishing' fleets that took soundings of harbours and charted shorelines. If they could use the Aleutians as stepping-stones to invade and gain a foothold on mainland Alaska, they would only be a three-hour flight from Seattle and its massive Boeing bomber plant. They could also use Alaska as a base from which to strike at Russia, just across the Bering Strait.

Despite being aware of this threat, the Americans did little to fortify the Aleutians, though they did have small garrisons on Attu and Kiska, and airstrips and naval facilities on eastern islands including Unimak

Fleet Admiral Isoroku Yamamoto, the Japanese commander whose plan for the Pacific War determined the course of conflict in the Aleutian Islands.

and Unalaska, which were closer to the mainland and easier to supply. After the attack on Pearl Harbor on 7 December 1941, however, most of America's attention was focused on the South Pacific and East Asia—even more so after the battle of the Coral Sea in May of 1942, which saw the Americans lose two aircraft carriers to the Japanese Imperial Navy. At this high point in Japanese fortunes, Admiral Isoroku Yamamoto was planning the coup de grace against the American navy, a top-secret plan known as the 'MI Operation'. The Combined Imperial Fleet would sortie to the vicinity of Midway Island in the Central Pacific, to destroy the remaining American carriers. At the same time, a large Japanese invasion force would head for the Aleutians, to threaten the United States. When the Americans realised this, they would leave their bases and race for the North Pacific—at which point Yamamoto would intercept them near Midway and destroy them.

THE TIDE TURNS AT MIDWAY

The question for Admiral Chester Nimitz, commander in chief of American naval forces in the Pacific, was, where would it do the most good to place his diminished naval forces. Dividing them would give him almost no chance of defeating Yamamoto at Midway, but leaving the Aleutians undefended would permit a Japanese invasion of Alaska and cut off important American shipping lanes in the Bering Sea. In the end, Nimitz opted for a compromise that would shape the course of the fifteen-month-long campaign in the Aleutians: he would send a small force there, just large enough to delay the Japanese, while he concentrated most of his navy, including his two remaining aircraft carriers, at Midway.

So began the most momentous few days in the history of the Pacific War. On 4 June, the Americans and Japanese clashed at Midway, in a large-scale naval action that turned out to be a disastrous defeat for Yamamoto—he lost all four of his aircraft carriers along with three hundred planes and over three thousand Japanese lives. The day before, the Japanese navy had approached the Aleutian Islands in force, bringing two aircraft carriers, six heavy cruisers, a screen of submarines and destroyers, and troop transports containing two and a half thousand Japanese marines.

The commander of the North Pacific Fleet was Admiral Boshiro Hosogaya. During the preliminary phase of his attack, he sent planes off to bomb Dutch Harbor, the main American base on Unalaska Island, causing considerable damage. But he subsequently received dispatches from Yamamoto describing the disastrous Japanese defeat at Midway; Yamamoto ordered Hosogaya and his carriers to steam south to protect the withdrawal of the battered Japanese fleet. Then, almost immediately, Yamamoto countermanded these orders; he had realised that even a small success, like the occupation of the Aleutian

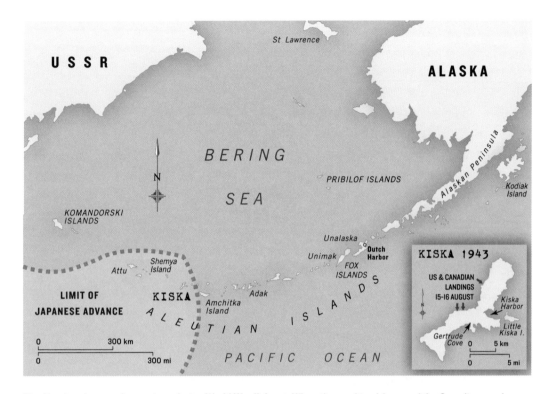

The Aleutian theatre of operations during World War II. Inset: When the combined forces of the Canadians and Americans attacked Kiska in August 1943, they were met with one of the biggest surprises of the war.

Islands, was needed now. So he ordered Hosogaya to occupy the islands furthest from the range of the American bombers based in Dutch Harbor and Unimak: Attu and Kiska.

THE FORGOTTEN WAR

The Japanese marines easily took Attu and Kiska—the former had no American forces, the latter only a small group of sailors manning a radio outpost. For the first time, Japanese forces were officially occupying U.S. soil. For the Japanese people—who were not told of the defeat at Midway—this was a momentous victory. For the Americans, it created, coming after more Japanese I-boat submarine attacks on the West Coast, a serious threat to national morale: if the Japanese had been destroyed at Midway, what were they doing in Alaska, and sending submarines to bomb coastal cities with impunity?

There were 2,600 Japanese troops on Attu and 6,000 on Kiska, but at first the war in the Aleutians was one of savage bomber attacks and fighter encounters, as each side sought to cripple the other, the Japanese forces flying east from Kiska and the Americans flying west from Dutch Harbor. Horseshoe-shaped Kiska Harbor bristled with anti-aircraft emplacements that made bombing runs there as perilous as any that occurred in the European theatre.

But, with the invasion of North Africa then taking place and battles raging in the Solomon Islands, the Aleutian front was quickly forgotten, and both sides suffered privations as a result. Supplies, including winter weather gear, had to be scrounged; fishing and hunting were permitted to supplement rations. The Japanese troops were perhaps better prepared, having warmer footwear; some of them even spent their spare time skiing. On Kiska, they lived in a huge underground base, to protect them from bombers: they also built three hospitals, a dental clinic and a telephone switchboard.

Gradually, however, the Americans built up their forces for a planned invasion of Attu, which took place eleven months after the Japanese occupied the island. On 11 May 1943, U.S. troops landed on the frozen island, expecting a three-day-long battle. It ended up taking three weeks. Japanese resistance was ferocious, finishing with a fierce banzai attack that caught the Americans by surprise. Of the 2,600 Japanese, only 28 survived. The Americans suffered 3,800 casualties, including 500 killed. Proportionate to the forces involved, Attu would end up being America's second most costly battle during the Pacific War in terms of loss of lives, the bloody assault on Iwo Jima being the first.

PLANNING THE WITHDRAWAL

The battle of Attu convinced American planners that they had not taken the Japanese forces in the Aleutians seriously enough, so when they planned for the invasion of Kiska, they allotted thirty thousand American troops and five thousand Canadians to the attack—more than twice as many as had landed on Attu—and set the date for mid-August.

The only problem was, the Japanese weren't planning on being there. In the summer of 1943, after the invasion of Attu, Aleutian-based bombers began raiding Japanese bases in the Kuril Islands, particularly on the fortress island of Paramushiro (now Russian-controlled Paramushir). The Kurils guarded the northernmost approach to Japan, and the Japanese high command became convinced that forces on Kiska would be better deployed there.

But how to get them off Kiska? The Americans were blockading the island and bombing it daily—it would only be a matter of time before they invaded. The Japanese began sending I-boats to Kiska, and eventually managed to evacuate about six hundred soldiers, but this was dangerous: the American fleet located three of the submarines and destroyed them, killing three hundred Japanese troops. Time was running out. Finally, Vice Admiral Shiro Kawase, by then in charge of Japan's Northern Pacific forces, concocted a daring plan. Back on Paramushiro, he put together an evacuation force consisting of three cruisers, eleven destroyers and a refuelling tanker. 'Taking advantage of dense fog', he wrote, he would 'evacuate all men [from Kiska] simultaneously'.

Fortunately, by this time in the war, the Japanese had changed their naval communications codes, so that the Americans, who had previously broken the top-secret Japanese ciphers, did not hear of this plan. The Japanese commander on Kiska, who had been preparing for the death of himself and all his men, was instructed that a rescue fleet would soon be arriving.

AN INVISIBLE MANOEUVRE

On 21 July, the Japanese evacuation fleet steamed south, making a wide circle below Kiska to evade American forces and planes. Reaching their assigned coordinates eight hundred kilometres south of Kiska, the ships waited for fog—for only under a thick cloak of cloud could they possibly approach the Aleutians, which swarmed with hostile American shipping preparing to invade the island.

On 26 July, the Japanese finally got the weather they needed. Vice Admiral Kawase and his fleet entered a large fog bank and moved with it to a point eighty kilometres off Kiska. Their luck held and the Americans failed to spot them, though the Japanese lost five of their ships in a multiple-ship collision in the fog, the damaged vessels being forced to limp back home. On the morning of 27 July, the weather worsened. Deciding he did not have enough time to wait for nightfall—the Americans were bombing Kiska furiously—Kawase sent the Japanese fleet steaming into Kiska Harbor.

The five thousand or so Japanese soldiers on Kiska were ready. They had destroyed gun emplacements, booby-trapped their underground facilities and scrawled obscene messages

---

TAKING THE WAR TO AMERICA

The invasion of the Aleutian Islands wasn't the only time during World War II when the Japanese attacked North America. While many people have heard about the German submarine incursions against America's East Coast, it is far less well known that a Japanese I-boat submarine succeeded in torpedoing and sinking an American freighter at the entrance to Los Angeles harbour in January 1942. A month later, another Japanese submarine surfaced outside Santa Barbara, California, and hurled twenty-five shells into an oil refinery. Later, the Japanese came up with the idea of attaching incendiary bombs to hot-air balloons and using the jet stream to carry them to Pacific Northwest forests. The balloons never started the massive forest fires the Japanese were hoping for, but one such device did kill four curious American picnickers in Oregon, who made the mistake of picking it up.

Allied transport ships bringing troops ashore on Kiska, on 15 August 1943. It would be a further three days, during which Canadian and U.S. troops frequently shot at each other, before the Allies realised the enemy had departed.

for the Americans on the walls. Now, in one of the most brilliant manoeuvres of World War II, two Japanese cruisers took off about 2,400 of the soldiers and six destroyers carried off the rest. By 7.30 pm, the evacuation had been completed—without a single injury. With the fog lifting, the Japanese fleet sailed at full speed out of Kiska. Four days later, Vice Admiral Kawase arrived, undetected by the Americans, in Paramushiro.

For two weeks before the 15 August date set for the invasion of Kiska, the Americans battered the island with hundreds of thousands of kilograms of high explosives. They even dropped leaflets calling on the Japanese to surrender—leaflets that fluttered down on a deserted island. Finally, on the morning of 15 August, thousands of American and Canadian troops stormed ashore in thick fog (with more following the next day). Booby traps exploded and jittery troops fired at movements in the fog. Other troops fired back. For days, small fire-fights occurred all over the island. Although many American commanders suspected from the start that the Japanese had left, others thought they were buried in the underground bunkers and needed to be dug out. In the three days before the Allies realised that no one was at home but themselves, over three hundred Americans and Canadians were wounded by friendly fire. Four Canadians and seventeen American soldiers died.

In a war that was now singularly devoid of victories for the Japanese, the retreat from Kiska was something they could finally point to with satisfaction, since they had tied up thousands of American troops and scores of American ships. For a people renowned for fighting to the death, it was a rare kind of victory.

- -

THE BATTLE OF THE PIPS: FOR THE BIRDS?

At about one o'clock in the morning of 26 July 1943—the day the Japanese evacuation fleet began its approach to Kiska—a U.S. naval attack force was returning from a ferocious, pre-invasion shelling of the island when the cruisers and the battleships simultaneously picked up seven 'pips', or bright spots, on their radar screens.

The pips were twenty-five kilometres away and moving towards Kiska, and the Americans assumed that this was the expected Japanese relief force. Immediately, they opened up in a stunning display of firepower that rent the night sky, continuing to fire until the last pip disappeared from the radar screens. They sent catapult planes into the sky to search for wreckage, but even in the clear moonlight none was found. Nor was any discovered the next day.

So what were the Americans firing at? It certainly wasn't the Japanese, who were nowhere near the area. For a long time, the U.S. Navy recorded the 'Battle of the Pips', as it became known unofficially, as a radar malfunction. But in his definitive book on the Aleutian campaign, *The Thousand Mile War*, Brian Garfield may have come up with the real answer. In the 1990s, he was contacted by an Alaskan captain who pointed out that the 'pips' were almost certainly flocks of dusky shearwaters, or muttonbirds. These birds migrate between Alaska and New Zealand. Summering in the Aleutians, they fly low in flocks of thousands, looking for plankton. The more primitive World War II radar would have 'read' these flocks as solid objects. Once the flocks found a good feeding ground, they would have settled onto the water and gradually spread out, causing the 'pips' to fade away.

PART TWO
WHO DARES WINS
courage, boldness and the element of surprise

'Screw your courage to
the sticking place,
and we'll not fail.'

Shakespeare, Macbeth, 1605

THE SNATCH: FRANCISCO PIZARRO KIDNAPS INCA KING ATAHUALLPA, 1532

THAT NOVEMBER DAY IN 1532, IN THE INCA TOWN OF CAJAMARCA, THE ODDS were laughable: one hundred and sixty-eight Spanish conquistadors against eighty thousand Inca troops. True, the Spanish had sixty-two horses, guns, and swords made of steel, all three of which the Inca—armed with wooden clubs, slings, bows and arrows, blowguns and spears—had never before encountered. And the conquistadors, whatever else one might think of men who seek to destroy civilisations for the sake of ready gold, were brave. But this was too much, even for them. As the Inca ruler Atahuallpa—considered a god by his subjects— approached with his special guard of seven thousand handpicked warriors, the Spaniards, as one of their chroniclers recorded, 'made water without knowing it, out of sheer terror'.

But the conquistador leader, Francisco Pizarro, second cousin to the more famous Hernán Cortés, conqueror of the Aztecs a decade before, had a trick up his sleeve. Pizarro was illiterate, completely untrustworthy and ruthlessly ambitious, but he was also cunning. In such a situation, the only tactic that made any sense from the point of view of the greatly outnumbered Spaniards was kidnapping, or, more colloquially, a snatch. In this case, the snatchee would have to be Atahuallpa himself, ruler of an empire that covered thirty-two degrees of latitude, making it, in 1532, the largest empire on earth.

Perhaps it would have been unwise for Francisco Pizarro to ponder just how large a chunk of the world he and his few score men were about to bite off—there are more pressing issues to deal with when you are outnumbered almost five hundred to one. But his actions would have larger consequences than most kidnappings, consequences which would include the decline of one empire and the rise of another.

Opposite: Spanish soldier and explorer Francisco Pizarro (1475–1541), in a sixteenth-century portrait. Like his cousin Hernán Cortés, Pizarro conquered an entire empire through ruthless use of kidnapping as a weapon of war.

FABLED CITIES OF GOLD

After landing on an island in the Caribbean in 1492, Christopher Columbus thought he had discovered a new route to the Indies. He had not. But he had found a world that would vastly enrich the Spanish masters for whom he sailed, putting them a step up in their race for global domination against the Portuguese and English. The first Spanish island possessions in the Americas—Cuba, Hispaniola and Puerto Rico—did not deliver up much in the way of the gold that the Europeans treasured, nor did Panama, settled by its discoverer, Vasco Núñez de Balboa, in 1512. But rumours of vast golden cities in the Americas persisted; two of the favourite legends were of the Seven Cities of Cibola, thought to exist in North America, and El Dorado in South America, where even the fountains in the plazas were said to be made of the precious metal. The conquistadors—meaning 'conquerors', the adventurers and soldiers of fortune who peopled the Spanish colonies—were, almost to a man, desperate to be the first to enter such a city. And in 1521, one of their number, Hernán Cortés, actually did so, conquering the fabulous city of the Aztecs in what is now Mexico, and enriching himself and Spain immeasurably.

CORTÉS CONQUERS MEXICO

Eleven years before Francisco Pizarro pulled his epoch-making snatch, his second cousin, Hernán Cortés, did much the same thing. A hot-headed, often intemperate conquistador, Cortés led an expedition from Cuba to Mexico in April of 1519, and landed near present-day Veracruz. Word soon got back to Montezuma II, ruler of the Aztecs' capital city of Tenochtitlán. Montezuma had one hundred thousand Aztec warriors at his command; Cortés's forces numbered five hundred. But Montezuma, like most Aztecs, was extremely superstitious and may have thought Cortés was the mythical god-king Quetzalcoatl, who, prophesy had it, would return to claim his throne in the Aztec year Reed-1—which happened to be 1519.

Cortés marched through Mexico, allying himself with the enemies of the Aztecs, and arrived in Tenochtitlán in November. Montezuma made the mistake of inviting Cortés and his men into the city, at which point Cortés kidnapped the Aztec leader. Montezuma was later stoned to death by his own people after Cortés forced him to address them from a balcony (at least, that is the Spanish version of events—it is also possible Cortés had him executed).

After two more years of intense fighting, Tenochtitlán fell. A band of five hundred men had defeated an entire empire thanks to modern weaponry, extraordinary daring and the rigidity of the hierarchical Aztecs, who had trouble acting independently when their all-powerful ruler was removed. Though Cortés defeated a much richer empire and reaped the rewards, it could be argued that Pizarro's achievement was even greater, for the land he conquered was more remote and he received no aid from indigenous allies. Both conquests, however, were incredible, never-to-be-repeated acts of military daring-do.

Cortés's discovery—which, in a way, proved that golden cities did exist—set off a race among conquistadors to be the first to discover another one. One keen competitor was Francisco Pizarro, who was actually a rather unlikely conqueror, as it happens.

Born in 1475 in Trujillo, Spain, he was the illegitimate son of an infantry captain. Neither his father nor his mother wanted much to do with him—he was apparently never schooled and so was illiterate all his life. By the time he was twenty-two, he had sailed to Hispaniola, where he made a living herding pigs—the basis for many of the epithets hurled at Pizarro by his enemies, who were legion (Pizarro had his cousin Hernán's smarts and reckless courage, but not his charm). Soon, however, Pizarro sought to enrich himself through adventure. He was with de Balboa when the latter hacked his way across the Isthmus of Panama and discovered the Pacific Ocean in 1512. He was in Panama in 1522 when another conquistador, Pascual de Andagoya, returned from the very first exploration of the shores of western South America recounting tales of an unbelievably wealthy country far to the south, called Pirú or Virú. Andagoya had become sick and returned without actually seeing this country, but the rumours were all Pizarro needed to hear. As if sensing his destiny in these fabulous tales, he made preparations to sail south.

THE LAND OF FOUR QUARTERS

The Inca Empire, tucked between the Andes and the western coast of South America and covering much of modern-day Ecuador, Peru and northern Chile, was one of the best-kept secrets of the early sixteenth century. It was a relatively new empire. The Inca tribe had taken shape around AD 1200, when a band of Indians from Lake Titicaca (on the border between present-day Bolivia and Peru) migrated south and founded the city of Qosqo (modern Cuzco) in the Andes Mountains. That the Inca thrived in this alpine environment, at heights of up to four thousand metres, where slopes averaged a steep sixty-five-per cent incline and where extremes of weather were common, was extraordinary in itself—the Inca were obviously a hardy lot. But even more impressively, beginning about 1350, they pushed their way out of their mountains, conquering neighbouring tribes, until they reached the Pacific Ocean, and then moved north and south. In a series of empire-building moves worthy of the Mongols, the Inca eventually acquired territory that stretched for four thousand kilometres, from high mountains to ocean.

In the Quechuan language of the Inca, their land was known as *Tawatinsuyu*, or 'The Land of Four Quarters', for the highly organised Inca had divided up their country into four different departments or administrative districts, all ruled by the Inca, which in Quechuan means 'lord' or 'royal person', from the capital city of Qosqo. To connect the

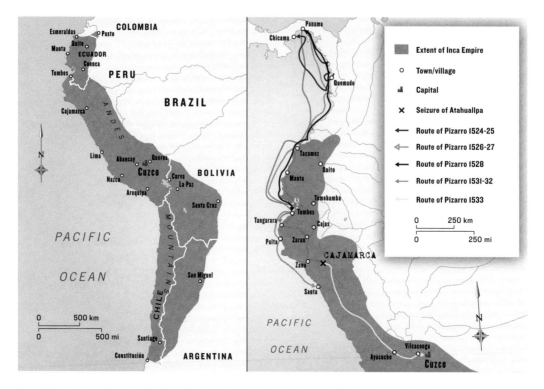

At left, the extent of the Inca Empire at its peak, prior to the arrival of the Spanish conquistadors. At right, the routes of Pizarro's four expeditions to western South America, which led him ever closer to the heart of the Inca realm.

different parts of their empire, the Inca put in forty thousand kilometres of stone roads. Everyone in the land of the Inca worked, at least part of the time, for the empire—building roads, making cloth, growing crops, mining guano on offshore islands or soldiering. The Inca ruthlessly practised relocation, moving conquered populations, where needed, from one end of the empire to the other. Some historians have even compared the Inca state to Soviet Russia: food and lodging were provided to all, but the masses were merely pawns in the games played by their rulers.

And what rulers they were. Ensconced in his fabled palace in Qosqo was the Inca himself, so all-powerful that even his bodily wastes and fingernail clippings were collected and saved by faithful retainers. He was considered immortal, which led to an Inca custom that fascinated the Spanish: whenever an Inca died—of course, he hadn't *actually* died, given his god-like status, simply shifted into an altered eternal state—his corpse was mummified. Since the Inca used sophisticated embalming methods and since the high air of Qosqo is almost perfectly dry, the mummy lived on forever. So the Inca capital was filled with mummy-corpses who ruled from their separate palaces, and had households full of relatives and retainers with their own political agendas. The place was as replete with intrigue as any Medici court, but it was all fomented by dead men. As Pizarro said: 'The greater part of the people, treasure, expenses and vices … were [sic] under the control of the dead'.

Controlled by the dead or not, the Inca world was a powerful one. By 1530, the empire had been at its fullest extent for about one hundred years. And then pale-skinned men arrived, unbidden, on its northern borders.

ENTER PIZARRO

Francisco Pizarro was nothing if not dogged. He made three separate attempts to reach the land of the Inca in 1524, 1526 and 1528. Each time, he and his expedition were turned back by various hardships, including hunger, skirmishes with hostile tribes and incredibly arduous terrain. But on his third expedition, Pizarro managed to land briefly at Tumbes, in what is now northern Peru; there, he saw local Indians wearing decorations of gold and silver and learned that the Inca Empire was a reality. Pizarro sailed back to Panama, and from there to Spain, where he showed Inca treasures to King Charles V, especially objects of worked gold and silver. He then received a charter to 'extend the empire of Castile'.

In 1530, Pizarro set forth with 168 men on his last expedition to the Andes. But when he arrived in Tumbes, he found the town empty and desolate. Tragically for the Inca (but quite luckily for Pizarro), the empire had experienced two plagues: one was smallpox, which ravaged Inca civilisation horribly in the mid- to late 1520s; the other was civil war. The great Inca ruler Huayna Capac had died in 1525, possibly of smallpox. Unfortunately, he had not appointed a successor. So his sons Huáscar and Atahuallpa began a bloody war to decide who would become Inca. In the summer of 1532, just before Pizarro and his men showed up, Huáscar and Atahuallpa fought a decisive battle in which Atahuallpa triumphed, leaving thousands dead on the battlefield. Huáscar was captured and sent as a captive to Qosqo.

Because of this great battle, Atahuallpa and his eighty-thousand-strong army were still in the vicinity of Tumbes when word of the arrival of a group of strange, pale-skinned men reached them. Atahuallpa was not overly concerned about such a small force, but the men were a curiosity he decided he wanted to see, and so he sent word that they were to meet him in the town of Cajamarca. Had Atahuallpa been in his high capital city of Qosqo, it is possible he might not have been so curious. It is also possible that, deep in the heart of the Inca Empire, Pizarro might not have attempted what he did.

RENDEZVOUS AT CAJAMARCA

When Pizarro and his men received word that the Inca wanted to see them, they journeyed the short distance to Cajamarca, and there spent a nervous night awaiting his arrival. It was almost certainly during this restless evening that Pizarro came up with the idea of kidnapping Atahuallpa. In this, he may have been inspired by the example of his cousin Cortés, who had seized the Mexican ruler Montezuma II in a similar fashion. But Pizarro's situation, as he recognised, was even more precarious than Cortés's, as he didn't have as many men, nor the Indian allies his cousin had recruited along the way. Pizarro warned his men that the slightest show of fear would cause the Inca to slaughter them. It was apparent to him that, in the face of the overwhelming number of Inca and with no prospect of any backup, the only way to turn the situation to their advantage was by a sudden, surprising and forceful move. And he set about devising a trap in which Atahuallpa himself would be caught.

Next day, 16 November 1532, Atahuallpa, brimming with confidence after his victory, showed up with his personal bodyguard of seven thousand Inca warriors. He was carried into the square on a litter decorated with jewels and feathers, surrounded by eighty nobles who were his personal retainers. Other retainers swept the plaza before the litter, while the

SMALLPOX, EUROPE'S SECRET WEAPON

A great aid to the European invasion of the Americas in the early sixteenth century was the dread disease of smallpox, against which the indigenous populations had absolutely no immune defences.

In December 1518, there was a relatively small outbreak of smallpox on the island of Hispaniola. The disease was carried to Central America, probably by Spanish soldiers or sailors, in 1520, where it decimated the Mayan population then spread north and south. It arrived in Tenochtitlán, capital city of the Aztecs, in 1521, in time to kill much of the population and hasten the Spanish victory.

Smallpox appeared in the high Andes Mountains in 1524 or 1525, and swept through the Inca like wildfire. At this point, the Inca had not yet even met a European and could have had no idea where the plague was coming from. They quickly fell ill with smallpox's characteristic high fever, vomiting and leaking blisters, and hundreds of thousands died. Smallpox was to revisit the Inca four more times in the sixteenth century, each time taking a devastating toll, as it was to do all over the Americas through to the late eighteenth century.

Europeans arriving after the epidemics greatly under-estimated the number of indigenous people who had dwelt there. Today, it is clear that there were far more people in North and South America before 1492 than previously supposed, and that smallpox and other diseases had killed most of them before Europeans arrived—up to ninety-five per cent according to some estimates.

During the surprise Spanish assault on the Inca in the village of Cajamarca, it was Pizarro himself who wrenched Atahuallpa from his litter—stunning the Inca leader's retinue—and then dragged him into captivity.

bodyguards roared songs in a language none of the conquistadors could understand. They understood the show of power, however, and were terrified, some of them even losing control of their bladders at this point, as one of their number recorded.

Cajamarca had a long central plaza surrounded on three sides by empty royal buildings. The Inca crowded the square, filling it to overflowing, while the Spanish lined the buildings on all three sides. From the beginning, the conquistadors sought to provoke Atahuallpa. Knowing that the Inca were afraid of horses—in fact, they thought them some mutated form of human being—the conquistadors pranced their steeds around the edges of the square, badly frightening many of the locals.

A friar, Father Vicente Valverde, who accompanied the conquistadors, was sent out by Pizarro to speak with Atahuallpa through an interpreter. He told the Inca that he must give

In this nineteenth-century Mexican painting of the funeral of Atahuallpa, an impassive Francisco Pizarro (second right) looks on as priests administer the last rites and conquistadors restrain weeping relatives of the Inca.

up his cherished beliefs and become a Christian. When Atahuallpa asked the friar what gave him the right to ask this of him, Valverde handed him his Christian breviary, his book of daily prayers. Atahuallpa held it to his head, listened for a moment and then snorted. 'This book does not talk to me', he said, and he threw it on the ground. Whether Pizarro had actually planned this little scenario with Valverde or not, it played right into Spanish hands.

Father Valverde shouted that the Inca had insulted the Christian faith. At which point, responding to a signal prearranged by Pizarro, a trumpet blew, guns fired, a small cannon belched flame and the conquistadors charged from beneath the shelter of the buildings in the square. These unfamiliar sights and sounds sent the Inca into a panic. They trampled over each other in an effort to escape, smothering some of their number and leaving mounds of dead in the plaza. A slaughter ensued. The Spaniards hacked away with their steel swords and rode down the Inca with their horses. Not only were the Inca shocked by this brutal onslaught, but most of the warriors present had come with only ceremonial arms and were not able to defend themselves effectively.

The Spanish conquistadors killed thousands. Pathetically, the Inca clustered around the litter bearing Atahuallpa, trying to protect him as they were killed one by one. Some of them carried the litter on their shoulders, even after having had their arms hacked off. Finally, Pizarro himself dragged Atahuallpa off the litter and made him captive. The immense Inca army stationed just outside the town joined the panicked bodyguards in flight after their ruler was snatched. One Spanish observer described the countryside around Cajamarca as being blanketed for kilometres in all directions with retreating, terrified Inca.

THE END OF AN EMPIRE

At first, the Spanish treated Atahuallpa well, giving him food and allowing certain of his retainers to see him. After a few days, he finally understood that what these men wanted was gold. To the Inca and his people, this was absurd. Gold decorated their shrines and the statues of their gods, but had no value aside from the fact that it was pleasing to the eye. (The Inca essentially had no economy and did not use gold or silver as barter.) So Atahuallpa promised the Spaniards an entire room full of gold—seven metres by five metres by more than two metres high—and another two rooms filled with silver, if they would let him go.

To this, Pizarro acquiesced. From December to May, cartloads of gold and silver made their way to Cajamarca, as the Inca stripped sacred shrines of the precious metals. While this was going on, Atahuallpa schemed. He sent word to his men to kill Huáscar, who was still a captive, and any of his other brothers who remained alive—he was trying to make sure that no one would conspire against him while he was imprisoned. Pizarro, in the meantime, waited for the gold to arrive and developed his own strategy. He familiarised himself with Inca society and politics and conspired with Tupac Huallpa, an ambitious half-brother of Atahuallpa. If Tupac Huallpa would take an oath of fealty to Spain, Pizarro would have Atahuallpa killed and support Tupac Huallpa as the new Inca. This would leave Pizarro with a friendly Inca rather than one who would almost certainly scheme revenge.

The deal was made, and Atahuallpa's fate was sealed. Pizarro then offered him a choice: he could either be burned to death at the stake as a heretic, or garrotted—the latter a mercy that would be given him only if he converted to Christianity. Faced with the fate of being burned, which would deny him immortal life as a mummy, Atahuallpa allowed himself to be baptised and was then garrotted in May of 1533.

With the malleable Tupac Huallpa installed as the new Inca, Pizarro then marched on Qosqo and assumed control of the region for Spain. With a little assistance from smallpox, which had greatly weakened the empire, Pizarro had done what seemed impossible: he had destroyed an entire culture and taken over a nation of five million people with a force of just 168 men.

The Inca would continue to resist Spanish rule through a guerilla war that lasted forty years, but the final outcome was never in doubt. Pizarro grew wealthy, but never gave up scheming—in 1541, he was shot dead in Lima by the son of a conquistador he had betrayed. As he died, Pizarro reached out a trembling finger and drew a cross on the floor in his own blood.

LES SAUVAGES' SECRET WEAPON: SAMUEL DE CHAMPLAIN DEFEATS THE IROQUOIS, 1609

'A BOUNDLESS VISION GROWS BEFORE US; AN UNTAMED CONTINENT; VAST wastes of forest verdure; mountains silent in primeval sleep; river, lake and glittering pool; wilderness oceans mingling with the sky.' Thus the great nineteenth-century American historian Francis Parkman described his vision of the country that opened up for French adventurers in the earliest days of European exploration of what was then called New France, and is now Canada. Parkman saw the beauty of this wild country with a romantic eye, but he was not blind to its dangers—for all its glory, New France was a 'churlish wilderness, [with] a pitiless climate', where, at any moment 'disease, misery and death' would fell the unwary.

New France was inhabited by Indians, whom the French invariably called *les sauvages*—'the savages', 'the uncivilised ones'. These 'savages' were populous and had made their home there for centuries. When the French under their great explorer and empire-builder Samuel de Champlain came upon the scene, the Indians of what is now eastern Canada—the Huron, Micmac and Algonquin peoples, among others—were engaged in a bitter war with the Iroquois of present-day New York State—a group of allied tribes, including the Cayuga, Oneida and Mohawk, who all spoke Iroquoian languages and some of whom had formed the so-called Confederacy of Five Nations.

In one of those marriages of convenience that so often marked early North American history, the Canadian Indians and Samuel de Champlain joined forces. Champlain, hoping to win the Indians' favour and thereby get them to guide him deeper into the interior of the continent, offered to help them defeat their enemies using his powerful firearms. The Indians, realising the potentially devastating impact of such weapons on the Iroquois—who had not seen white men, let alone faced their guns—agreed. And so, on a July day in 1609, they delivered Champlain, hidden in the bottom of a canoe, covered with animal skins, to the site of a small battlefield on the shores of one of the 'wilderness oceans' Parkman wrote about, and North American history changed forever.

AN INHOSPITABLE LAND

The less hospitable northern part of the American continent took longer to feel the colonising touch of Europeans than the Caribbean, Mexico or South America. Although the Viking Leif Eriksson sailed from Greenland to discover Newfoundland in about AD 1000, it was a long time before John Cabot voyaged back there to claim it for England, in 1497. For decades after that, French and Portuguese fishermen came to harvest cod in the teeming coastal waters of Newfoundland, but never stayed more than a few weeks at a time.

In 1524, Giovanni de Verrazano, in the employ of the French king, voyaged as far as Newfoundland, but it was not until the three voyages of Jacques Cartier, from 1534 to 1541, that France made a real effort to build a colony that rivalled those of its enemy Spain, to the south. Cartier sailed along the St Lawrence River as far as present-day Quebec, where he twice tried, and failed, to build a permanent settlement. Although a great explorer, he became obsessed with finding something called the Kingdom of Saguenay, a mythical land far to the north filled with gold and diamonds, and made a fool of himself in the process. His other signal failure was to instill hatred in the hearts of the Indians, who could have been his allies, by kidnapping some of them and taking them back to France. When Samuel de Champlain arrived in the wilderness of New France some sixty years later, he vowed not to make the same mistakes as Cartier.

Samuel de Champlain was born around 1570, in Brouage, a seaport town on the west coast of France, south of Brittany. Relatively little is known of his early life, and the first

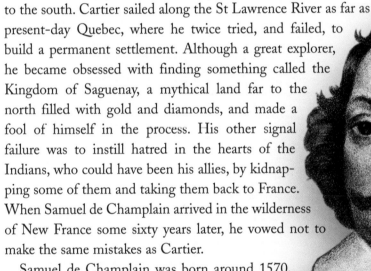

A skilled sailor and talented writer, Samuel de Champlain gained lasting fame for founding the city of Quebec and exploring the Great Lakes.

record of him is as a soldier fighting in the French army of King Henri IV against the Spanish, in 1594. When the war ended four years later, Champlain signed on as a sailor with ships plying their trade in the West Indies. After at least six transatlantic voyages, he emerged a well-rounded figure: a brilliant sailor who wrote the widely read *Treatise on Seamanship*; a chart-maker so exacting that his maps can be followed today; an artist who sketched with proficiency all the extraordinary sights of his long life; and a man who, though a warrior, was far more compassionate than most of his contemporaries to the indigenous peoples he encountered.

In 1603, Champlain sailed with a French company with instructions from King Henri IV to develop the existing fur trade with the Micmac, or Montagnais, Indians. Between 1604 and 1606, Champlain made several more voyages to New France with fur-trading groups chartered by the king to form monopolies. Given his own ship, he explored the American coastline as far south as Cape Cod, in present-day Massachusetts. He made charts, which he illustrated, sought places useful for trade or settlement, and, above all, studied the native people that he met.

- -

THE CONFEDERACY OF FIVE NATIONS

The alliance of eastern woodlands Indians known as the Confederacy of Five Nations was one the most extraordinary of Indian organisations. The five tribes that made up the confederacy were the Iroquoian-speaking Seneca, Mohawk, Oneida, Onondaga and Cayuga, who roamed most of present-day central New York State, south as far as Pennsylvania's Susquehanna River, and west to the Lake Erie region of Ohio.

The confederacy was an early form of democracy, governed by the Grand League of the Iroquois, at which each tribe was represented and where absolute unanimity of opinion was required for every action the league took. The league passed laws, punished the guilty, settled disputes and made decisions on whether or not the tribes would go to war. However, in typical Indian fashion, the individual tribes in the confederacy could, in the long run, follow their own path and decide not to take actions dictated by the league. The Indians of the confederacy did not call themselves Iroquois—which may be derived from a Huron insult meaning 'black snake'—but instead referred to themselves as the *Haudenosaunee*, which meant 'people of the long house', for they normally dwelled in communal bark houses, each containing five fires and five families.

Despite their advanced political system, the Iroquois were aggressive and territorial. So-called 'Mourning Wars' were fought, whereby the Iroqouis would attack and kidnap other Indians to replace Iroqouis who had died. Fighting on the side of the British, the Iroquois were able to reap the benefits of victory in the French and Indian War, but not in the War of American Independence, in which their British benefactors were defeated. After that conflict, many Iroquois headed north to Canada to take advantage of land grants from the Crown.

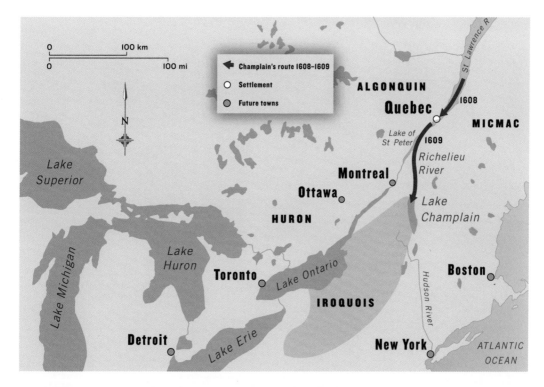

The homelands of the various Indian peoples of northeastern North America, and the route followed by Samuel de Champlain and his Indian allies to confront the Iroquois on the shores of the lake that now bears his name.

The Indians were a bundle of contradictions. The men could spend days in energetic canoeing and hunting, then might lie on their back for a week almost without moving, stuffing themselves with food until they became ill. They were incredibly obscene: their talk often resembled rough, bawdy bar banter today, and one of their favourite tricks was to stand just outside of missile range, pull down their pants and moon their enemies. Yet they were, in their own way, extraordinarily spiritual. They believed in the power of dreams and paid close attention to what those dreams seemed to foretell. For them, the wilderness was not just trees, rocks and water, but a place where good and evil spirits dwelled, into which the dead disappeared after they died, and where voices could be heard whispering of the future.

The Indians may have been uncivilised from a French point of view, but they were not stupid. They refused Champlain's entreaties to take him further into the interior, to the source of the furs they traded. A frustrated Champlain went back to France and returned to North America, in July of 1608, with a company of thirty men and another charter from the

The Quebec house of Samuel de Champlain, as sketched by the explorer himself around 1629. Champlain favoured Quebec as a site for the capital of New France because of its strategic position on the St Lawrence River.

king to seek out those elusive furs. He sailed up the St Lawrence to the site of modern-day Quebec (the name comes from the Micmac word *Kebec*, meaning 'the place where the river narrows') and built a *habitation*, a three-storey house surrounded by a moat, and tried to lay in food and crops for the winter. But, though he knew the cold weather could be severe, Champlain was unprepared for the terrible winter of 1608–09. By the time it was over, only eight of the twenty-four Frenchmen who had begun the winter there were alive, the rest dying of malnutrition and scurvy. Despite his lack of food, Champlain made it a point to feed a band of Micmac Indians who had crossed the St Lawrence on ice floes, so desperate were they to find food. The Indians were grateful for his kindness, but it was not enough to get them to help him explore westwards. Soon, however, Champlain came up with a plan.

In the spring of 1609, he offered to help the local Indians in their fight against the Iroquois if, in return, they would take him west, to the present-day Great Lakes. He pointed out to the hesitating chiefs that by employing his firearms—specifically, the arquebus, an early matchlock firearm—they could alter forever the balance of power between themselves and their traditional enemy. Finally, the chiefs, who had seen what the arquebus could do, assented.

ADVANCING ON THE IROQUOIS

In the middle of June, the Hurons and Algonquins came from further west and north to join the Micmacs and form a great force of perhaps two thousand Indians. Champlain led this army west on the river, sailing in a two-masted shallop while the Indians paddled in canoes against the St Lawrence's powerful current. They travelled through the Lake of St Peter, before finally reaching the mouth of the River des Iroquois, now known as the Richelieu River, which would take the battle force into Iroquois territory in northern New York State. Here, frustratingly, after a great feast and war dance festival that lasted two days, most of the allied Indians decided they didn't feel like fighting after all, traded some goods with their fellows and disappeared back into the woods.

Champlain proceeded anyway, but soon realised that he was faced with rapids so turbulent his shallop would never be able to traverse them. Since the ship was too heavy to portage, he sent it back to Quebec with most of his men, taking with him only two volunteers. The Indians who remained were only sixty strong, and they had twenty-four canoes among them.

A KILLING MACHINE

The weapon used by Samuel de Champlain, the arquebus, first came into general use in the early sixteenth century. Although it was a much inferior weapon to a crossbow or even a longbow in terms of accuracy, it could be fired very quickly and loaded (as Champlain loaded it) with more than one lead shot, thus giving it far more killing power than an arrow.

The arquebus was a matchlock weapon, meaning that a pan held a fuse (or match) in a lock at the breech of the gun. When the fuse was lit, powder ignited and the gun fired. The range of the arquebus was short—perhaps thirty metres or so—but it could be a devastating weapon when several thousand arquebusiers massed together to fire their weapons, as happened at the battle of Pavia in 1525, when three thousand Spanish arquebusiers defeated eight thousand French knights.

Gradually, however, the drawbacks of the arquebus began to tell—for example, you had to keep the match lit at all times in order to be ready to fire, which might give away your position at night—and, by the mid-seventeenth century, technology had moved in the direction of the musket.

Champlain emerges from among his Huron allies to fire on the Iroquois. The Iroquois would have been astonished, not only by Champlain's appearance (few of them had seen a white man) but also by the devastating impact of his weapon.

Champlain travelled with his Indian allies until he reached the vast lake that today bears his name: Lake Champlain. To the west were the snow-capped Adirondacks. Early on the morning of 29 July, as they paddled their canoes along the shores of the lake, Champlain and the Indians saw dark shapes across the water: the canoes of the Iroquois. Both sides spotted each other at the same time, and began shouting insults, trying to outdo each other with offensive references to ancestors and scatological inventions. This went on for some time, Champlain drolly noted, for all the world like 'the besiegers and besieged in a beleaguered [European] town'. Finally, representatives of both sides met and decreed that the fight would take place on the shore, in the morning.

'THE IROQUOIS WERE MUCH ASTONISHED'

When morning came, Champlain and his allies looked across the lake to see the Iroquois waiting for them, brandishing their weapons. There were perhaps a hundred of them. Although Champlain had supplied the secret weapon, it was the Hurons who furnished the battle plan. They instructed Champlain and his two French companions to lie down in the bottoms of their canoes, and covered them with furs. Then they paddled the canoes across to meet the Iroquois, who were arrayed in a small meadow on a point of land where Fort Ticonderoga—a much-contested citadel in American history—would later be built.

When the canoes landed, the Hurons and their allies leaped out and arrayed themselves in a battle line. Then, at the behest of the Hurons, Champlain arose from his covering of furs. He was wearing a doublet and long hose, over which he had placed armour consisting of a breast and back plate, and cuirasses to protect his thighs, all made of steel. On his head he wore a helmet with a white plume.

Champlain ordered his two volunteers to crawl into the woods on the side of the meadow. Then he advanced behind his allies towards the enemy. The Iroquois were armed with bows and arrows and shields made of wood and hide. Their chiefs, who wore long white feathers in their headdresses, had previously been pointed out to Champlain as prime targets by the Hurons. The Canadian Indians now parted into two groups to let Champlain through. Champlain loaded his gun with four balls of lead and moved ahead until he was only thirty metres from the enemy. In a moment redolent with drama and significance, the Iroquois, Champlain wrote later, 'halted and gazed at me and I at them'.

When he saw them make a move to draw their bows, he aimed his arquebus at the chiefs and fired. Two of the Iroquois leaders fell dead; another was mortally wounded. 'The Iroquois were much astonished', Champlain wrote, 'that two men could be killed so quickly' and that their thick shields, effective enough in warding off arrows, were no match for this flaming and explosive weapon. There was an exchange of arrows, and then Champlain's compatriots fired their arquebuses from the woods. This so dismayed the Iroquois that they turned and fled.

ONE HUNDRED AND FIFTY YEARS OF ENMITY

The shot from Samuel de Champlain's gun changed the face of warfare in North America. The Iroquois hurried to purchase arms from Dutch traders in New York. They remained not only enemies of the Hurons, Micmacs and Algonquins, but also became sworn foes of the French, as well. In the battles that would culminate in the French and Indian War of the mid-eighteenth century, the Iroquois would side with the British.

In the short term, the victory boosted the fortunes of Champlain and his Indian allies. With their help, he would subsequently explore North America as far west as the Great Lakes, pioneering a lucrative empire for France until his death in 1635. For the Hurons and their allies, the triumph was not a lasting one, but it was extremely satisfying. On the night after the battle, they took great pleasure in torturing and burning to death Iroquois prisoners. Champlain was horrified and even insisted on the right to shoot one poor captive to put him out of his misery. Undeterred, the allied Indians cut off the arms and legs of one of the Iroquois Champlain had slain in the battle and presented these grisly trophies to him—with the understanding that he would take them back to France and offer them to his king.

ATTACK IN THE EYE OF THE STORM: THE BATTLE OF QUIBERON BAY, 1759

THE YEAR 1759 HAS LONG BEEN KNOWN AS THE ANNUS MIRABILIS IN BRITISH HISTORY—the 'Year of Victories', in which Great Britain defeated its enemy France in four major battles in a two-front war, and set the stage for the creation of its global empire. None of the victories of 1759 was as remarkable as the battle of Quiberon Bay. Perhaps the only large-scale naval battle in the age of sail to take place in gale-force winds, Quiberon was initiated and dominated by a determined British admiral named Sir Edward Hawke. Demonstrating amazing courage and incredible seamanship, Hawke raced his twenty-three ships straight through an Atlantic storm to shatter a French fleet that was about to partake in an invasion of the British Isles. Hawke's dashing victory not only kept Britain safe, but also helped ensure the country's ultimate triumph in the Seven Years' War.

A WAR ON TWO FRONTS

The Seven Years' War began in 1756 and centred on two locales: western Europe, where Frederick the Great of Prussia, with help from his ally, King George II of Great Britain, fought against France, Austria, Russia and Sweden; and North America, where Britain was locked in a struggle with France for domination of rich colonies in Canada, New England and the West Indies, a struggle that became known as the French and Indian War.

Ancient rivals, Britain and France had been fighting more or less continuously for over a century. In 1759, France had twenty-five million people, Britain perhaps seven million; yet the French were then at the point of military defeat. In North America, Quebec, the centrepiece capital of New France, was threatened by an advancing British army under James Wolfe; in Europe, the French saw their forces defeated at the battle of Minden, in northern Germany, by a combined Prussian and British army—the first triumph in the Year of Victories.

Edward Hawke, the British admiral whose victory at Quiberon Bay foiled French plans to invade Britain during the Seven Years' War.

In order to take back the initiative, King Louis XV decided on an extraordinary step: the invasion of Great Britain. Unfortunately, due to rivalries between various French commanders, the invasion plan became needlessly complicated. Forty-eight thousand French troops gathered in southern Brittany in the Gulf of Morbihan, inside Quiberon Bay, ready to board three troop transports that would carry them across the Channel. But the warships that were to escort the transports and protect them against the powerful British navy were located in two different places: the Mediterranean fleet in Toulon, and the northern fleet, under the French admiral, Count de Conflans, at Brest. When the Mediterranean fleet sailed to rendezvous with Conflans, however, British warships under Admiral Edward Boscawen routed it at the battle of Lagos Bay, off the coast of Portugal, on 7 August—the second of the great British victories that year.

Despite this, Louis XV insisted that the invasion go ahead, with only the protection of Conflans's fleet. The problem was that whenever Conflans looked to sea from his port in Brest, he found his way blocked by a remarkable commander: Admiral Edward Hawke.

RETURN OF THE HAWKE

Even the historian Frank McLynn, who is generally sympathetic to Edward Hawke, calls him 'a tactless, indiscreet prima donna with no political skills or personal charm'. Fifty-five at the time of Quiberon Bay, Hawke had a personal friendship with King George II, which kept his career alive, despite the dislike many in the British Admiralty carried for him. He had been a hero of the battle of Finisterre, in 1747, during the War of Austrian Succession, when he had destroyed a French fleet off the northwestern coast of Spain. However, in 1758, he had thrown a fit of pique during a raid on the French, when he mistakenly thought he was being relieved of command, and withdrew his flagship and wrote a nasty letter to his superiors, for which offence he was forced to retire.

Hawke later apologised for his error of judgment, but thereafter he burned with a desire to redeem himself in the eyes of those who said he was a coward. However, those who knew him well never doubted two things about him: his courage and his seamanship. He was not some political appointee, but a true seaman, a widower with little or no personal life who lived to be on the ocean. So, in the early summer of 1759, the Admiralty, seeing the French build-up across the Channel, called Hawke back into service to lead a fleet of twenty-three warships to blockade Admiral de Conflans in Brest. In what has been called the first successful long-term blockade of an enemy naval base (as opposed to an enemy city or coastline), Hawke kept Conflans bottled up, while occasionally sending small forces on raids to destroy French shipping, and intercepting and turning around merchant shipping heading for France.

As the autumn winds began to assail the Channel, the blockade became more difficult, however. When storm-force winds blew up that Hawke knew would keep the French fleet at harbour, he would beat back to Torbay on the English coast and replenish his supplies, while watching for any change in the weather that might allow the French to begin their invasion.

Meanwhile, on 13 September 1759, a British army led by James Wolfe defeated French forces on the Plains of Abraham outside the city of Quebec—bringing about the third great British victory of the year and opening up all of New France to British rule. In late October, an anxious Louis XV ordered Admiral de Conflans to escape Hawke's blockade, drive south to rendezvous with the troops transports in the Gulf of Morbihan and begin the invasion.

On 10 November, gales forced Hawke to put back into port at Torbay. By the time conditions improved enough for him to sail forth, on 14 November, Conflans had, as Hawke learned from British supply boats, left Brest with his fleet of twenty-one ships and was on his way to Morbihan. Hawke immediately gave chase. Moving with incredible speed in his hundred-gun flagship, the HMS *Royal George*—he wrote to the Admiralty that he had carried 'a press of sail all night with a hard gale at S.S.W.'—he caught up with Conflans near Belle Isle, the rocky island off the coast of the Quiberon Peninsula.

- -

NAVAL ARSENALS

Ships of the line of the late eighteenth century had innumerable ways in which to deal death to their enemies. The most tried and true method, of course, was the cannonball: solid shot of varying size (generally, from three to twenty kilograms) delivered by the ship's cannons. The ship's cannons also fired grapeshot (tin boxes of musket shot) as an antipersonnel weapon at close range. When ships drew alongside each other, they also fired 'dismantling shot', chains and star-shaped pieces of metal that were intended to shred the enemy's sails and impede its manoeuvrability.

At the beginning of the eighteenth century, a typical warship had about fifty cannons—twenty-five on each side. But then an arms race ensued that pushed the number up. In 1759, Admiral Hawke's flagship, the *Royal George*, had one hundred guns; he also had three ninety-gun ships, as well as numerous ships with seventy-four, seventy, sixty-four and sixty guns. Conflans's fleet possessed no one-hundred- or ninety-gun ships, but had four eighty-gun ships—which operated with two gun decks instead of three.

Relatively few eighteenth-century naval battles ended with ships blowing each other up with cannon fire, unlike twentieth-century engagements, which almost always ended this way. Instead, either a ship, unable to fight back or manoeuvre, struck its flags and surrendered, or it was boarded and a bloody fight occurred using weapons familiar to any land-based army: muskets (fired once and then wielded as clubs), pistols and cutlasses.

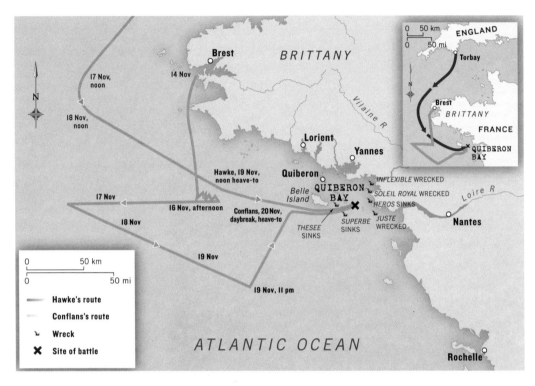

Main map: Pursued by Hawke, the French commander, Conflans, desperately sought the shelter of Quiberon Bay, but Hawke intercepted him and the battle was joined. Inset: The British fleet's route from England to Quiberon Bay.

CHASING AWAY THE DEMONS

As Hawke arrived off Quiberon Bay, the weather began to deteriorate even further. Gales blew from the west and north-northwest, and the sky turned deeply stormy and grey, so much so that it almost appeared that night was coming on at noon. Seeing Hawke's warships, Conflans decided to run his vessels into Quiberon Bay. He later came under much criticism for making this decision, with the court of Louis XV accusing him of cowardice, but it was not a bad one: he was marginally outnumbered, having two fewer vessels than the British total of twenty-three, and outgunned, having a total of 1,532 guns to the British fleet's 1,666 guns. Conflans's plan was to reach the somewhat more sheltered lee of the Quiberon Peninsula (the east side), and form his ships into a battle line with the wind behind him to make his ships more manoeuvrable. In any case, as Conflans later explained, he did not really think that the British would dare to sail into Quiberon, with its rocky shore-line and numerous reefs and shoals, in the middle of a full November storm. But he had not reckoned on Admiral Hawke.

So intent was Hawke to catch and destroy his enemy—perhaps to clear his name with the Admiralty once and for all—that he directed his ships to sail straight into Quiberon, in hot pursuit of the French. Many of his officers were aghast when they received this order—battles did not take place in gale-force winds, if at all possible—but they could do nothing but obey. It was obvious that Hawke would have no second thoughts, even for an instant, believing that the slightest reticence might bring on again the taunts of his detractors.

The seventy-four-gun *Magnanime* led the way, followed closely by Hawke in the *Royal George*. He told his officers to set his top-gallant sails—a risky manoeuvre in high winds, as these topmost sails might, caught in a powerful gust of wind, tip the ship over. When that didn't pour on enough speed for him, he set his sidesails. In those days, the sidesails of a vessel were used only when the wind was extremely light, in order to catch the faintest breeze. To use them in the midst of a storm was akin to turning on the afterburners of a rocket—they thrust the *Royal George* along at enormous speed. Hawke's men followed in his other ships, terrified. With their gun ports open and ready to do battle, any water pouring in could easily capsize the vessels and send them quickly to the bottom of the ocean.

Conflans watched with amazement as Hawke's ships entered the bay. Because of the aggressiveness with which Hawke pursued the French, Conflans did not have time to bring his ships into a line of battle. Before he knew it, the British were among his fleet, blasting away.

AN APOCALYPTIC SCENE

The battle that took place in Quiberon Bay on November 20, 1759, was depicted numerous times by British painters fascinated by its extraordinary atmosphere, with nature seeming to echo the apocalyptic fighting going on. As the forty-odd warships did battle and thousands of spectators watched from the shores, waves rose as high as the ships' quarterdecks, the water appeared dark green—almost black—and fast-moving storm clouds occasionally obscured all vision. The rocky coast that surrounded the warships was stark and dangerous, and enormous white-capped breakers crashed down on the beaches and broke against reefs.

After about two hours, Conflans decided to make a break for the open sea in his flagship, the *Soleil Royal*. Hawke, recognising his adversary's vessel and taking this combat very personally, ordered his master to lay up alongside the French ship. A battle between the *Royal George*, the *Soleil Royal* and two other French warships ensued, with Hawke bombarding relentlessly and being hit by volley after volley in return. The two other French ships, *Intrépide* and *Superbe*, seeing that Hawke had manoeuvred his vessel into position to rake Conflans with a full broadside, bravely sailed into the path of fire: the *Superbe* sank almost immediately, killing the 630 Breton sailors who manned it.

In the meantime, the numerous other actions taking place in the storm-tossed bay resulted in the destruction or disablement of five French ships, with one, the *Héros*, striking its colours and surrendering. By five o'clock, however, darkness had descended, and it became far too perilous for ships of either side to move. The two enemies anchored, without lights, and waited for daybreak.

Both forces had a horrific night, as gale-force winds tore through their rigging and the ships tossed and turned, each rough movement causing wounded sailors to shriek in agony. As light came, seven French ships headed for the safety of the Vilaine River, where the heavy tides and the onshore gale had raised the water high enough for them to make it over the sandbar at its mouth. On the river, they were safe from the heavier British vessels, but isolated and unable to assist the other French ships.

Come daylight, the *Soleil Royal* received a rude surprise: it lay at anchor surrounded by British ships. Before the British seamen could bring fire to bear on the French ship, however, Conflans ordered its anchor lines to be cut, and it drifted to shore and ran aground. A ship Hawke sent after it, the *Essex*, hit shoals and also ran aground, becoming one of just two British ships to be lost in the battle (the other, the *Resolution*, also ran aground; both crews were, however, rescued and taken aboard other British ships).

Soon all the French ships had been destroyed, run aground, or scattered, but still Hawke hadn't finished with them. He tried to convert lifeboats to fire ships in an attempt to float

THE SAD FATE OF THE ROYAL GEORGE

After its gallant performance at Quiberon Bay, the HMS *Royal George* took part in operations against the Americans during the War of Independence, and against the Spanish at the battle of Cape St Vincent in 1780. On 29 August 1782, it was being outfitted at Spithead, in the south of England, before taking part in a routine patrol to Gibraltar. Aside from the crew, there were a good many visitors on board, including hundreds of relatives of crew members, many of them women and children. The ship was heeled to port to allow repairs below her waterline. At the same time, casks of rum were being loaded.

Unfortunately, in the excitement and confusion, with so many visitors and so much going on, someone forgot to secure the gun ports on the gun deck, the lowest of the *Royal George*'s four decks. Very quickly, the gun deck flooded and, ironically and tragically, the ship that had survived the swells of the Channel in the battle of Quiberon Bay sank. In what remains the Royal Navy's worst peacetime accident, eight hundred people died, including three hundred women and sixty children.

The wreck of the *Royal George* subsequently presented a hazard to navigation and was ultimately destroyed by explosives in 1840.

One of many British paintings made to commemorate the glorious victory at Quiberon, this one shows Hawke's flagship HMS *Royal George*—flying the St George's Cross—engaging a French ship, possibly the *Soleil Royal*.

them over the sandbar at the mouth of the Vilaine River and torch the ships there. When weather conditions didn't permit this, he made sure his men fired on and destroyed the grounded *Soleil Royal* and also the *Héros*—which had attempted to flee in the night but become stuck on a sandbar. To some, this might have seemed like overkill, but Hawke, who kept his political enemies in mind at all times, wanted his already amazing victory to be as complete as possible. As he later wrote: 'When I consider the season of the year, the hard gales on the day of action, a flying enemy and shortness of the day, and the coast they were on, I can boldly affirm that all that could possibly be done has been done.'

GLORY, REWARD - AND SATISFACTION

Hawke's triumph at Quiberon sealed a hugely successful year for Britain and helped ensure its ultimate triumph in the Seven Years' War, though victory was not confirmed until 1763, when the war ended and the Treaty of Paris was signed. Hawke's reward was to be made First Lord of the Admiralty in 1766—sweet revenge on the men who had once slighted him. After he retired in 1776, he was also bestowed with a baronetcy. Covered with honours, his enemies silenced at last, the man who had single-handedly saved Britain from foreign invasion died in 1781.

KITCHENER'S GAMBLE: THE BATTLE OF OMDURMAN, 1898

FIELD MARSHAL HORATIO HERBERT KITCHENER, FIRST EARL KITCHENER, more commonly known as Lord Kitchener, was not one of those commanders whom you could, by any stretch of the imagination, think of as beloved. People who knew him spoke of him as ruthless, forbidding and stern. If you doubt it, just take a look at his picture on one of the most famous military recruiting posters of all time, the World War I era 'Lord Kitchener Wants You!' advertisement, in which he is depicted pointing a sternly admonitory finger at any non-military men who might be shirking their way down the street. Enough to make you jump into uniform, just to escape his steely gaze.

On top of this, Kitchener was described as 'machine-like' in his decision-making, and such a micromanager that, while still a field commander, he refused to employ a chief of staff, making even the most insignificant decisions himself.

He had little personal life and never married, although he was engaged for a time to a woman who died of typhoid fever in Cairo. Modern historians have spent many thousands of words speculating that Kitchener—with his love of ceramics and flowers—was gay and that he had an affair with his long-time aide-de-camp Captain Owen Fitzgerald, but he was probably more interested in work than love.

This dedication to his role resulted in some impressive achievements. Not the least of these was his extraordinary success in the Sudan at the battle of Omdurman, where he commanded a force that destroyed Islamic power in the region. The bloody fight at Omdurman is in itself a remarkable tale, but the way Kitchener got to the Dervish capital was an extraordinary physical as well as tactical achievement.

Opposite: The stern visage of Lord Kitchener stares out from this famous British recruitment poster of 1914. The image inspired other recruitment campaigns including the 'Uncle Sam' posters designed in the United States in 1917.

DEFYING THE MAHDI

The Sudan is the huge area south of Egypt and the Red Sea, traversed by the White and Blue Nile rivers, which join at Khartoum to form the Nile. In area, Sudan is today the tenth largest country in the world; nine other countries touch its borders. For centuries, it was known for trading in ivory and slaves. In 1820, Muhammad Ali, ruler of Egypt, conquered the country and its population of Islamic tribesmen and Coptic Christians. When Egypt became a British colony in 1882, the new rulers inherited this vast region with its imposing landscapes: dry deserts in the north, swamps and rain forests in the south, endless flat plains and jagged mountain ranges.

Just as Britain was taking over, a large faction of the Sudanese were in rebellion because Egypt had been trying to abolish the country's lucrative slave trade. The leader of these rebels was one Muhammad Ahmad ibn 'Abd Allah, a Sunni Muslim holy man who styled himself the Mahdi, 'Divine Holy One'. The Mahdi and his holy army (forerunners of today's jihadists) had destroyed the Egyptian army and were in the process of retaking the entire country. When the British sent in Major General Charles Gordon to evacuate the remaining Egyptian forces in 1885, he was surrounded in Khartoum and killed.

The Mahdi himself was killed in the summer of 1885, but the outnumbered British in Egypt effectively ceded control of the Sudan to the Mahdi's successor, the Khalifah ('deputy') 'Abd Allah, despite popular outcry in Britain to avenge Gordon's death. The dervishes of the Mahdist cause—the term was almost universally applied to the soldiers of the Mahdi and the Khalifah, although strictly speaking, a dervish is an ascetic Sufi holy man—attempted to invade Egypt, but the British pushed them back and then left them alone. By the mid-1890s, however, Lord Salisbury, the British prime minister, had become concerned that the growing militant Islamic power of the Mahdists would cause an

THE WAR IN THE SOUDAN

SCENE 3º. WAR IN THE SOUDAN, WITH TERRIFIC ENCOUNTERS, ASSAULTS, NAVAL COMBATS & WARLIKE EPISODES.

This dramatic late-nineteenth-century depiction of a fierce battle between British soldiers and dervish fighters shows how British military adventures in the Sudan captured the popular imagination.

uprising in other Muslim parts of the British Empire, like India. This, along with a fear that Islamic Sudan might ally itself with the French, or even interfere with British access to the Suez Canal, which had been built in 1869, caused Salisbury to plan a British invasion of the Sudan.

KITCHENER, AT YOUR SERVICE

Horatio Herbert Kitchener was born in 1850, the son of an army man. After the death of his mother when he was fourteen, he grew up shy and inward. At the behest of his father, he went to a military academy—not the glamorous training grounds of future military heroes at Sandhurst, however, but the Royal Military Academy at Woolwich, where he found the study of military engineering suited his precise mind. After graduation, he joined the Royal Engineer Corps and served in the Middle East, where he learned Arabic and made a name for himself as a bright, ambitious young officer.

Eventually, he transferred to Egypt, served on the expedition that sought unsuccessfully to relieve Charles Gordon at Khartoum, fought in numerous battles against the Mahdist forces (in one, a glancing dervish bullet left a slashing scar across his face, adding to his formidable appearance) and was rewarded, at the age of forty-two, by being named *Sirdar* (Commander) of the Egyptian Army in 1892. He was still in this position when Lord Salisbury ordered the destruction of Mahdist forces in Sudan in 1896.

The key to this operation was taking the Mahdist capital of Omdurman, on the west bank of the Nile River, across from Khartoum, for whoever controlled Omdurman controlled the river and the entire Nile Valley. But how to get there from Egypt? One reason for the failure of Charles Gordon's expedition was that he and his men had had to drag boats south down the Nile, which was marked at stages by treacherous rapids and waterfalls. Essential supplies and men were lost in this arduous process. But the only alternative for Gordon would have been to march his men straight across the Nubian Desert, an arid, sandstone plateau of four hundred thousand square kilometres, with virtually no rainfall and no oases, and where the average daily temperature in June (the hottest month) is 43 degrees Celsius.

Kitchener, with his passionless but exacting engineer's eye, saw this as a fascinating challenge. After carefully studying maps of the region, he decided that if he could at least take his army down the Nile to the point where the cataracts made it virtually impossible to continue, he could then strike off across the Nubian Desert and reach Atbara, six hundred kilometres away, where the Nile became navigable again. Not that Kitchener's army would walk through the blazing landscape of this arid land. They would ride.

THE SUDAN MILITARY RAILWAY

Kitchener had decided that he would build a railway across the desert. Most commanders would not even have thought of attempting this feat, but Kitchener considered it the obvious thing to do. And he took his time about it. He first built up his Anglo-Egyptian force until it was a formidable one. Although still outnumbered by the roughly 50,000 dervishes the Khalifah could field, Kitchener's army eventually consisted of about 8,200 British regulars and 17,000 Egyptian and Sudanese soldiers. Knowing that the railway would only take him to Atbara—still over three hundred kilometres from Omdurman—Kitchener also ordered armed river steamers, made in London in prefabricated sections, to be carted along on the railway once it was built and assembled at Atbara. These gunboats carried extraordinary firepower—thirty-six artillery pieces and twenty-four Maxim guns—the like of which no Mahdist army had ever seen.

The building of the railway began on 1 January 1897, using forced labour provided by Egyptian troops and convicts. The journalist G. W. Steevens surveyed the construction at first

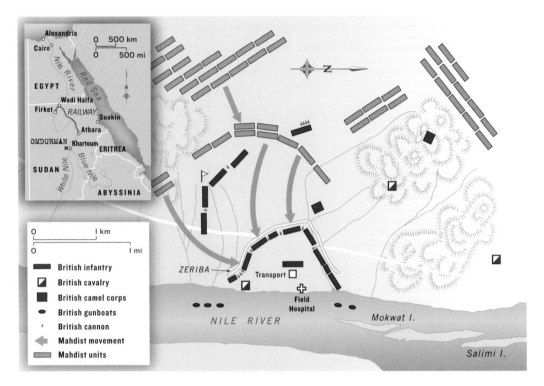

Main map: The positions of British and Madhist forces at the battle of Omdurman. Inset: The route of the Sudan Military Railway across the Nubian Desert, from the Nile cataracts to Atbara, a distance of six hundred kilometres.

hand, noting that Kitchener's 'machine-like precision' gave him the confidence to be daring: 'He actually launched his rails ... into the desert while the other end of the line [Atbara] was still held by the enemy'. As progress on the tracks went forwards, the men suffered severely from thirst, despite some water being found in deep wells bored in the ground.

It was slow going; the railway had to carry not only supplies for those thousands engaged in building it, but also the raw materials for the tracks, since there was no wood for ties, let alone metal for rails, where the railway was going, just, according to Steevens: 'yellow sand to the right and left ... stretching away endlessly'. Kilometre after kilometre, day after day, the railway moved forwards. The Khalifah heard of its progress, but apparently did not quite believe that the British could pull this off—there had been other, abortive attempts at railways across the Sudan. Steevens saw old engines and rusty parts strewn in the yellow sand, reminders of what could happen to this attempt.

After about a year, by the beginning of January 1898, the railway was 240 kilometres from Atbara. The Khalifah had finally begun to believe the stories that Kitchener was coming across the Nubian Desert, and started to organise against him. On 8 April, sixteen thousand dervishes attacked a British force that had arrived to secure Atbara in advance of the railway. After a fight, the Mahdist army was bloodily repulsed, and thereafter the Khalifah decided to risk everything on a massive pitched battle when the British arrived outside his capital of Omdurman.

Finally, on 14 July 1898, the Sudan Military Railway reached Atbara. This extraordinary feat of engineering meant that British troops and supplies that might previously have taken at least four months to make it south from Cairo could now arrive in eleven days. Winston Churchill, travelling with the expedition as a war correspondent, later declared that 'the Khalifah was conquered on the railway'.

FIREPOWER WINS THE DAY

After the railway arrived at Atbara, Kitchener assembled his formidable flotilla of gunboats. While it sailed down the Nile, the bulk of the Anglo-Egyptian army marched, by foot and camel, to Omdurman, and set up an encampment on the west bank of the Nile, north of the

---

KITCHENER'S MYSTERIOUS END

During World War I, Lord Kitchener was appointed Secretary of War. In late May of 1916, he departed England aboard the armoured cruiser HMS *Hampshire*, on his way to the Russian port of Arkhangelsk, where he intended to confer with Russian officials about the progress of the war. He never got there. On 5 June, the *Hampshire* struck a mine laid by the German submarine *U-75* and sank west of the Orkney Islands. Six hundred and forty-three British sailors and passengers died, leaving only twelve survivors. Lord Kitchener's body was never found, nor was the body of his rumoured homosexual companion, Captain Owen Fitzgerald.

Kitchener was presumed to be another random casualty of war, but then a German spy named Fritz Joubert Du Quesne claimed to have sabotaged the *Hampshire*. German records show that Du Quesne—a Boer who hated Kitchener for his merciless policies during the Boer Wars—assumed the identity of a Russian duke, boarded the *Hampshire* and then signalled the *U-75* that Kitchener was on board. The submarine laid a mine in the cruiser's path—but not before Du Quesne escaped on a raft. Du Quesne received an Iron Cross from Germany for his feat.

But did he really do it? His long and colourful life (he did not die until 1956) included escaping from a British prison on Bermuda and making his way to America, where he worked as Theodore Roosevelt's shooting instructor and as a film agent for Joseph P. Kennedy, John F. Kennedy's father. He also tried to organise a German spy ring in New York during World War II, for which crime he spent time in an American prison. All of which is to say that he was adventurous enough to have pulled off the Kitchener killing—and creative enough to have dreamed the whole thing up.

capital, in early September. There, Kitchener constructed a typically methodical defence: a 1.5-kilometre-long, semicircular *zeriba*, a wall made of mimosa thornbushes, anchored against the river, where his patrolling gunboats made sure that no one tried to attack from the east bank. His troops stood guard behind the *zeriba* in a classic British formation: two lines of soldiers, the front line kneeling, the back line standing directly behind. Inside the *zeriba* were field pieces and Maxim machine guns (in addition to the ones on the gunboats). The infantry were armed with the Lee-Medford MK II rifle, the finest infantry weapon in the world at the time, a repeating rifle that a trained soldier could fire fifteen times a minute.

The Khalifah had certain choices: instead of fighting the British here, he could retreat, drawing them into a war of attrition in the desert; or he could attack them at night, when their advantage in firepower would be diminished. But, instead, he chose a glorious but fool-hardy tactic: a massed attack in broad daylight. At dawn on 8 September, holding some of his forces in reserve, the Mahdist leader sent about twelve thousand screaming dervishes against the British lines. It was an extraordinary sight. Most of the dervishes were infantry, dressed in jihadist white, carrying swords, spears and, in many cases, rifles. Leading them were their emirs, on black Arabian stallions, carrying gigantic banners.

British artillery opened up when the Mahdist warriors were just over two kilometres away, found the range quite easily and began blowing them to bits—a watching Winston Churchill

OUR MAN IN OMDURMAN

Winston Churchill is most famous as the British prime minister whose leadership pulled his people out of the darkest days of World War II, but before his lengthy career in politics and government, Churchill was a renowned war correspondent, covering the action in Cuba and India before pulling strings to get himself assigned as a lieutenant to Kitchener's army as it made its way to Omdurman. There, the twenty-three-year-old Churchill took part in one of the last truly significant British cavalry charges, that of the Twenty-first Lancers against the dervish forces, which nearly destroyed the regiment.

Churchill made his way back to the banks of the Nile River after the attack, and in his *The River War: An*

Historical Account of the Reconquest of the Soudan, published in 1899, unforgettably described the effect of modern firepower on the dervish charge: 'With another officer I built a pile of biscuit-boxes on the edge of the slope, and, climbing thereupon, obtained some view of the plain. Eight hundred metres away a ragged line of men was coming on desperately, struggling forwards in the face of the pitiless fire—white banners tossing and collapsing; white figures subsiding in dozens to the ground; little white puffs from their rifles, larger white puffs spreading in a row all along their front from the bursting shrapnel. The picture lasted only a moment, but the memory remains for ever.'

saw shells obliterating five Sudanese warriors with every burst. Then the Maxim guns, firing at five hundred bullets per minute, tore huge holes in the Mahdist lines. Still the enemy kept coming. When the dervishes were a kilometre distant, the Anglo-Egyptian infantry opened up with their rifles. Now, with all the modern weapons available to them, the British wreaked a truly horrific toll. Not one dervish made it to within three hundred metres of the *zeriba*. Finally, about two hours later, Kitchener, in typical fashion, ordered the firing to stop: 'Cease fire, please. Cease fire! Cease fire! What a dreadful waste of ammunition!'

'THE MOST SIGNAL TRIUMPH'

The battle was not yet over. Kitchener, trying to avoid street-fighting in Omdurman, moved his forces out to chase the retreating dervishes, where they were ambushed by the rest of the Khalifah's infantry. The Twenty-first Lancers, young Lieutenant Winston Churchill's regiment, was nearly annihilated because it attacked prematurely, launching a dramatic cavalry charge. But here, too, superior firepower won the day. In the end, the British took Omdurman, driving the Khalifah out (he was chased down the following year and killed), and their takeover of the Nile Valley was complete. The Mahdists lost 10,000 dead, 16,000 wounded,

5,000 captured—a horrific 65 per cent casualty rate; the Anglo–Egyptian army suffered 48 men killed and 382 wounded.

The victory at Omdurman was, according to Winston Churchill, 'the most signal triumph ever gained by the arms of science over barbarians'. He was referring not only to modern firepower tearing apart men charging with spears and swords, but also to Kitchener's amazing feat of building a railway across a trackless desert and transporting an army across it. Even today, Kitchener's creation of the Sudan Military Railway ranks as a remarkable achievement in engineering, as well as an ingenious military strategy marked by vision and daring.

Though ill-advised and costly in terms of casualties, the charge of the Twenty-first Lancers at Omdurman won the regiment three Victoria Crosses for bravery.

ADMIRAL TOGO'S U-TURN: THE BATTLE OF TSUSHIMA, 1905

UNTIL THE ADVENT OF THE AIRCRAFT CARRIER DURING WORLD WAR II, twentieth-century naval battles were dominated by clashes between fleets of massive steel battleships, characterised by shrieking shells, huge geysers of water, flaming hulls and stricken ships slowly keeling over and sliding beneath the waves. Though iron battleships appeared as early as the mid-nineteenth century and steel was used from the 1870s onwards, the first major clash of these behemoth vessels did not take place until 1905, in the chilly waters of the Tsushima Straits off Korea, when the Japanese destroyed Russia's mighty Baltic Fleet with a perfect storm of two thousand high-explosive shells a minute, fired from unheard-of distances.

As well as being the first great naval engagement of the twentieth century, the battle of Tsushima had major and lasting implications. It helped Japan become a world power, a country the West was forced to deal with on equal terms. It began a race among the world's great navies to build bigger, more powerful battleships, resulting in the mighty dreadnoughts that would clash in World War I. And it dealt yet another blow to the prestige of the faltering Russian Romanoff dynasty, which would collapse just over a decade later.

But one of the most fascinating things about the battle was the successful strategy employed by the commander of the Japanese force, a British-educated son of a samurai named Admiral Heihachiro Togo. He took his entire fleet and made a U-turn in front of the Russian fleet. If you or I do a U-turn in traffic, we run the risk of being hit broadside by an oncoming car. That was the same risk Admiral Togo took, except on a much larger scale, for the vulnerable flanks of his ships might easily have been devastated by tonnes of powerful twelve-inch (thirty-centimetre) shells. That he lived to triumph is one of the great stories in the history of naval combat.

A NAVAL EDUCATION

Tsushima has been called—by historian Edmund Morris—'the greatest naval engagement since Trafalgar'. That's fitting, since Togo, the chief architect of this victory, was a great admirer of Admiral Lord Nelson, commander of the British fleet in that 1805 battle. Togo was born in 1848 in southern Japan, at a time when the country was still isolated from the West—as it had been for two hundred years—and ruled by a shogun. Togo's father was a *daimyo*, a samurai warrior with the status of a feudal lord. During his early life, Togo saw Japan, and ways of making war, change with dramatic speed. The American Commodore Matthew Perry visited Japan in 1853; his fleet included two steamships that astonished the cloistered country, whose only vessels were wind-driven. Trade with the West began after this, as did conflict. When samurai warriors murdered a British merchant who had slighted a Japanese lord, the British Royal Navy paid a visit to the port of Kagoshima, near Togo's home village, and demanded that the killers be executed. The Japanese refused and the fifteen-year-old Togo then watched as the British destroyed most of the town in six hours of concentrated gunnery. It was a lesson not lost on him, or on Japan. Soon after, a civil war began, in which the shogun was deposed by forces loyal to the Emperor Meiji, the beginning of the imperial government of modern Japan. The opposing forces developed small fleets of paddle-wheel steamships, and Togo fought as a gunner and third mate in these battles, gaining valuable experience.

In 1871, the Japanese government sent the young officer along with a group of his peers to study naval tactics in Great Britain. Despite the fact that British cadets taunted him as 'Johnny Chinaman' (they were unable to tell one Asian from another), he excelled and graduated second in his class from the Thames Nautical Training College, where he trained and lived aboard a Royal Navy vessel. He also gained experiences few other Japanese naval officers at the time were allowed—in 1875, for example, he circumnavigated the globe as an able seaman. It was in Britain, too, that Togo first learned about Nelson and his famous and unorthodox victory at Trafalgar, when rather than adhering to the convention of drawing his ships up parallel to the enemy, Nelson drove them straight at the opposing fleet. The success of the tactic relied entirely on speed—something Togo would always remember.

BUILD-UP TO WAR

In the twenty-five years between 1880 and the battle of Tsushima, Japan's navy grew to become one of the most powerful in the world. There was plenty of opportunity for the expanding Japanese navy—and Togo—to practise tactics. During the Sino-Japanese War in 1894, Togo saw combat with the Japanese fleet that destroyed a larger Chinese armada in the Yellow Sea. Suing for peace, China was forced to cede Japan a good deal of territory, including Formosa (present-day Taiwan) and to give up its claim to Korea. Then the Russians stepped in to grab territory, including large amounts of land in Manchuria and Korea. It was only a matter of time before the two burgeoning powers would clash.

By 1904, when Togo was named commander in chief of the Combined Fleet of Imperial Japan, the Japanese navy had six battleships (purchased from Great Britain), twenty-four cruisers, twenty destroyers and fifty-eight torpedo boats, and was ready to do battle. At the beginning of that year, a series of confrontations escalated tensions between Russia and Japan, and the two countries broke off diplomatic relations on 6 February. Two days later (and two days before war was officially declared), obviously prepared for this, Togo launched a surprise attack against the Russian Pacific Fleet, at harbour in Port Arthur, Manchuria. Ten destroyers attacked and damaged two Russian battleships and a cruiser—not as critical a blow as the Japanese were to strike in another surprise attack at Pearl Harbor, thirty-seven years later, but enough to put the Russians on notice that this upstart new power was not to be trifled with. In August of that year, the Pacific Fleet, bottled up in Port Arthur by Togo's ships, attempted to make a break for the port at Vladivostok, 2,500 kilometres north, but Togo intercepted it and, in the battle of the Yellow Sea, fighting with a squadron of only four hastily assembled battleships, forced the Russians to return to Port Arthur.

Despite these initial Japanese naval victories, however, the land war in Manchuria bogged down in a bloody and lengthy World War I-like conflict of attrition, with the Japanese

NELSON'S EXAMPLE

One hundred years before Admiral Togo, Admiral Lord Nelson earned his place in the history of naval tactics for his bold victory at the battle of Trafalgar. In this crucial encounter of the Napoleonic Wars, an outnumbered British fleet faced off against a French–Spanish armada near Cape Trafalgar, in southern Spain. The British under Nelson had twenty-seven ships of the line, compared with their opponents' thirty-three.

For weeks before the battle, Nelson prepared his commanders, by drilling them to take the initiative against the enemy and attack in small groups, almost like guerilla fighters. Nelson didn't want to fight an orthodox, parallel-lines conflict, in which the superior firepower of the Spanish and French was likely to win the day. Instead, he ordered his ships to fly directly into battle as soon as they were ready, breaking through the line of enemy ships and wreaking havoc. Although Nelson was killed by sniper fire at the battle, his tactics were wholly successful. The French–Spanish fleet lost 4,400 killed, 7,000 prisoners and 24 out of 33 ships, and Trafalgar ushered in a century of British dominance of the high seas.

The Japanese naval squadron under Admiral Heihachiro Togo steaming to bombard the Russian enclave of Port Arthur in the surprise attack that opened the hostilities in the Russo-Japanese War of 1904–05.

unable to destroy the Russian army. All of this meant that the impending confrontation between the rest of the powerful Russian fleet and the Japanese under Admiral Togo would be crucial to the outcome of the war.

FACING OFF

Even after the destruction of its Pacific Fleet, the Russians remained a formidable sea power. The Russian fleet stationed in the Baltic, under the command of Admiral Zinovy Petrovich Rozhestvensky, was renamed the Second Pacific Fleet and ordered to sail to Port Arthur and confront the Japanese navy. Beginning on 15 October 1904, the Baltic Fleet made a truly incredible thirty-thousand kilometre journey: through the North Sea and the English Channel, past Spain and Portugal, all the way down the west coast of Africa, around the Cape of Good Hope, past Madagascar, across the Indian Ocean and into the Pacific. It was an extraordinary but exhausting accomplishment. The tired sailors' morale wasn't helped any when the Russians learned that Port Arthur had fallen to Japanese infantry and that the remains of the Russian fleet there had been destroyed by land-based Japanese artillery.

Still, as it steamed into the Pacific, Rozhestvensky's proud yellow-and-black-painted armada was a redoubtable sight. The Second Pacific Fleet had fourteen large warships (eleven battleships and three cruisers), as well as destroyers and torpedo boats, compared to

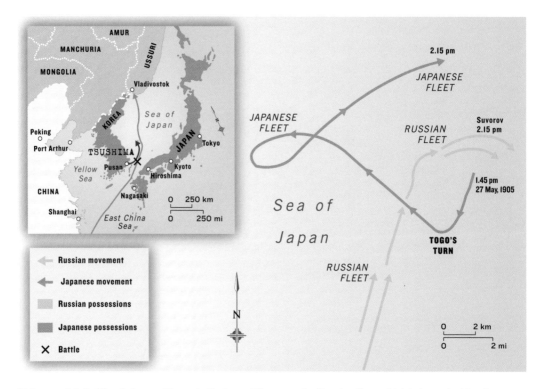

Main map: Admiral Togo's famous U-turn in the face of the oncoming Russian fleet, which led to a decisive Japanese victory. Inset: The Straits of Tsushima, where the Japanese and Russian fleets finally clashed.

Japan's twelve warships (four battleships, eight cruisers). But the more significant difference was qualitative. Togo had placed a premium on speed for his battleships and they could outrun most of the Russian ships by at least three or four knots. In addition, the Japanese had developed a new type of shell containing a material they called *shimose* (essentially, the highly inflammatory and sensitive explosive substance called melnite). These had four times the explosive force of Russian shells and, while not armour-piercing, released clouds of a poisonous gas containing picric acid on contact. The Japanese were also better gunners than the Russians, trained incessantly to the point where they could hit targets accurately from kilometres away while firing at twice the rate of the Russians.

Knowing that the fleet at Port Arthur was destroyed, Admiral Rozhestvensky's goal was to link up with the remaining Russian fleet in Vladivostok, now the only port open to him. In order to do this, he could travel east of the Japanese islands, or he could take a much more direct passage through the Tsushima Strait, which lay between the southeastern corner of the Korean Peninsula and the island of Tsushima. Given his lack of fuel, the Tshushima Strait was the better option, perhaps his only one. The problem was, the Japanese had already figured he would take this approach, and Togo's fleet was patrolling the waterway in force.

Late on the night of 26 May 1905, the Russian ships entered the strait, travelling at nine knots, under blackout conditions. They managed to get past the first line of Japanese cruisers and destroyers, but then two Russian hospital ships, lagging several kilometres behind and fully lit up (according to international rules), were spotted by a Japanese cruiser. The captain immediately sent word to Admiral Togo at his base on the southern coast of Korea, opposite Tsushima Island: 'Enemy's smoke in sight'. The main Japanese fleet immediately set out to intercept the Russians.

Leading the Japanese fleet around to the north of Tsushima Island to meet the Russians, who were approaching from the south, Togo, in his battleship *Mikasa*, spotted the Russian fleet about thirteen kilometres away. It was 1.45 pm. The big Russian battleships led the way, divided into two columns, moving at about ten knots. Admiral Togo sent out a signal: 'The fate of the empire depends upon this event. Let every man do his utmost'.

DARING TO CROSS THE 'T'

Togo was now headed right at the enemy; if he kept on in the direction he was going, he ran the real risk of placing his line of ships right between the double line of Russian vessels— and being blasted out of the water from salvoes on each side. Yet if he moved his warships to the east, the Russians could easily slide right by him and head north, aiming for sanctuary in Vladivostok. This Togo would not allow.

Most commanders in this situation would have turned their ships in place so that Japanese ships could head north in a battle line parallel to that of the Russians. But in doing so, the normal Japanese battle line would have been reversed, and Togo's weakest ships, his cruisers, put under the withering fire of the powerful Russian battleships at the head of the enemy line of battle.

Togo assessed this in just a few minutes, and then made a daring and now famous strategic move. To the astonishment of the watching Russians, he first ordered his ships, beginning with the *Mikasa*, to turn across the line of the advancing Russian fleet. This manoeuvre was known as 'crossing the T', the approaching Russians forming the stem of the 'T' and the Japanese, with their movement, creating the horizontal line at the top. It was a highly risky manoeuvre, for it allowed the Russians a perfect opportunity to pour fire into the flanks of the turning ships, while the Japanese had only the Russian bows to aim at, a much smaller target.

The Russians on the lead battleships watched with amazement. Commander Vladimir Semenoff later wrote, 'I looked and looked and, not believing my eyes, could not put down my glasses'. The Russians hastened to take advantage of this apparent gaffe on the part of Togo, and began firing from a range of six thousand metres, but, as Semenoff recorded, the marksmanship either went awry or shells exploded without effect (many of the Russian shells turned out to be duds). Meanwhile, the Japanese moved so quickly that, before the Russians knew it, the enemy ships were well off their port bows. Once there, and with the open-mouthed Russian sailors looking on, the entire Japanese battle line made a U-turn and swiftly aligned itself parallel to the Russian fleet. Semenoff wrote: 'The enemy had finished turning. The twelve [Japanese] ships were in perfect order at close intervals, steaming parallel to us'. The Russian ships, poorly handled by their inexperienced crews, bunched up in confusion. At 2.15 pm, Togo ordered the Japanese to open fire at a distance of over six kilometres. This was an extremely long distance for accurate fire at this time, but Togo knew that he could rely on his well-trained gunners, and that this, indeed, was his trump card. Having outman-oeuvred the Russians, he knew he could pick them apart at long range.

The accuracy of the Japanese gunners was astounding. The incendiary *samose* shells exploded ferociously, tearing apart the Russian ships and killing and maiming the Russian sailors. The first to sink was the *Oslyabya*, followed by Admiral Rozhestvensky's flagship, the *Suvorov* (Rozhestvensky transferred to another ship), followed by the battleships *Alexander III* and *Borodino*. By seven o'clock that evening, the Russian fleet had been destroyed. After mopping up operations on 28 May, which included capturing a severely wounded Rozhestvensky, the Japanese could claim an extraordinary victory. Out of 42 Russians ships, 31 had been captured or sunk, including every battleship. The Russians lost 4,830 dead and 5,917 captured. Japanese losses were 3 torpedo boats and 116 dead.

HMS DREADNOUGHT

The success of Admiral Togo's big ships and their twelve-inch (thirty-centimetre) guns fired at long range inspired the British to build even bigger battleships. The first of this class, the HMS *Dreadnought*, was constructed between October 1905 and December 1906. The *Dreadnought* was the most heavily armed ship in history up to that point, with ten twelve-inch guns, twenty-four three-inch (eight-centimetre) guns and five torpedo tubes. It was also thickly armoured and could reach a speed of twenty-one knots—in the early twentieth century, this was the fastest ship afloat. As a result, its name came to be used for an entirely new class of ships.

In an ensuing arms race, Great Britain and Germany both built *Dreadnought*-class ships and a super-*Dreadnought* class was to follow next. But even though these mighty battleships saw action in both World Wars, they were soon rendered obsolete by submarines and the aircraft carrier.

Russian Admiral Rozhestvensky transfers from his sinking flagship to a torpedo boat as the Russian fleet goes down to overwhelming defeat. The Japanese later captured the wounded admiral, then returned him to Russian hands.

A TURNING POINT

The defeat at Tsushima forced the Russians to make peace, resulting in significant territorial gains for Japan—the Treaty of Portsmouth, which ended the war and was signed in September 1905, essentially gave Japan control of Korea and much of Manchuria. This, plus the immense prestige given by the victory, made Japan the pre-eminent power in Asia, and set the stage for its territorial expansion in the late 1930s. Admiral Togo's victory also marked the beginning of a new naval era dominated by massive steel battleships and their big twelve-inch guns, which could be fired at much greater ranges than any previous guns and could, on their own, utterly annihilate lesser ships. And, finally, it marked Togo out as a brilliant and innovative strategist, on a par with his great hero, Admiral Lord Nelson.

KING ALBERT RISKS ALL: THE FLOODING OF FLANDERS, 1914

IF YOU LOOK AT A MAP OF WESTERN EUROPE, YOU CAN SEE THE PROBLEM: Belgium is located between France, Germany and Britain, so that when these countries decide to wage war, 'poor little Belgium' (as it was dubbed during World War I) gets caught in the middle. In the middle of the middle, as it were, are the Belgian plains of Flanders, an area that, historically, extends from northern France to northern Belgium along the North Sea coast. It is a low-lying land, divided north to south by the Yser (IJzer) River, crisscrossed with canals and prone to flooding—Flanders, indeed, means 'flooded land' in Flemish.

This region, particularly the area between the Yser and the North Sea, was a pretty, pastoral, contented sort of place before October of 1914. It was a country of rich pastures, picturesque villages, ancient battle towers, belfried churches and low, white farmhouses capped with red-tiled roofs. Much of the land was *polders*—tracts reclaimed from the sea. Along the coast were fashionable resorts like La Panne and Saint-Idesbald, where the ruling French-speaking elite of the country went to vacation, but, inland, Flemish peasants continued to till the soil as they had done for generations.

Just four short years later, Flanders would be a war-torn wreck, what the American historian Winston Groom has called 'a gigantic corpse factory', a place where hundreds of thousands of British, French, German, Belgian and American soldiers had given their lives—so many that their blood soaked deep into the rich soil. The carnage came to be symbolised by the red poppies that grew prolifically in this bloodstained earth, as described in Canadian writer John McCrae's famous poem 'In Flanders Fields':

> In Flanders fields, the poppies blow
> Between the crosses, row on row ...

And had it not been for the Belgian king, Albert I, who summoned the North Sea in to inundate his rich land, the slaughter would have been even worse.

THE SHADOWS OF WAR

World War I was the almost inevitable result of a military build-up that began at the end of the Franco–Prussian War of 1870–71. Germany's victory in this war encouraged it to expand its army and navy in the hope of becoming a major world power, and made a bitter enemy of its neighbour, France. Coming to power in 1889, Kaiser Wilhelm II, the young, militaristic German ruler, feared that a hostile France might ally itself with Russia to the east and hem Germany in. He also realised that Britain, too, saw Germany as a threat, particularly to its traditional naval dominance, despite the strong ties between the countries' two royal families— Kaiser Wilhelm was a grandson of Queen Victoria and therefore first cousin of the British king, George V.

With tensions soaring, all countries began to arm themselves, and Germany continued to lead the way. The effect of its bellicose stance was to reinforce alliances between France, Britain and Russia aimed at containing it. Regarding this containment as a suffocating encirclement, Germany developed detailed plans for an attack on

King Albert I. Not yet forty when war began, Albert quickly demonstrated his determination to fight off the German threat.

France and Russia. The precarious situation in the Balkans, where Russia vied with Germany's traditional ally Austria for control of Serbia, soon provided a justification for war.

After a Serbian anarchist assassinated Archduke Franz Ferdinand, the heir to the Austro–Hungarian Hapsburg throne, in Sarajevo on 28 June 1914, Austria invaded Serbia, with Germany's support. Russia mobilised against Austria and Germany, leading Germany to declare war on Russia. With France obliged by treaty to support Russia, the two bitter enemies of the Franco-Prussian War lined up against each other again.

Germany's war plan was known as the Schlieffen Plan, after its creator, Count Alfred von Schlieffen, German Chief of Staff from 1891 to 1905. Perfected by the time of his retirement in 1905, it called for a blocking force to hold the heavily fortified French border while a much larger force marched through neutral Luxembourg and Belgium to the North Sea coast, then swung south around Paris. Inspired by Hannibal's success at Cannae, Schlieffen saw the final outcome as a huge encirclement of the French army, which would be attacked on France's eastern border from front and rear, and destroyed. When the French were safely pacified, the Germans would turn their attention to their enemies in the east: the Russians.

Speed was of the essence. For his plan to work, Schlieffen calculated that the conquest of France had to be completed in six weeks. Belgium was the only major obstacle, and he foresaw few problems there: it was a small, relatively weak nation, and its defences would be easily overcome—if it even attempted to defend itself at all.

'A NATION, NOT A HIGHWAY'

Belgium had been created in the 1830s from a conglomeration of Flemish states, mainly at the behest of Great Britain. The formation of the new nation was a victory for Britain and its secretary of state, Lord Palmerston, because it kept France from annexing the country, but this victory came at a price: by treaty, Britain promised to come to the aid of Belgium if ever the country were invaded.

King Albert I was the third king of the Belgians. He came to the throne young, in 1909, and was still just thirty-nine years old when World War I broke out in 1914. He was a handsome, dark-haired young man, whose informal mode of dress and comportment brought him into the twentieth century ahead of most royalty of the time. Albert was quite religious, and known for being taciturn, but he was not someone who readily gave in to bullying. When Germany's Kaiser Wilhelm (who was, in fact, a distant royal relative) tried to force Albert to allow German troops to move through Belgium on the eve of World War I, Albert famously replied: 'I rule a nation, not a highway'.

German infantry in Brussels preparing for an attack on Antwerp in August 1914. In the early stages of their advance into Belgium, it seemed that the Germans would be unopposed and that the Schlieffen Plan would be fulfilled.

Unfortunately, Belgium was a neutral country and had not participated in the arms build-up of Germany, Britain, France and Russia. Belgian soldiers, while brave, were severely outnumbered and ill-prepared, compared to the Germans. Many units dressed like nineteenth-century grenadiers. They had few machine guns and those they did have were pulled by teams of dogs.

German Chief of Staff Field Marshal Helmuth von Moltke commanded seven armies totalling about 1.5 million men. As per the Schlieffen Plan, two of these armies were arrayed in a line from the city of Metz all the way to Switzerland, as a blocking force should the French attack. The rest moved north. On 4 August 1914, the German First and Second Armies, totalling nearly six hundred thousand men, crossed the Meuse River and moved against the Belgian fortress of Liège. That same day, Britain, honouring its obligations to Belgium, declared war on Germany.

The Belgians put up an unexpectedly strong resistance, using machine guns and artillery to kill thousands of Germans making frontal attacks (the first of the great slaughters of the Great War) until Major General Erich Ludendorff took one brigade and managed to capture Liège. The two German armies then advanced, pushing the Belgian field army back further and further. Brussels was abandoned and the Germans entered the city in triumph on 20 August, while Belgian forces under King Albert retreated towards Antwerp. What should have been the beginning of a glorious German victory, however, was marred by a series of outrages towards Belgian civilians; moreover, the unexpected resistance of the Belgians had slowed the German advance considerably.

Huge crowds of refugees fled before the German armies. Now and again, the Belgians would turn and fight a delaying action in the blazing hot August weather, with rifles and machine guns chattering. King Albert rallied his troops enough to give the French army time to attack from the south, while the British Expeditionary Force (BEF) crossed the Channel, landed at Le Havre and immediately threw itself into the fray. But the better-prepared Germans began to push the French and British south, and the Belgians were forced to retreat north and west, towards the sea.

By the end of August, five German armies—about a million men—were stretched from Liège to the outskirts of Paris (German officers could see the Eiffel Tower through binoculars). But then Moltke, seeking to strengthen his right wing, which was fighting furthest to the north, in Belgium, withdrew forces from the area around Paris, and the French counterattacked. In the battle of the Marne, Moltke was defeated, suffered a nervous

THE RAPE OF BELGIUM

Very shortly after the Germans invaded Belgium in August of 1914, the atrocities began. On 4 August, the German army shot six hostages near the Meuse River and burned down an entire village. Within a month, there were at least three large-scale massacres of Belgian civilians—in one town 211 dead, in another 384, in still another 612. The victims, who included women and children, were lined up against walls and machine-gunned or bayoneted.

In committing these atrocities (in fact, simply by invading neutral Belgium), the Germans were in violation of the Hague Convention of 1907, which all the combatants had signed. They claimed that they had been sniped at by Belgian civilians, but nothing could excuse their actions, which included burning down a priceless library of rare volumes in the city of Louvain—known as the 'Oxford of Belgium'—as well as murdering many of the town's inhabitants.

Allied propagandists had a field day with the German excesses, placing stories in newspapers that said the Germans were impaling babies on bayonets and mutilating and raping virgins and nuns. These were almost certainly exaggerations, but hardly a month into World War I, the Germans had become the enemy of civilised people everywhere, and had no one to blame but themselves.

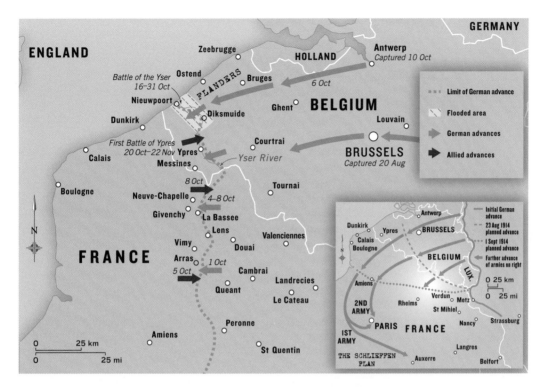

Main map: By flooding the area around Nieuwpoort and Diksmuide, Albert managed to halt the German advance and secure the Yser sector for the Allies. Inset: The Schlieffen Plan, Germany's original invasion strategy.

collapse and was replaced. It was now mid-September and the Schlieffen Plan, which was supposed to have taken six weeks to complete, was hopelessly stalled. Moreover, both the Germans and the Allies realised that their northern flanks were not anchored—that they had not reached the North Sea, in other words, and were thus unprotected.

A DESPERATE RACE

There now began what became known as the Race to the Sea. In an amazing series of manoeuvres, the armies of the British and French and those of the Germans began to leapfrog each other as they moved back north. They dug in as they went, seeking to place themselves one step ahead of the enemy. The Germans wanted to turn the Allied flank and reach the Channel ports; the Allies wanted to keep the Germans from doing that and, if possible, turn their flanks. Ten separate battles occurred as the antagonists clashed bitterly.

The manoeuvres took the warring armies straight back into Belgium, where King Albert had emplaced his army around Antwerp and was strongly resisting the German advance.

After a ferocious German artillery attack set the city of Antwerp ablaze in early October 1914, King Albert was forced to evacuate the city. He took refuge on the Belgian coast, where he then had to make a brave and fateful decision.

Everyone knew the fighting would not stop until one of the armies breached the other's flank—or they reached the North Sea. If no flank was turned, the entire front would more than likely be gripped in a stalemate.

German forces ranged in on Antwerp on 27 September with their huge howitzers and began battering the city in an awesome display of modern firepower. The poet Rupert Brooke, a lieutenant with the BEF, watched the destruction and called it 'one of the greatest crimes of history'. Thousands of civilians and Belgian soldiers were slaughtered until King Albert abandoned the city on 6 October and evacuated west to the sea with his five weary Belgian divisions.

By then, the forces of all antagonists were concentrated in Flanders—formerly lovely, quiet, pastoral Flanders—a total, historians later estimated, of almost three hundred thousand Allied soldiers and five hundred thousand Germans, facing each other on a battlefield about sixty-five kilometres long. Although the soldiers dug trenches, they were not the elaborate variety seen later in the war; these were simply connected foxholes, or shallow ditches. Sometimes the men on both sides simply sheltered behind trees and in ruined houses, since the water tables in Flanders (water underlay everything, up to a metre beneath the soil) made serious digging difficult.

German and Allied forces were concentrated most strongly around the central Flanders town of Ypres, a city renowned for its cloth merchants. On 20 October, the first battle of Ypres took place (there would be two more during the war, which would claim in total over a million lives) as the British and French sought to pulverise the German right flank and drive it away from the North Sea. In a bloody coincidence, the Germans opened their own attack at the same time to try to break through to the English Channel. Wave after wave of German troops met the Allies in desperate fighting along the Yser River.

Young German soldiers died by the thousands at the hands of the French, British and Belgians, but their overwhelming superiority in numbers began to tell. By 21 October, the Allied forces were being pushed back everywhere across the Flanders plains. Beleaguered BEF forces and Belgian soldiers held a line from Ypres to the village of Diksmuide, but between Diksmuide and the coastal town of Nieuwpoort was a wide gap through which the rallying German forces would almost certainly attack, turning the Allied flank.

AN AGONISING DECISION

King Albert, who had retreated to a Belgian seaside village, knew that if something wasn't done, Belgium was lost and the Allied cause in peril. Along the coast, the Germans were being held back only by the fierce fire of British battleships in the North Sea. A small force of Belgian soldiers and Flemish sailors held Diksmuide, but then, on 21 October, the Germans opened up their powerful guns and reduced that village to rubble. The way to Nieuwpoort was opening up, along with the all-important railway line that ran between Diksmuide and the seaport.

There is some question as to whose idea it was to open the sluices and floodgates to inundate the land and thereby create a water barrier to the German advance. Some historians attribute the plan to a Belgian general, others to Flemish civilians. But once it was brought to King Albert, he did not hesitate. Even though he knew that flooding the land would cause incredible hardship for his people in years to come, on 27 October he ordered that the floodgates be opened, that the sea be let in.

The people of Flanders had spent much of their history keeping the sea out, and now they were allowing the water to inundate their land, so this was no small thing. Many, if not most, of the Belgian civilians in the areas to be affected had already fled the conflict, but those who had not yet evacuated were now forced to leave their homes, in the certain knowledge that their farms and businesses would be severely affected by the rising water (and in fact it would not be until 1920 that the land would grow crops again). Yet the Belgian people knew they had no choice, and most supported their king's decision: without this desperate gambit, they would be overwhelmed by the German forces, whose reputation for cruelty now preceded them.

The Belgian army, with the aid of the civilian engineers in charge of the sluices and flood-gates, went into action. The night of 29 October saw a full moon, which created the right tidal conditions—as high a tide as possible was needed, in order to ensure that the waters rushed in with maximum effect. The main sluices of the canal system were at Nieuwpoort, and these were exploded with large dynamite charges. Other, smaller ones, had to be held openly manually in order to let enough water flow out. In the meantime, Allied troops took up high positions on canal walls and riverbanks.

The first sign the Germans had of the operation was when water began to flow into their trenches. Yet even as the waters were rising, they made a last desperate attack, sloshing

POETRY AND FLANDERS

The battle for Flanders, as well as spawning human death on an almost unheard of scale, brought forth poetry. John McCrae was a Canadian soldier and medical officer in World War I. The sights he saw at the first battles in Flanders—particularly the vision of bright-red poppies waving over the graves of his dead comrades in arms—led him to write a poem (published in *Punch*, in 1915) that is recited to this day, often at Remembrance Day ceremonies. 'In Flanders Fields' is a cry from dead and buried Allied soldiers for others to 'take up our quarrel with the foe / To you from failing hands we throw / the torch' of a crusade to defeat Germany. At the same time, the poem reminds us of the inhumanity of war, of a time when 'the larks, still bravely singing, fly / Scarce heard amid the guns below'. McCrae died on the western front in 1918, of pneumonia.

Another famous poem to come out of Flanders was written by Rupert Brooke. Unlike McCrae, Brooke was a poet first and a soldier second. Part of the British Naval Division stationed at Antwerp, he was inspired by what he saw in Flanders to write the poem, *The Soldier*, whose beginning was later recited by generations of English schoolboys:

If I should die, think only this of me:

That there's some corner of a foreign field

That is for ever England ...

Brooke, on his way to Gallipoli in 1915, was also felled by disease after a mosquito bite became septic.

Later, once the full effect of the war had been felt by all participants, such patriotic poetry was supplanted by the more morbid offerings of the likes of Siegfried Sassoon and Wilfred Owen. For now, however, the sacrifices in Flanders were used to inspire still more sacrifice.

After the opening of the Flanders floodgates, German army units found themselves surrounded by deep water and under fire from Allied forces. This contemporary illustration depicts the scene in a hamlet south of Nieuwpoort.

through ankle-deep sheets of water. But they were beaten back by the better-positioned and better-prepared Allies. Within about a week, the North Sea floodwaters had risen to cover the land from Nieuwpoort to Diksmuide, a distance of sixteen kilometres. The water was more than three kilometres wide and more than a metre deep. Even if the Germans had been able to find sufficient shallow-draft boats to transport thousands upon thousands of troops, they would have been sitting ducks for Allied artillery and machine-gun fire.

Belgium—and the entire Allied line—was now safe from being outflanked. Indeed, the Germans were never able to overcome this artificial water barrier for the duration of the war. Effectively stalemated, they were forced to engage in the long, attritional campaign that came to characterise World War I. The Belgians—outnumbered and outgunned—had done extraordinarily well. As one British diplomat put it at the time: 'In this fine defence, which did honour to all the troops and commanders engaged in it, the Belgians performed a signal service to the Allied cause'.

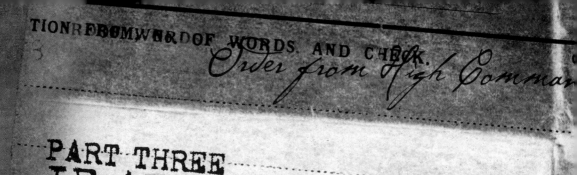

PART THREE
IF AT FIRST YOU DON'T SUCCEED
persistence, resistance and the art of siegecraft

'I propose to fight it out on this line, if it takes all summer.'

General Ulysses S. Grant, telegram to Abraham Lincoln, 11 May 1864

CYRUS STOPS THE WATERS: PERSIA OVERWHELMS BABYLON, 539 BC

CYRUS II, OR CYRUS THE GREAT, AS HE WAS ALSO KNOWN, IS THE SUBJECT OF numerous Persian and Mesopotamian mythic stories, most of which have to do with savage rulers waking up in a cold sweat, realising that their days of glory are about to end with the arrival of Cyrus and his army. Cyrus is also mentioned, at least twenty times, in the Old Testament. There he is named as the man whom the Lord anointed to free the Jews from their Babylonian captivity, and plays a part in one of the most famous biblical stories, in the Book of Daniel, when a spectral hand appears at a feast and writes words on a wall that foretell the downfall of the ruler of Babylon, Belshazzar.

Such dreams and portents may not have occurred, but Cyrus, in his own words, 'King of the World, Great King, Legitimate King of the Four Rims of the Earth', was quite real. Born around 580 BC, he founded the Persian Empire by conquering most of the known world. Even more astonishing, he was a just king, with a record for human rights some modern-day rulers might envy. And in 539 BC, in what is the most mythic story of all—and yet a true one—he came to Babylon and conquered this supposedly impregnable city, by diverting the flow of an entire river. Who needs moving fingers when you have Persian engineers and a king with a good head on his shoulders?

EMPIRES OF THE NEAR EAST

Prior to Cyrus and the rise of Persia, the empire that controlled most of the ancient Near East (today's Middle East) was Assyria, whose charioteers had thundered across the plains of what is now northern Iraq to subject the peoples of the region. The Assyrians could hardly be described as enlightened: their favourite tactic was to utterly crush conquered peoples, not only abducting them as slaves, but also transporting entire ethnic groups from their homelands to other areas of their vast empire. As King Sargon II of Assyria put it, in the eighth century BC: 'Grovelling they came to me, for the protection of their lives. Knowing that otherwise I would destroy their walls, they fell and kissed my feet'.

Among the ethnic groups conquered by the Assyrians were the nomadic tribes collectively known as the Medes, who lived in the mountains of western Iran, and whose fine horses the Assyrians took as tribute, which, in turn, helped make the Assyrian cavalry the best fighting force in the world. In the seventh century BC, the different tribes of the Medes formed a coalition to resist the Assyrians. Joining forces with other tribes on Assyria's eastern border, they swept down from the mountains and, within a decade, had done the incredible: they had destroyed the great Assyrian Empire.

The Medes then went on to conquer present-day Turkey, Syria and Armenia, and set themselves up as the new rulers of the

A seventeenth-century French depiction of Babylon, dissected by the Euphrates River. At the time of Cyrus's attack, Babylon was one of the world's largest cities.

Fertile Crescent (roughly modern-day Syria and Iraq) and all lands to the north, east, west and south. They were, however, not much better than the Assyrians when it came to human rights, treating most captive peoples as little better than chattel and demanding a crippling yearly tribute. Finally, one day, a young man rose out of the east to smite them.

Cyrus—a Latinising of the old Persian *Kuros*, which may mean 'like the sun'—was born, possibly in 580 BC, in what is now western Iran. He was a member of a tribe known as the Parsuans, the original Persians, and the son of a king. After his father's death in 559 BC, he became king and mounted a campaign against the Medes, who were ruled by his grandfather (although some sources say Cyrus simply inherited the kingdom). Within ten years, the Medes had gone the way of the Assyrians, and Cyrus became master of much of the Near East. But instead of selling the Medes into slavery and tossing their wives and daughters into his harem, Cyrus allowed them to stay in their homes in their capital city, even to look after their own affairs, which caused them to love and respect him. After subduing other local nations—including the Lydians, who were led by the fabled King Croesus—Cyrus turned his eyes, in 539 BC, to the rich and fertile land of Babylonia.

A FABULOUS CITY

Babylonia lay in Mesopotamia, the 'land between the rivers' (the Tigris and Euphrates), and was a former province of the Assyrian Empire. However, the Babylonians had made the smart choice in the war against the Assyrians, allying themselves with the Medes, and their power had grown accordingly. The centre of Babylonia, and almost synonymous with the empire, was the city of Babylon, which had existed since at least 2300 BC and had been the largest metropolis in the world since at least the mid-seventeenth century BC.

Babylon was a fabulous city by all reckonings. Built on both sides of the Euphrates River (its ruins lie about eighty kilometres south of present-day Baghdad), it could be seen, and the noise of its 250,000 people heard (the world was then a very quiet place!), from several kilometres away. It was surrounded by a wall that was, in fact, two walls: a double row designed so that if the outer wall were breached, the inner would still provide a formidable barrier to any attacker—especially since a moat ran through the space between the walls. At regular intervals along the outer wall were watchtowers, which projected outwards so that archers could fire down on anyone scrambling up a siege ladder. The Greek historian Herodotus claimed the wall was almost ninety kilometres around, one hundred metres high and twenty-five metres deep. Modern archaeology fixes it at possibly thirty metres high and about sixteen kilometres in circumference. It was said that two chariots could be driven side-by-side along the road on top of the wall, so it was probably at least fifteen metres wide.

Within Babylon could be found numerous ziggurats and temples, though probably not the famous Hanging Gardens of Babylon—there is little archaeological evidence of their existence. The city had a polyglot population unlike any in the world, for the Babylonians, under the great King Nebuchadnezzar II, had conquered numerous peoples and, following the practice of the Assyrians, had enslaved them and brought them back to Babylon. One such population consisted of the artisans, craftsmen and nobility of the Judaeans, whose city of Jerusalem Nebuchadnezzar had destroyed in 586 BC.

TAKING THE WATERS

At the time of Cyrus's advance on Babylon in the autumn of 539, Nabonidus, son of Nebuchadnezzar, was the king of Babylonia. He was something of a mystic and spent much of his time in meditation and worship. Because of this he had named his son Belshazzar as

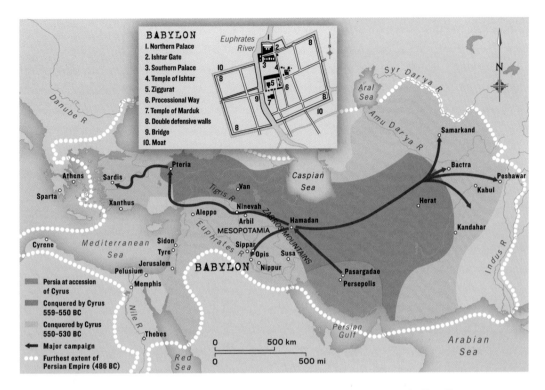

Main map: Within thirty years, Cyrus the Great established a large and lasting empire in the Near East.
Inset: A plan of Babylon around 539 BC showing the major features of this large and magnificent city.

coregent, and left him in charge of the defence of the city. As Cyrus's forces came over the Zagros Mountains and made their way down onto the plains of Mesopotamia, people fled before them. The Babylonians noted that the Persian army was moving quite slowly, stopping to harvest grain and fruit, and seemed unprepared for war. Yet when Babylonian forces attacked the Persians at the northern towns of Opis and Sippar, they were thrown back handily by the Persian horsemen, who seemed to be everywhere with their bows and arrows.

Despite this, Belshazzar was little concerned by the approach of Cyrus, since the city gates were safely closed and the walls bristling with soldiers armed with spears and arrows. But Belshazzar did not quite understand his predicament. For, as Cyrus advanced with his army, he was co-opting the entire Babylonian population. Much of the grain he harvested, and the animals he took, he gave back to the people. He had messengers run before his army, crying that the Babylonians' liberation from their tyrannical rulers was at hand and that they need not be afraid. Cyrus even asserted that he had been sent by the chief Babylonian god, Marduk—the patron god of Babylon itself—to restore the city to its former glory, and to free its oppressed inhabitants. Criers from Cyrus's forces called out as they went: 'By [Cyrus's] side Marduk walks. His hand Marduk holds'.

But although Cyrus was well aware of the power of such supernatural notions on a fearful populace, he would not depend on the gods to find a way through the daunting walls of Babylon. Instead, he would look to his own genius and military experience—and a little bit of luck. A few kilometres from Babylon, he found what turned out to be the key to the city.

Cyrus's scouts, knowing that their leader was searching for something—anything—that might reveal a way into the city, showed him an old reservoir that was dry and overgrown with weeds. From it branched off canals, also dry and disused, that led to the Euphrates River. At the time, irrigation canals were widespread in Babylonia. The reservoir and canals had probably been built many years before, for use in periods of approaching drought: at such times, water would be diverted from the Euphrates into the reservoir, to be stored as a back-up supply.

As he looked at the dusty drainage system, it dawned on Cyrus that there might be another use for it—that by draining the river he might create a way into the city. He instructed his engineers to shore up the walls of the reservoir, seal the bottoms of the canals with stone and cut new canals. Finally, late in September, men in each canal broke down the walls leading to the river. Slowly at first, then faster and faster, water poured along the new and refurbished canals. The men and their king watched with grim satisfaction as the water

THE MOVING FINGER

The most famous biblical story relating to Cyrus's seizure of Babylon is reported in the Book of Daniel. It describes how, as Cyrus's soldiers were sneaking into the city, Belshazzar feasted drunkenly with his friends. To mock the Jews, he called for the sacred gold and silver drinking vessels which had been looted from the Holy Temple in Jerusalem; he and his companions filled them with wine and mead and made toast after toast to the cups themselves, and to the gods of silver and gold and bronze.

Suddenly, to the revellers' great dismay, a finger appeared in the air and began to write strange words on the wall, in a language none of them recognised. Finally, they called for a young Jewish scribe, Daniel, to see if he understood the language. He did—it was presumably Aramaic—and he translated the words for Belshazzar as follows: 'God has numbered the days of thy kingdom and finished it. Thou are weighted in the balance and found wanting. Thy kingdom is divided, and given to the Medes and Persians'.

Balshazzar and his guests were aghast at these words and refused to give them credence. But then word reached them of Cyrus's arrival. The story gave rise to the saying 'the writing is on the wall', now used widely to suggest that someone's or something's demise is inevitable.

The fall of Babylon was a favourite subject for painters from the Romantic period through to the late nineteenth century. This rendering of Belshazzar's feast, by the English artist John Martin, dates from 1820.

level of the reservoir rose and that of the Euphrates fell. Were any of these soldiers prone to musing on irony, they might have considered the fact that the Euphrates, which had long provided life and succour to Babylon, was now about to be the city's undoing.

CELEBRATIONS COME TO AN END

It was the time of the harvest festival in Babylon, and despite the presence of the enemy army, the people of the town were celebrating. Belshazzar's spies had told him that Cyrus's forces were camped several kilometres away, and seemed to be having a festival of their own, with much singing and dancing, so Belshazzar continued to celebrate with his friends. It's unlikely many people noticed the water level dropping during the night; even if some did, it's the kind of thing that people think they're imagining, or to which they might attribute other, more mundane causes, such as, in this case, a failed lock system.

In Babylon, there was an archway over the point where the Euphrates entered the city. Waiting in the darkness there, under the high walls, was a handpicked force of Persian commandos, probably armed only with swords, which they hid under dark cloaks. When the

Hebrews pay homage to Cyrus after his decision to release Babylon's enslaved peoples. Captive since Nebuchadnezzar's razing of Jerusalem in 587 BC, the Jews subsequently returned to their homeland to help rebuild their holy city.

water dropped low enough—according to Herodotus, just up to the men's thighs—they slid into the river. Then they waded through the water and into the city.

Climbing quietly out of the canal, the Persian shock troops seized sentries near one of the city's large gates, cut their throats and then opened the gates to let in the rest of Cyrus's army, which had come up under the cover of darkness and waited silently outside the walls. The army then rushed through the gates and into the streets, overwhelming the surprised soldiers, seizing strategic points and heading for the coregent's residence.

Belshazzar was told of the attack by panicked sentries. Leaping up and grabbing a sword, he led a poorly armed group of noblemen (mostly half-drunk) against the intruders. In a fight that went on for much of the night and spattered the halls and stairways of the luxurious residence with blood, the cream of Babylonian nobility, including Belshazzar, was slaughtered.

Because of Babylon's great size, much of the population did not even know the city had been invaded. When the citizens awoke the next morning, no doubt with a huge collective hangover, they found themselves subjects of Cyrus the Great.

A BENEVOLENT RULER

There were worse things than that, it turned out. Noting that Babylon had become a festering breeding ground of slavery, Cyrus had the populations of captured nations released.

These included many ancient peoples—the Phoenicians, Amorites, Elamites and the Judaeans, who had been enslaved for forty years. (The Babylonian captivity of the Hebrews and Cyrus's deliverance of them became a part of Jewish legend and was taught to countless generations of Jewish children.)

Not only had Nebuchadnezzar enslaved all these peoples; he had enslaved their gods, as well. So Cyrus decreed that everyone returning to their homeland was free to take the statues of those beings they worshipped along with them. It must have been quite a sight to see gods of so many descriptions bobbing along on wooden carts or strapped to the backs of horses.

Cyrus's empire was now reaching its pinnacle. His strong desire to conquer the Greek cities and thus have an opening to the Mediterranean had still not been realised—seeking to achieve these aims, his son Darius and grandson Xerxes would later do famous battle with the Greeks. Yet by the time Cyrus died in battle in 530 BC, in a meaningless border war against a small Iranian tribe, he had created the world's first real empire.

As for Babylon, the city began to lose its luster after Cyrus built a new provincial capital at Pasargade, in the province of Pars. Alexander the Great would die in Babylon in 323 BC, but after that the city was virtually forgotten, until excavations began in the twentieth century that would reveal something of its former glory.

A NOBLE DECLARATION

On the first day of spring in 538 BC, when he was crowned king of all Babylon, Cyrus the Great issued a proclamation that was highly unusual in the ancient world. A man who was the ruler of the entire known world, who had dictatorial powers, stood on the steps of the great temple of Marduk, the ancient Babylonian god, and declared that all the captive people of Babylon could go free, that their captive gods were also free and that the cities in Babylon ruined in warfare by the Persians would be restored.

Messengers spread this message throughout the huge, sprawling city. Later on, a scribe took a stylus to a clay cylinder and put down a brief summary of Cyrus's words:

My soldiers went about peacefully, widespread through the extent of Babylon. In all Sumer and Akkad I let no man be afraid. I devoted myself to the internal condition of Babylon and all the other cities. I freed the dwellers from the yoke that was ill-placed upon them. Their dilapidated dwellings I restored. I put an end to their misfortunes.

The cylinder was then baked in an oven to preserve it, and placed in a record storehouse. And there it stayed until 1879, when an Iranian archaeologist, Hormuzd Rassam, rediscovered it while digging in the remains of the ancient city. The cylinder, twenty-five centimetres long and now in the British Museum, is probably the first declaration of human rights ever recorded.

THE ROAD ACROSS THE OCEAN: ALEXANDER THE GREAT'S EXTRAORDINARY CONQUEST OF TYRE, 332 BC

ALEXANDER THE GREAT WAS, TO PUT IT MILDLY, A PIECE OF WORK. HIS FATHER, Philip, king of Macedonia, was a violent drunk who set out to conquer the known world, ended up settling for overpowering the Grecian city-states and then was murdered, supposedly by a spurned male lover, but quite possibly by Alexander and his mother Olympias, Philip's third wife out of four. Olympias, aside from fulfilling the role of Jocasta in Alexander's real-life Oedipal triangle, was a knockout beauty who was part of a Dionysian sect of snake-worshippers and liked to take large reptiles to bed with her. Modern shrinks would love to have Alexander on the couch: he referred to Philip as 'my so-called father' and was convinced that his true progenitor was Zeus, who had come down to earth and impregnated Olympias.

But Alexander also had a few things going for him. As a boy he was tutored by Aristotle, whom we know mainly for his philosophy, but who was also an expert on constitutional law, music, medicine, astronomy, optics, zoology and even bees: who better to give the future conqueror of the world a full sense of the world's possibilities? And, for better or worse, being Philip's son gave Alexander invaluable military training and, when Philip died, control of a ready-made army of thirty thousand superb Macedonian fighters.

Alexander's genius and ambition were all his own, however. He was the most deeply intuitive of all the great generals of history (Napoleon is perhaps his only rival in this department), seemingly able to read the minds of enemy commanders across the field from him, time and time again deceiving them and thwarting their well-laid plans.

Opposite: The *Alexander Mosaic*, located in the House of the Faun in Pompeii, Italy, depicts the Alexander, wearing a breastplate painted with a portrait of Medusa, defeating Persian king Darius III at the battle of Issus, in 333 BC.

Alexander had a reputation for being generous to brave enemies, but he didn't like anyone who refused to show him respect. Thus, in 332 BC, when the Phoenician city of Tyre—which sat almost a kilometre out into the ocean and was thought to be impregnable—thumbed its nose at him, he employed all his military wisdom, guile and vast resources to teach it a lesson. He decided that if Tyre wouldn't come to him, he would come to it. And in one of the great engineering feats of his age, he built a road across an ocean to destroy the city.

TAKING ON THE WORLD

Though one of his most marvellous victories, the taking of Tyre would be just one in a long series of triumphs for Alexander, which began after Philip's death by an assassin's sword in June of 336 BC. It was then that Alexander decided to fulfil his father's plan of conquering the known world. In this period, that meant, essentially, destroying the Kingdom of Persia, under King Darius III, which extended from the Euphrates River in present-day Iran all the way to Afghanistan.

At the time of his father's death, Alexander was twenty. He is described as being ruddy-cheeked, blonde-haired, short of stature and having (an interesting observation made by numerous ancient chroniclers) very small, very pointy teeth. The army he commanded was fearsome, comprising a fast-moving cavalry and an extraordinarily well-drilled infantry that fought in phalanxes eight men deep, with each man being equipped with a *sarissa*, a spear that was almost six metres long. When properly lowered and employed, the *sarissas* formed an overlapping hedge of murderously sharp points almost impossible to penetrate.

Before setting out to do battle with Darius and his Persians, Alexander had to first secure his northern borders, just across the Danube River, where a rebellious nomadic tribe, the Illyrians, posed a threat to his rear. The ease with which Alexander dispatched these hardened fighters gave notice to the world that he was someone to be reckoned with. At one point, he and his army found themselves on a small plain in front of an Illyrian fortress, surrounded on three sides by rugged slopes full of barbarians. Alexander extracted himself from this perilous position by setting a brilliant trap. He marched his *phalangites* out onto the plain and had them give a close-order drill demonstration in full view of the enemy. The phalanxes manoeuvred in complete silence, communicating only by hand signals. At one command, they would lift their *sarissas* vertically; on another, they would depress them to horizontal position, and wheel left, then right, then march straight ahead. So transfixed were the savage Illyrians by this strange, silent display that they crept down from the mountains to watch—and were immediately set upon and destroyed by Alexander's forces.

The threat to his northern borders removed, Alexander and his army marched into Asia Minor in 334 BC, invading the homelands of Darius III. Carrying a copy of Homer's *Iliad* with him, Alexander crossed the Hellespont (now the Dardanelles) self-consciously tracing the route of Homer's ancient and noble Greeks, and marched through present-day Turkey, liberating the Greek cities under Persian sway. The Persian army, with Darius at its head, arrayed itself in a defensive position on a broad plain near the Granicus River (now known as the Kocabas). Alexander, surrounded by hundreds of his elite mounted bodyguard, the Companions, routed the Persians and sent their king fleeing. Despite the fact that he received a serious head wound, Alexander had achieved his first success against a major power.

Before dealing a final blow to Darius, Alexander turned south and west to protect his flanks. He fought his way through what is now Syria, where Damascus surrendered to him, and then down the coast of what is now Lebanon to the mighty city of Sidon, which fell without a fight in the winter of 333 BC. At that point, all that stood between him and the treasures of Egypt was the ancient mercantile city of Tyre, today situated in southern Lebanon, close to the border with Israel.

BUCEPHALUS: ALEXANDER'S SECRET WEAPON

When Alexander was about twelve years old, he came upon his father and numerous grooms trying to tame a horse. The horse had been given to Philip during a campaign in the Balkans, and was a beautiful animal, much taller and more elegant than the average Macedonian pony. But every time someone tried to mount him, the animal would throw them.

Alexander watched this for a while and then spoke up, saying that it was too bad no one knew horses well enough to properly approach this animal. His father, embarrassed in front of his men, challenged Alexander to see what he could do about it. Alexander had noticed that the horse was highly skittish when it came to shadows, so he entered the ring, took the stallion by its reins and simply pointed it in the direction of the sun. The animal almost immediately calmed down; after a few minutes of stroking the horse and talking gently to it, Alexander mounted it and, to everyone's astonishment, cantered around the corral. Philip was so pleased he gave the horse to his son.

Alexander named his steed Bucephalus, which means 'ox-head', possibly because of an unusual marking on the animal's skin. For twenty years, man and horse were inseparable. Alexander would ride no other horse into battle. Bucephalus never flinched from combat; indeed, in the battle of Gaugamela, he took Alexander so close to Darius's chariot that he was nearly able to kill the Persian king.

The aging Bucephalus finally died of wounds received in the battle of Porus, in 326 BC in India, and Alexander mourned the animal deeply, even establishing a city named after him: Bucephala.

AN ISLAND FORTRESS

When Alexander rolled up to Tyre, the city was already a thousand years old and had a reputation as one of the premier mercantile centres in the world. It was an old Phoenician city that had at first been located on the seashore; then, after repeated sieges on the part of the Babylonians, it was moved to a small island, five kilometres in circumference, just offshore.

Alexander and his forces arrived on the mainland in November of 333 BC, and stared out across the waters at Tyre. The island was a valuable piece of real estate, containing two natural harbours, which the Persians would be able to use as a base for their fleet, should they choose to come after Alexander when he moved south. Tyre could not, therefore, be bypassed.

However, it was widely held to be unconquerable. Alexander was told how Nebuchadnezzar, the ancient king of the Babylonians, had attempted to besiege Tyre for twelve years before giving up and going away. Hearing about this was like catnip to Alexander, since the thing that pleased his ego most was surpassing legends of the past and creating his own.

Alexander had only a very small navy, however, and thus no real way of making an amphibious landing at Tyre. He stalled for time by asking the Tyrians if he might simply be allowed to enter the city to worship at their famous shrine of Melkart, the Tyrian version of Hercules. The Tyrians refused, telling Alexander that no Macedonians would be allowed in the city. They also asserted that Tyre was officially neutral in the war

----

BARGAINING WITH ALEXANDER

During the siege of Tyre, Alexander received a letter from Darius III, whose family Alexander had managed to capture and was holding. Darius offered Alexander ten thousand talents—a huge ransom—for the safe return of his family. Not only that, but Darius proposed that he and Alexander divvy up the Middle East: Alexander would get all the land west of the Euphrates, and—here's the kicker—he would also receive the hand of Darius's daughter in marriage.

When Alexander's companion Parmenion saw this offer, he said: 'I'd take it, Alexander, if I were you'. To which Alexander famously replied: 'If I were you, so would I. But I'm Alexander'.

His reply to Darius was pure Alexander, too. He said Darius could have his family anytime he wanted, for no ransom at all. All he had to do was come and take them. He also said that there was no point in being offered half of Asia Minor—he already had half, as it was, and intended to take the rest whenever it suited him. As for Darius's daughter, he would marry her if he chose to, with or without Darius's permission.

All of this was more than mere posturing. Alexander knew that it was the right time to take on a weakened Darius; if he and the Persian king struck an alliance, a stronger foe might arise in Babylon to attack the Macedonians in the future.

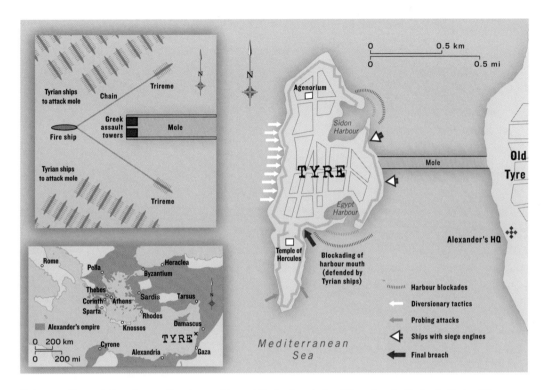

Main map: Alexander's mole steadily advanced toward the besieged city of Tyre, despite the best efforts of the defenders, who at one point sent out a fire ship to destroy it (upper inset). Lower inset: Alexander's empire.

between Darius and Alexander and that no Persians would be allowed in, either. The Tyrian reply was as disingenuous as Alexander's request to worship at the shrine.

Alexander then decided to send the Tyrians an ultimatum: surrender or die. When the Macedonian general's heralds reached the city, the Tyrians took them high on their walls, making sure the Macedonians on the mainland could see them. Then they killed them and threw their bodies into the sea. Watching this savage scene, Alexander was enraged. He prided himself on treating conquered enemies well. The only fitting response to this affront was to destroy the city. But how?

Alexander had a cadre of Greek engineers with him, and he set them to studying the problem. Tyre had stone walls rising to a height of forty-five metres. It was out of the range of any type of catapult and could not be taken by surprise. The water between the city and the mainland was mainly shallow and reef-strewn, although near the island the channel deepened to six metres. Even if Alexander could raise a fleet to invade, a landing would still be difficult: Tyre's harbours could be quickly closed, either by harbour boom or ship blockade. It seemed that the only way to get inside the city was to knock down or otherwise breach her walls, but there was no way to get close enough.

Then it came to Alexander that the city did have one weakness: it could not move away. Its inhabitants could not retreat. He could take all the time he liked. So he decided to build a bridge to the island, along which his army would march to Tyre, and conquer it.

THE WAY TO TYRE

More properly, what Alexander decided to build was a causeway, or mole, a sort of landfill, sixty metres wide—so that he could pour his phalanxes over it in breadth as well as depth—and three-quarters of a kilometre in length. Materials were readily available in the old city, and Alexander had his men rip it apart for its ancient stone. Then his engineers marked out a path across the water with stakes, and filled the area between the stakes with sand, limestone or crushed rock. Initially, they made rapid progress. They were out of reach of Tyre's fortress walls, which bristled with catapults, and the water was too shallow for Tyrian vessels. But as soon as the work progressed far enough and the channel deepened, the Tyrians launched ships filled with archers to harass the workers. Alexander responded by building two wooden towers. Between them, he stretched a huge hide screen. The screen was moved in front of the work as it progressed and provided some protection for the workers—until the Tyrians, remarkable military innovators themselves, sent in the fire ship.

This large vessel was heavily weighted aft, so that its bow stood up in the air. Atop the raised bow, timbers and piles of straw, which had been covered with highly flammable pitch, were stacked high. Three huge masts were affixed to the front of the ship, as well, and between these masts hung huge cauldrons filled with brimstone and oil. The Tyrians waited for a windy day, then towed this strange and unwieldy boat out into the harbour. As the wind pushed its upraised bows against the head of the mole, brave Phoenicians set it afire then dived into the water just before the boat crashed into the hide screen. The cauldrons tipped, flames shot up into the sky and Alexander's wooden towers and hide screen, and numerous Macedonian lives, were lost in a firestorm.

But Alexander would not be deterred, no matter what the setback. For six months, the work continued, with thousands of Alexander's men taking part in this extremely hazardous duty. Alexander sent to Sidon for more ships. When they arrived, he attempted to force the Tyrians out from their harbour to do battle, but they refused and blocked their harbour

Opposite: A relatively bloodless representation of Alexander leading the final and extremely violent assault on Tyre.

An eighteenth-century oil painting of Alexander's glorious entry into Babylon in 331 BC. Eight years later, following conquests that extended deep into Asia, Alexander returned to that fabled city and died there, aged thirty-two.

entrances as foreseen. Alexander then had catapults built on the ships, anchored them off the island and began to bombard the city walls, hoping to knock them down in increments. Tyrians swam out at night with knives between their teeth and cut the anchor ropes. When the Macedonians began to use anchor chains, the Tyrians catapulted huge rocks onto the siege ships to wreck them. And whenever the Tyrians captured a Macedonian, they would bring him up on the walls, disembowel him and throw his body into the sea.

As this very strange siege continued, yet stranger things began happening. According to accounts in ancient chronicles, a sea monster arose from the ocean and crashed into the causeway—which the Tyrians took as a favourable omen. However, it did not harm the work being done and immediately slid back into the sea—and this the Macedonians considered to be a point in their favour. In the meantime, Alexander had a dream in which Hercules himself stood on the walls of Tyre, like a Macedonian prisoner about to be sacrificed. He was waving his hands and imploring Alexander to come to his rescue.

MARCHING ACROSS THE WATER

Finally, after seven months of extraordinary trial and difficulty, in August 332 BC, the causeway was close to the walls of Tyre. Alexander did not attempt to finish the last stretch of the mole, since it would reach a part of the city walls that had been so heavily fortified as to be impregnable. Instead, he brought catapults to the end of the mole and used them to hurl huge stones at the walls on either side of the reinforced area. Together with the ship catapults, they managed to breach the walls of Tyre in several places.

Then, in a carefully planned assault, Alexander sent his newly reinforced navy to break through one of the harbour booms in the south of the island, and floated landing craft carrying huge towers up to the breached walls. Men fired arrows from the towers, while others poured through gaps in the walls. The Tyrians put up a desperate, ferocious and highly inventive defence, which included increasingly terrible weapons such as barbed grapples on long ropes that could grab assailants climbing siege ladders and drag them screaming up the wall to be murdered, and tubes that discharged molten lead in blazing streams upon the attackers. Most feared of all were the huge metal bowls the Tyrians filled with sand and gravel and heated to a red-hot consistency before tipping over any Macedonians in range. The Greek historian Diodorus wrote of the sand: 'It sifted down under their corselets and their clothes, searing their flesh with intense heat … they screamed entreaties like men under torture and none could help them, but with excruciating pain they went mad and died'.

Finally, however, the city fell. Alexander ordered his men to murder its inhabitants, except those few who were able to take refuge in the city's shrines, which Alexander considered sacred. Eight thousand Tyrians were killed and thirty thousand taken captive and sold into slavery. Two thousand of those put to the sword had their bodies hung from crucifixes, as a reminder to anyone who might see them of the likely fate of those who defied Alexander. As a capstone to the victory, Alexander had his men finish the causeway. After that, he had them haul his biggest siege catapult to the temple of Hercules and placed directly in front of the shrine. Then Alexander knelt and gave thanks to Hercules for his great victory.

TRACES OF AN EMPIRE

Soon after, Alexander conquered much of the known world. He went from Tyre to Egypt, where the inhabitants received him as the man who would save them from the Persian threat. He was hailed as a Pharaoh, even given the sacred symbols of the crook and the flail. After lingering in Egypt, Alexander turned back east, where, in 331 BC, he defeated Darius at the battle of Gaugamela. All of Persia was then Alexander's, but still he was not satisfied and continued east to invade India in 328. After fighting there for two years, he journeyed back to Persia, where he died, of fever, alcohol overdose or poisoning by one of his many enemies—there are numerous theories—in June of 323.

Alexander's empire fell apart shortly after he died, mainly because he had named no heir, and although his name will be forever remembered, there are few tangible reminders of his presence. However, if you choose to, you can go to Lebanon and visit Tyre, and there you can see, though they are now part of a much wider causeway, the remains of Alexander's amazing road across the ocean.

PUTTING UP WALLS: CAESAR TRIUMPHS AT ALESIA, 52 BC

THERE HAS NEVER BEEN A MILITARY LEADER LIKE JULIUS CAESAR. ENDLESSLY inventive, personally brave, he was apparently able to inspire loyalty in the most cynical and battle-weary legionary. And he seems to have enjoyed more than his fair share of good fortune. Indeed, so convinced of his luck was he that in one battle—wearing his distinctive *paludamentium*, or scarlet general's cloak—he stood out in front of his faltering army and allowed the enemy to rain iron spears down directly on him and him alone. Hundreds fell. Not one touched him.

Campaigning in Gaul from 58 to 52 BC, Caesar needed all the luck and skill he could muster, especially when he fought the last and most decisive battle of the war against a charismatic young leader commanding a tribe of fierce warriors in a supposedly impregnable hilltop fortress. Caesar's ambitions could have ended on the muddy earth of what is now south-central France, but, drawing on all his expertise (as well as his seemingly bottomless well of hubris), he managed to save the day for his legions and for himself.

But it was a near thing.

A RUTHLESS LEADER

After his assassination on the Ides of March in 44 BC, Caesar was officially declared a god, but his origins were somewhat more humble, if not without privilege. He was born in the year 100 BC (via Caesarean section, supposedly) to an aristocratic but relatively impoverished Roman family. After the premature death of his father, the sixteen-year-old Caesar became

Opposite: Gaius Julius Caesar was one of the greatest military commanders in history. His management of the Roman forces at the siege of Alesia would display to the full his brilliant talents for organisation and innovation.

the head of his family. Caught up in a civil war raging at the time, he made some powerful enemies. He escaped into the army and spent two years campaigning in foreign countries, then returned to Rome and began building his reputation as a master politician and orator.

Yet he remained, first and foremost, a ruthless military man. During a journey to Rhodes in 75 BC, he was kidnapped by Sicilian pirates who held him for a ransom of fifty talents of gold. (They had intended to ask for twenty, but Caesar told them it was too little.) Caesar swore he would see them all crucified. They thought he was joking, but after he was ransomed, he returned, captured every one of them and hung them out to die on crosses.

In 63 BC, he became military governor of Iberia (Spain), where he quelled rebellious tribes. He returned to Rome in triumph to reign as co-consul along with the weak-willed Marcus Bibulus; the true ruling power of the country lay with what became known as the First Triumvirate, made up of Caesar and his political allies Pompey and Licinius Crassus. When, after five years, Caesar's term of office was over, he became governor of most of Gaul. He immediately set out in 58 BC to assert his authority over the territory.

AMONG THE GAULS

Gaul was, very roughly, modern-day France and Belgium, and, as Caesar famously wrote, it was divided into three parts, consisting of the Belgae people (in the north), the Celts in central France and the Aquitani to the south and west. Caesar marched into Gaul in 58 BC with the four veteran legions that had been given to him as governor, plus two others that he had raised in northern Italy. The Romans had already subjugated part of Gaul, particularly around the area of modern-day Provence, but the tribes to the north and west of the Rhône River were troublesome. Caesar may have decided to take them on because he wished to gain territory and the booty and glory of war, but it is also likely that he wanted to erase a hostile presence on Rome's northern borders—at an earlier time, about three centuries before Caesar's birth, Gauls had marched on Rome and sacked the city, and Rome had never forgotten this.

Although the Gauls were members of different tribes, they shared certain characteristics. They were fierce warriors who practised animism, the worship of natural objects such as lakes, trees and mountains. They were physically striking, most having long, flowing hair (northern Gaul, where Caesar reckoned the tribes to be the wildest, because they were so far from the civilising influence of Rome, was sometimes called *Gallia Comata*, or 'long-haired Gaul'). There were about three hundred tribes in all, numbering in the millions. The Romans were nearly always outnumbered, but usually managed to defeat their enemies by virtue of superior fighting tactics and clever politics—much of Caesar's campaigning involved turning certain tribes into Roman allies, while conquering others by force.

Caesar quashed the Belgae in the north and the tribes along the Atlantic seaboard in the west. He invaded Britain with two legions in 55 and 54 BC, invasions which some historians think were unnecessary, except to increase Caesar's prestige back home, which they certainly did. By then, all of Gaul appeared to be under control, though there was the occasional insurrection, as occurred in the winter of 54–53 BC, when Gauls in what is now Belgium nearly captured an entire garrison, until Caesar intervened. But such revolts were nothing compared to the one that would end the war—the one led by the great warrior Vercingetorix.

PREACHING INSURRECTION

Caesar later wrote in his *Commentaries* that, by the winter of 53–52 BC, 'Gaul was now tranquilised'. But Caesar was retrospectively justifying his departure, and this was not, in fact, the case. In the mountainous country of the Averni tribe, in south-central France—the modern Auvergne—a charismatic young nobleman named Vercingetorix was fomenting rebellion.

Vercingetorix's father had been a powerful Gallic chieftain who had tried to become king of his tribe and had been murdered by rivals. Vercingetorix had apparently inherited some of his ambition. In January of 52 BC, the Carnute tribe near modern Orléans rose up and massacred Roman settlers who were coming to occupy the land. A wave of rebellion swept over France and Vercingetorix, then probably in his early twenties, decided to ride it.

- -

GATES COME TUMBLING DOWN

To study Julius Caesar's conduct in battle is to observe a fertile military mind in action, for the Roman general was always thinking of new and improved ways to deceive the enemy. In the winter of 54–53 BC, tribesmen in the area that is now modern Belgium arose in revolt against the Romans. After slaughtering nine thousand Romans marching through the region, they besieged the Seventh Legion, under General Quintus Cicero, younger brother of the famed orator. Caesar immediately set out from his winter camp to relieve the siege, and when the Gauls found out he was coming, they turned and marched in force in his direction. In classic Roman fashion, Caesar hastily threw up a fortified camp with high walls of dirt and logs. But he instructed his men to make the camp gates very thin, so that while they appeared strong, they were in reality quite fragile.

When the Gauls arrived and made to storm the fort, they didn't even bother to attack the gates, which were normally the strongest part of Roman camps. Then, all of a sudden, a Roman trumpet blew—and the supposedly unyielding gates blew outwards, as if from an explosion. Massed Roman cavalry had charged straight through the thin dirt barriers and into their enemy, who were so taken by surprise that they were slaughtered where they stood, or had to run for the hills to save themselves.

He began preaching rebellion against the Roman yoke, which scared the elders of his tribe so much that they ousted him from the Averni capital of Gergovia and its environs. From there, Vercingetorix wandered the countryside, fomenting insurrection. He appears to have been a compelling and magnetic figure, described as having curly reddish-blonde hair and moustache, and being eloquent of speech. Going from village to village, he recruited so many to his cause that he was able to return to Gergovia and oust the elders who had ousted him. He now claimed the prize that had been denied his father: leadership of his people. He ordered that arms be made—spears, swords, axes—and spent a good deal of time receiving the groups of warriors who arrived daily in response to his emissaries.

Next, Vercingetorix marched with thousands of men upon the tribes in the south of France who were loyal to Rome. The Romans had to react quickly, because these tribes protected Rome from northern barbarians. So Caesar raced from his winter quarters in northern Italy, picking up legions along the way, in order to cut off Vercingetorix and make him do battle.

SCORCHED EARTH

As Caesar pushed him back, Vercingetorix adopted a scorched-earth policy, burning all the settlements in the Romans' path, so that the countryside was filled with the smoking ruins of crops, farms, even entire towns. Vercingetorix retreated with his army to a camp outside Avaricum, the region's capital city (modern Bourges). He wanted to burn the city,

ROMAN LEGIONS: THE RE-ENLISTMENT FACTOR

Unlike most modern armies, to which soldiers are recruited regularly for short periods, Roman armies carried out mass recruitments of thousands of men at a time and these men stayed in their units for long periods—sixteen years in Caesar's time and, later, twenty years. At the end of their service, all the veterans would be pensioned off together and given land (usually in the Roman colony where they had served), and a new mass enlistment would begin.

This system had evident advantages and disadvantages. One advantage was that these men—recruited at the age of roughly twenty—bonded strongly and became a co-ordinated fighting unit. However, as casualties weakened their number, no new recruits were brought in, although non-Roman citizens from the frontiers often formed auxiliary units that aided understrength legions in battle. Thus a legion, which on paper numbered about six thousand men, could be whittled down to several hundred. In addition, Roman commanders (including Caesar) often faced revolt if they refused to allow legions whose enlistment time was up to go home during times of war. Usually, large bribes were needed to get the men to stay on for more campaigning.

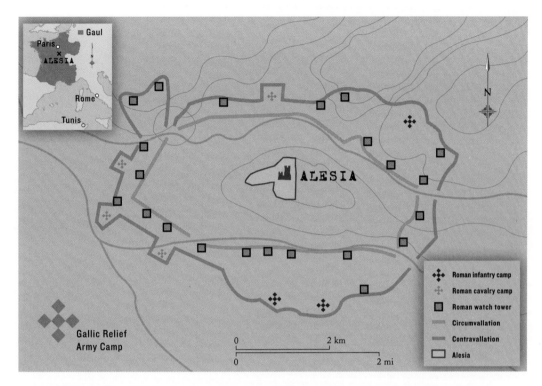

A plan of the Roman forces and constructions around the town of Alesia during the prolonged siege of 52 BC, showing the inner wall (circumvallation) and outer wall (contravallation) constructed by Caesar.

but when those who lived in the region protested, he instead sent ten thousand men to help the city's forty thousand inhabitants hold out against Caesar.

Caesar's legions besieged Avaricum for twenty-five days, most of which were plagued by driving rains. Since the walls, made up in large part of great stones, were too tough to be knocked down by battering rams, the Romans tried to break the stones off one by one using huge hooks attached to long poles. The Gauls, in reply, lassoed the hooks with long ropes and winched them over the walls by means of windlasses. When the Romans tried to tunnel under the walls, the Gauls replied by digging their own tunnels to undermine the Roman ones. But eventually, the Romans were able to build a huge siege-tower, push it against the wall and climb into the city. Furious at having been stymied for so long, the legionaries slaughtered, according to Caesar's count, forty thousand men, women and children, while only eight hundred managed to escape to join Vercingetorix.

The armies of Vercingetorix and Caesar then raced each other to the Averni capital of Gergovia; Vercingetorix won by a nose, quickly fortified the city and was able to repulse the

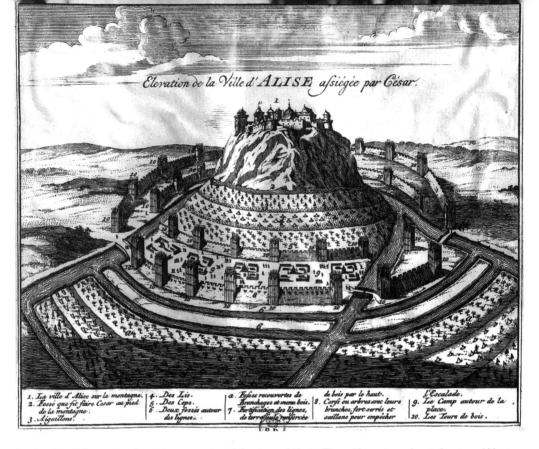

Elevation de la Ville d'ALISE assiégée par César.

1. La ville d'Alise sur la montagne. | 4. Des Lis. | a. Fosses recouvertes de | de bois par le haut. | L'Escalade.
2. Fossé que fit faire César au pied | 5. Des Ceps. | Branchages et menu bois. | 8. Cerfs ou arbres avec leurs | 9. Le Camp autour de la
   de la montagne. | 6. Deux fossés autour | 7. Fortification des lignes, | branches, fort serrés et | place.
3. Aiguillons. | des lignes. | de terre seule renforcée | saillans pour empêcher | 10. Les Tours de bois.

A rather fanciful seventeenth-century engraving of the siege of Alesia. The settlement was located on top of Mont Auxois, above the present-day village of Alise-Sainte-Reine in the Bourgogne region.

Romans and inflict heavy losses—Caesar's first defeat in battle. Vercingetorix's victorious troops chased after the retreating legions and were only stopped by the legendary Legio X, which Caesar rallied personally to stand in the way of the advancing Averni. Even so, as the Gauls withdrew to Gergovia, they could still savour a great victory. They had in their possession several of the sacred standards of the legions and had, according to some historians, wiped out at least six thousand Roman troops.

Caesar left the area of Gergovia and marched south, while more and more tribes flocked to Vercingetorix's side. Feeling powerful, the Averni leader attacked Caesar's cavalry with his own but was badly beaten during a pitched battle near modern-day Dijon, in part because the Roman army had been reinforced with German mercenaries from across the Rhine. Vercingetorix's troops were sent reeling back, and Caesar, sensing the advantage, followed quickly with his sixty thousand troops.

Unwilling—wisely—to meet Caesar on an open field of battle, where the trained fighting power of the legions would more than make up for the fact that the Gauls outnumbered them, Vercingetorix then took his eighty-thousand-strong army to the town of Alesia, on a plateau about fifty kilometres from modern Dijon. There, he would make his stand.

A FIELD OF HORRORS

Situated on Mont Auxois, Alesia was a fortified town, bulwarked by deep trenches and heavy, stone walls. To assault it would have been suicidal, and Vercingetorix thought, correctly, that Caesar did not have enough men to invest it effectively. It was now September of 52 BC. If Vercingetorix could hang on for a few months, Caesar would have to retreat to a winter camp and Vercingetorix would be seen by all his people as the victor. But the Averni leader, as brave and charismatic as he was, had not counted on Caesar's perseverance and ingenuity.

Caesar immediately set to work building one of the most extraordinary siege works that has ever been built, a wall that ran all the way around Alesia. It was the kind of construction known in military terminology as a circumvallation, and it was designed to make sure the Gauls were blockaded inside their fort and to protect the besieging Romans from raiding parties from Alesia. Caesar's palisade was four metres high, sixteen kilometres around, with twenty-three small forts along its circumference. The walls were made of thick tree trunks from trees cut in nearby forests. Sharpened branches—'like stag's horns', Caesar wrote in his *Commentaries*—were affixed to the outer walls every metre or so to impale anyone trying to climb.

Between the city walls and the palisade, for about four hundred metres directly in front of their lines, the Romans created a field of horrors for any enemy troops trying to cross no-man's-land. Nearest Alesia, they placed rows of *stimuli*, wooden blocks fixed with iron spikes thirty centimetres long. Outside these were fields of ironically named 'lilies'—sharpened stakes in pits. Closes to the palisade were two deep parallel trenches, one of them filled with diverted stream-water, the other empty.

Vercingetorix, looking out from his battlements, would have realised that the Romans were here to stay and known, too, that his men had only thirty days' worth of rations. He ordered his cavalry out to attack the Romans and try to halt their construction work, but the German mercenaries once again swept in and routed the Gauls. As, after three weeks, the Roman fortification neared completion, Vercingetorix sent more of his cavalry out under the cover of darkness to try to break through; though most were killed, a few managed to escape the ruthless German mercenaries.

WALLING THEMSELVES IN

Caesar found out from captured Gauls that the escapees had asked other tribes to help Vercingetorix. Caesar knew that if the Gauls attacked in number from the rear, the Romans could be obliterated. Despite having little time to analyse the situation fully, he came up with what one historian has called 'one of the most brilliant siege tactics in the history of warfare'. Caesar had a second wall built behind the first, facing outwards, in the direction that the relief forces might come. This second wall, known as a contravallation and similarly made of wood, entirely encircled the first wall; its wider circumference made it twenty-five kilometres round. Between the two walls, there was room for the entire Roman army. After completing the second wall in a few weeks, Caesar waited. In the meantime, conditions inside Alesia were terrible, with thousands of women and children starving alongside their warriors. When the Gauls sent them outside the walls of Alesia, hoping the Romans might let them through, to food and safety, Caesar, unable to risk opening his wall, left them where they were, starving.

In late September, reinforcements came thundering up the valley to aid the Gauls. Caesar wrote that 250,000 barbarians arrived to support Vercingetorix, but most historians place the number at around 100,000. This relief force immediately attacked the outer Roman wall, while Vercingetorix launched an attack from within Alesia on the inner wall. The hard-pressed Roman legions were forced to fight two fronts, but at least had protection on both sides. Had Caesar not erected the second palisade, it is almost certain that the legions would have been massacred. The battle raged all day with Caesar, sporting his *paludamentium*, seemingly everywhere, on both ramparts. By sunset, neither side had gained the advantage.

The next day, 2 October, the last attack of the battle of Alesia was launched. The Averni had discovered a weakness in the Roman walls—a place where, because of the irregular shape of the slopes of Mont Rea, the mountain that abutted Mont Auxois near Caesar's defences, the palisades did not quite meet. The Gauls of the relief force and Vercingetorix's forces had managed to communicate well enough to launch a co-ordinated attack against this place and, in desperate fighting, the Romans were nearly overwhelmed, in some places being outnumbered six to one. Vercingetorix's Gauls came prepared: they filled the trenches with dirt, and, locking their shields over their heads, made it to the rampart walls, where they hurled grappling hooks over the palisades and tried to pull them down. The Romans threw iron spears down on their heads from above.

Every soldier, both Roman and Gaul, knew that this battle was the one that counted—there would be no quarter given to the loser. The relief forces attacking down the slopes of Mont Rea had great momentum and came crashing against the outer walls, shaking them to their foundations, while Gauls who had come down the slopes from Alesia, on the other side of the Roman enclosure, hurled spears into the palisades, killing hundreds of Romans.

Then, when the battle seemed most desperate, Caesar did what Caesar always seemed to do: threw himself in harm's way and saved the day. Sensing weakness in one flank of the

Vercingetorix arrives at the Roman camp ready to surrender to Julius Caesar, as depicted in this nineteenth-century oil painting. The palisades and watchtowers of the Roman fortifications are visible in the background.

Gallic relief force, Caesar personally led Roman cavalry and infantry *outside* of the ramparts to flank the Gauls. The surprised enemy was routed, with thousands killed and captured, and Vercingetorix retreated to his fortress, knowing he had to surrender.

THE END OF GAUL

The next morning, in a celebrated scene, Vercingetorix rode a dashing charger in a full circle around where Caesar and his officers sat. Then, leaping down, he hurled his sword and spear to the ground—and then sat in front of Caesar in submission. Surviving Averni were given to Caesar's triumphant legions as slaves—each Roman received one Gaul.

Vercingetorix became Caesar's prisoner and was taken to Rome in chains and imprisoned for six years. Then, after Caesar was named emperor in 46 BC, Vercingetorix—by then a wasted wreck of his former self, although probably no more than thirty years old—was paraded before the Roman people before being garrotted.

The war in Gaul was more or less over, although the Gauls would rise in rebellion from time to time. But ultimately, they became staunch Roman allies until the fall of the Roman Empire in AD 476. All thanks to Caesar's quick thinking and the double row of palisades he built across a muddy hilltop.

FINDING A WEAK SPOT: TAKING CHÂTEAU GAILLARD, 1203-04

THESE DAYS IT'S CALLED TRASH-TALKING, BUT PERHAPS IN THE THIRTEENTH century it had a different name—castle-bashing, king-kicking? In any event, around 1198, two regents, Richard I of England (the famous Lionheart) and Philip II of France, exchanged words over the extraordinary castle that Richard had built in Normandy—Château Gaillard, a fortress that held such a special place in the legendary English king's affections that he referred to it as 'my fair daughter'.

King Philip scoffed: 'I would take that castle if its walls were made of iron'.

To which, when he heard it, Richard replied: 'And I would hold it if its walls were made of butter'.

Look out! Fighting words. But this barbed exchange captures the essence of medieval warfare in western Europe, which consisted for the most part not of armies clashing on open fields or knights engaged in hand-to-hand combat, but of siege warfare in which huge, elaborately constructed fortresses were assaulted by armies carrying with them siege engines of equally elaborate construction. The name of the game in this type of warfare was coming up with new and better castles—rather than an arms race, a sort of 'castle race'—to which attacking forces would respond by looking for new and better ways to breach these fortresses. Besieging a castle involved certain, almost routine actions, such as setting up siegeworks and blockading the area. But the shrewdest campaigners also spent a good deal of time simply studying the castle, looking for a flaw, something the castle builders had overlooked.

Opposite: King Richard I of England, the so-called Lionheart, who waged war against Saladin in the Holy Land, then was ransomed from desperate imprisonment before coming home to build the greatest castle of the era.

King Philip's subsequent siege of Château Gaillard—a castle that not only King Richard considered impregnable—took place over the course of roughly seven months, from August of 1203 to March of 1204. This was not an especially long time for a siege, but the whole affair might have taken much longer had it not been for the keen senses of a French commoner by the name of Ralph, who was nicknamed Snubnose. Snub it may have been, but Ralph's nose was acute, for it sniffed out a latrine chute, by means of which the French would capture the supposedly impregnable castle and, thereafter, the entire English kingdom of Normandy.

KINGS, FRIENDS - LOVERS?

Richard and Philip, separated in age by eight years—Richard, born in 1157, was the elder—were once the closest of companions. Through his mother, Eleanor of Aquitaine, Richard had close ties to France. Philip had helped him to rebel against his father, King Henry II, and seize the throne of England in 1189; the French king also took part in the Third Crusade against the Saracens who held the Holy Land, although he left the campaign early due to illness. The two men were so close that, one contemporary chronicler put it, they 'ate from the same dish and at night slept in one bed', and there has been some speculation among historians that they had a homosexual affair.

As is well known, passionate love is just a bowshot away from its obverse, ardent hatred. When Richard came back from the Crusades and his long imprisonment—he was captured on the way home and held for ransom by Henry VI, Holy Roman Emperor—he discovered that his treacherous brother John, in league with Philip II, had offered the Emperor eighty thousand marks to *continue* to hold Richard captive. (Fortunately for Richard, his mother, Eleanor, topped the offer with one hundred thousand marks and finally

King Philip II of France. Despite Richard's death, Philip remained determined to destroy the English king's treasured Normandy stronghold, Château Gaillard.

freed him in 1194.) From Philip's point of view, this made great sense. John was a weaker ruler than Richard, easily manipulated, and Philip's ultimate goal was to regain French territory (which included Normandy) currently in the hands of the English.

From this point on, Richard and Philip were sworn enemies. In order to foil Philip's designs on Normandy, Richard decided to build a castle, and he made sure to pick just the right spot for it—a cliff high above the point where the Seine and Gambon Rivers flow into each other, right on the frontier between the Angevin territory and the rest of France. The castle would guard important river crossings, without access to which Philip would be unable to campaign in Normandy. And to make sure Philip was well and truly stymied, Richard would spare no expense to make sure the castle was completely unconquerable.

'HOW BEAUTIFUL SHE IS!'

Richard ordered that the fortress be built in great haste and it was. In an astonishing feat of construction, the English castle was all but completed in one year, 1197–98. Six thousand workers toiled ceaselessly to make the impregnable outpost a reality. In a sign of how important the project was to him, Richard spent 12,700,000 ducats on its construction, a sum that equalled or surpassed the English crown's annual income at that time.

But what a castle it was! Shaped roughly like a triangle, Château Gaillard was built on a narrow promontory that rose one hundred metres above the Seine. Sheer cliffs led down to the water on the broad base of the triangle. At the southern end—the tip of the triangle—

- -

MEDIEVAL SIEGE WEAPONS

In the Middle Ages, large armies besieging a castle normally had a number of fearsome weapons at their disposal. Many relied on a sudden release of tension, like that which fires an arrow from a taut bowstring. A catapult worked, for example, by pulling a rope as far back as possible then releasing it, to propel a huge boulder through the air.

Smaller catapults were used as antipersonnel weapons. In this category were the ballista (from the Latin, meaning 'to throw'), which looked like an enormous crossbow and shot thick iron bolts the size of spears, and the mangonel, which looked like a huge spoon set on a frame and fired rocks.

One way of getting close enough to a castle to make an assault was by using a belfry, a huge mobile tower on rollers. Covered with dampened animal skins to ward off attempts to set it on fire, the belfry was filled with men and pushed close enough to the walls to let a drawbridge down upon the battlements, across which attackers would rush en masse. Since ramparts were only wide enough for two or three lines of defenders, a massed charge of this sort stood a good chance of success.

the castle's outer court faced a gently sloping plateau, the main approach to the fortress. Here there was a moat ten metres wide and twelve metres deep, spanned by a drawbridge that was pulled up flush with the castle wall at the first sign of trouble and protected by a portcullis, a screen of heavy beams banded and tipped with iron, which slammed into notches in the ground.

The castle wall at this leading edge was ten metres high and two to four metres thick, and guarded by five cylindrical watchtowers cut with arrow slits. Between the outer court and the wider middle court were two more walls, each ten metres high and two and a half metres wide, separated by a deep moat. Even if attackers got over these defences and into the middle court, they were then faced with the massive walls of the inner court of the castle. These walls were embossed rather than smooth—that is, they were made up of nineteen semicircles joined together. Not only did this shape help deflect projectiles, which tended to glance off the arcs, but it allowed for enfilading fields of fire—in other words, archers could shoot sideways through slits to protect any point on the wall. There were no blind angles.

The only way into the inner court was through a single narrow gate, which was protected by drawbridge and portcullis and built on land six metres higher than the middle court. Attackers would find themselves being shot with arrows or having burning oil poured on them from a great height.

Finally, inside these walls, at the very top of the cliff, was the castle's innermost defence, the keep, or donjon. This huge tower had battlements at the top and only three tiny windows. Its walls were more than three metres thick and were sloped outwards at the base ('battered' in castle-building-speak) to make them difficult to climb. Deep grooves were carved into the side of the keep, down which burning oil or boiling water could be poured on anyone foolhardy enough to attempt to climb up.

THE LEGEND OF THE LIONHEART

It was during the last decade of Richard's life that the legend of Richard the Lionheart began to take shape, when he went off to fight the Muslims under Saladin, beginning in 1190. Arriving in the Holy Land in 1191, he defeated Saladin at the battle of Arsuf, although he was unable to take Jerusalem and ended up negotiating only a three-year truce with the Saracens and safe passage for Christian pilgrims. After his capture and imprisonment at the hands of Henry VI, and later after his death, poems and songs were written that celebrated Richard's bravery in battle and gave rise to the nickname of Richard the Lionheart. The great warrior was, however, a less successful ruler: in all, Richard spent only six months of his reign actually in England.

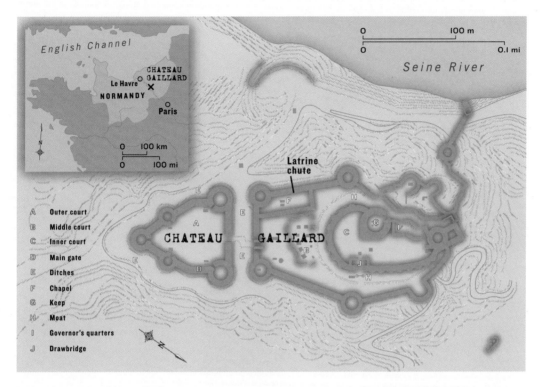

Main map: A plan of Château Gaillard. The besiegers advanced from the left, or south, where the land rose gently to the walls of the outer court. Precipitous slopes bounded the other sides. **Inset:** The location of Château Gaillard.

When Richard saw the castle completed in the summer of 1198, he is said to have exclaimed: 'How beautiful she is, my one-year-old daughter! What a *gaillard* castle!' By *gaillard* Richard meant 'well-built,' but the word also has the meaning of 'bold' or 'saucy', so many at the time began calling it the Château Gaillard, or Saucy Castle.

But Richard had little time to enjoy his daughter. During a minor campaign in France, he was wounded by an arrow and died after gangrene set in, on 6 April 1199. His brother John succeeded him and inherited his castle. John made only one modification: he ordered that another toilet be built in the chapel. This type of toilet was called a garderobe—essentially, a small L-shaped room, little more than a metre wide, built right into the castle wall. A garderobe of this sort normally had a seat, which may or may not have featured a wooden cover (to help out a bit on those freezing mornings). The toilet emptied into a long chute which dumped the waste outside the castle walls, probably into a pit or barrel. Many castle-builders remembered to put iron bars at the base of the chute, to keep out invaders. But this was one detail the otherwise meticulous builders of Château Gaillard managed to overlook.

A fourteenth-century naive-style painting on vellum of the siege of Château Gaillard. Note the looks of consternation and puzzlement on the faces of the French besiegers—Gaillard was a tough nut to crack!

PROBING THE DEFENCES

With John installed on the throne, Philip II decided that it was time to reclaim French territory held by the English and so began a campaign that ultimately brought his armies to the foot of the promontory upon which Château Gaillard was built, in August of 1203. King John was not then present. Commanding the castle garrison was a well-known English soldier named Roger de Lacy, who considered himself to be in a very favourable position. He had ample supplies for a year, a deep well and a small cadre of trained soldiers—his force may have been at most five hundred strong, but that was intentional: the point of the castle was to be able to hold out with few men against many.

Deciding, at first, that the castle was too strong to take by direct attack, Philip settled down to besiege it, after first capturing the small towns that lay along the base of the cliffs. One of his first stratagems was to release one thousand of these villagers and send them to the English castle, hoping that their presence would deplete de Lacy's food supply. But the English would not let these poor people into Gaillard, and, as the autumn turned to winter, they began to perish, until Philip finally relented and allowed them back through his lines.

Since the English had destroyed all local bridges across the Seine, hoping to cut off the French supply lines, Philip commanded that a sort of pontoon bridge, built of boats lashed together and protected by floating towers filled with archers, be constructed. He then had his men build a 'covered way' leading to the castle—basically a deep trench with a wooden roof. This allowed the French to get close enough to the moat to begin filling sections of it with wood and stones. Philip also ordered that the tops of nearby hills be levelled, so that catapults could be set upon them. When this was finished, in early 1204, he began raining huge boulders down upon the English inside Gaillard. Meanwhile, King John sent two relief forces to try to break the siege, but both were turned back with heavy English losses.

During the winter, the French began to build belfries—towers that could be rolled up to the castle walls. The first such attacks took place in February 1204. As catapults arched stones into the castle, the French pushed the belfries against the castle walls, allowing French soldiers on top to rain arrows down upon the English defenders. At the same time, other French soldiers attempted to scale the walls with ladders or even by gaining footholds in the rough stone.

The French had also been secretly digging, under the protection of the covered way, a deep tunnel under the walls of the outer courty, shoring it up with wooden beams. Now they lit a fire in it. The point was not to explode something in the tunnel, as soldier-miners in later centuries did, but to weaken the foundation of the castle wall. First the fire would burn the wooden beams shoring up the tunnel, and then the tunnel would collapse—and so too, hopefully, would a portion of the wall, which was at the same time being battered by cata-pults. This was, in fact, what happened—a portion of one tower crumbled in a huge cloud of dust, French soldiers rushed in and after fierce hand-to-hand fighting, the English retreated to the middle court.

Philip had conquered his first obstacle, but now faced others yet more daunting. He was prepared to bide his time and continue the siege, however, no matter what the cost. He sent his soldiers out to look for weak points, the Achilles heel by which Gaillard might fall. And soon, indeed, one was found.

BY A NOSE

Into our story at this point comes a character whom Shakespeare might have invented, a French common soldier named Ralph, who had the wonderful nickname of Bogis, or Snubnose. Not much is known about him, though we can assume that his proboscis must have been abnormally bobbed to receive such a sobriquet. He and a few of his fellow soldiers were examining the castle walls after the first courtyard fell, seeking an easier way to get into the middle court than direct assault. While other soldiers kept the English troops occupied by hurling both missiles and curses (a vital part of besieging castles was seeing who could insult his enemy's ancestors most cuttingly), Ralph suddenly noticed a dark hole low down on one side of the castle wall. Following his nose, he soon realised that it was a toilet chute.

Ralph would undoubtedly have reported back to his superiors that the latrine chute was not barred in any way. No one knows whether he was ordered to climb up the chute or volunteered, along with a few other unfortunate (or brave) souls, but we do know he was first to make the entrance.

What he experienced can only be imagined. The garderobe chute was probably just wide enough for a small man to squeeze through, and the only way to climb its length of ten metres or so would have been to grab hand- and footholds in the rough masonry and pull oneself laboriously along, no doubt smearing excrement along face and body. And, of course, one can only hold one's breath for so long.

When Ralph and his besmirched and besmeared fellows got to the top and exited the garderobe, they found themselves in a chapel (where perhaps, being religious sorts, they might have crossed themselves before continuing). The men were spotted almost the minute they ventured out of the chapel, but such was the shock of their assault (and possibly of their appearance) that the English reacted in a panicked way. Trying to drive the French out, they set fire to the section of wall with the chapel in it; the flames spread into adjacent buildings and smoke poured over the parapets of the middle court, inhibiting their own actions. In a panic, the soldiers retreated to the final circle of defence, the keep, as Ralph and his men opened the middle court gates and let the remaining French forces pour through.

NORMANDY REGAINED - AND RALPH REWARDED

On 6 March 1204, after repeatedly battering the keep wall with catapults and once again mining underneath it, the French managed to create a hole in the masonry large enough for French forces to pour through. Old custom indicated that once a 'practicable breach' was opened in a final fortification, the garrison could surrender with honour, and that is what Roger de Lacy, down to 140 men, did, in order to avoid needless slaughter.

The ruins of Château Gaillard are today a popular tourist attraction. In this photograph, the castle keep, at top right, rises above the embossed walls of the inner court. The Seine River is visible in the background.

The siege of Château Gaillard had lasted seven months, but it had only been a month since Richard's pride and joy had been under active attack—King Philip II had managed to reduce her in record time. After this, he campaigned through Normandy, taking the city of Rouen and pushing to the coast. King John's prestige and position were weakened by the humiliation of losing a supposedly impregnable castle to the French; indeed, it could be said that the loss of Gaillard began the long process that eventually led to the Magna Carta, for it was disgust at the king's military weakness that led the English barons to rebel and force him to sign this momentous document in 1215.

And what of the 'beautiful', 'well-built' Gaillard? The castle stood sound for the next two centuries and even protected French forces under English attack during the Hundred Years War. But by 1573, it was designated by the French a 'ruined castle, fallen down and uninhabited'. Armed gangs used it as a hideout, and French authorities gave permission for Capuchin friars to dismantle parts of it and use the material to repair their churches. However, much of the castle was spared, and it is now a popular tourist attraction.

There is no memorial to Ralph the Snubnose, but the curious will be glad to know that King Philip rewarded him with a 'knight's fee' for his dirty service—that is, while there was no question of this mere peasant becoming a knight, he was given sufficient land and money to *act* as if he were one. Which must have made Ralph wrinkle his nose in satisfaction.

DEATH IN THE AIR:
THE SIEGE OF CAFFA, 1347

ONE DAY IN THE SPRING OF 1347, A MONGOL KHAN ON THE SHORES OF THE BLACK Sea made a desperate decision. For months, he had been watching his men die around him from a terrible disease which raised egg-like swellings in the armpits and groin, bruised the skin in spots until it was purple and black, brought on horrible, quivering fevers and caused men to shriek hysterically as they died, reeking of bilious vomit and excrement. Yet, if Janibeg—for that was the khan's name—looked to the shining walls of the city his army was besieging, he could see his enemies, apparently unaffected, laughing at his weakening and dying warriors, and thanking God that they had been spared this pestilence that was decimating their foe.

The Mongol army was becoming feeble—at least half of its forty thousand men had died. It no longer had a hope of defeating the Christians holed up in their whitewashed port city. But, in true Mongol fashion, Janibeg decreed that his antagonists would not escape unscathed—that the curse that God had visited upon his people would also be felt inside the city.

Commanding those men who could still function, he set them to their catapults and trebuchets. Instead of having them mount rocks or containers of naphtha, ready to be lit, in the slings, he had them load up the gruesome corpses of their deceased comrades-in-arms, men who had died of this strange plague before they were able to inflict a blow on the enemy. At least in death, they might do some good.

Janibeg raised his arm. When he brought it down, the reeking corpses flew tumbling and turning through the air, like twisting, life-sized puppets, into the town of Caffa, where they landed with a splatter and a spray of blood.

And so began one of the most extraordinary episodes of biological warfare on record.

FLOURISHING THROUGH TRADE

In the mid-thirteenth century, Caffa (now Feodosiya in the Ukraine) was a sleepy fishing village on the north shore of the Black Sea, which had the misfortune to occupy a strategic location at a time when the West and the East were vying for control of the region. Caffa was part of the great Mongol Empire, begun by Genghis Khan in 1206, which had spread across China, the steppes of Russia, Central Asia and Asia Minor, and right to the edge of Europe. Much of Europe had been horrified by the Mongol threat—these so-called Tartar hordes had retreated in 1241 only because the great khan Ögödei, son of Genghis himself, had died— but not the intrepid merchants of the Italian city-state of Genoa. From the very beginning, these men had seen the incursions of the Mongols as an opportunity for unprecedented trade.

Located on the northwest coast of Italy, Genoa was a small but powerful city-state, one of the peninsula's maritime republics, and the Genoese were known far and wide as brilliant seafarers and crafty merchants. By the 1250s, they had made trading agreements with the burgeoning Mongol Empire and in 1266 they leased the village of Caffa from the Tartars and set about making it a major trading centre.

Caffa was perfectly situated to receive goods from all points of the compass: timber and furs from the north; silk and spices and diamonds from Indonesia; silver, gold and cotton from the west; and slaves from all over, for under the Genoese Caffa became one of the biggest slave markets in Europe, a place where Mongols, Muslims and Christians could both unload and purchase human flesh. Within eighty years, the population of Caffa had grown to about seventy thousand, and the settlement had become one of the most influential port cities in the known world.

'DREADFUL SIGNS AND PORTENTS'

The early fourteenth century was a time of terrible portent in Europe. The so-called Little Ice Age had begun, bringing frigid weather and massive blizzards that lasted well into the spring and destroyed crops. In about 1315, a terrible famine hit northern Europe, and humans as well as livestock died, and those who did not die were severely weakened by malnutrition. As if that wasn't enough, reports of strange and disturbing events came out of the East. Gabriel de' Mussis, the Italian scribe and notary who would later record the horrors of Caffa for history, wrote: 'In the Orient at Cathay … where the world's head is … dreadful signs and portents have appeared'. Supposedly, there were immense swarms of locusts, torrential rains followed by blistering droughts, earthquakes that swallowed cities and mountains whole and entire provinces assailed by poisonous snakes and scorpions. In fact, while some of these reports were fantasy and exaggeration, there *was* massive upheaval in China at this time. The country had been involved in a lengthy rebellion against the Mongol conquerors, which caused widespread suffering and death, with large swaths of land laid utterly to waste.

Even more ominously, a strange pestilence had arisen, one that seemed to emerge out of nowhere to wipe out an entire village before reappearing in the next village with the same mortal force. Historians now know that this was the bubonic plague, the so-called Black Death, which was soon to kill one in every two people in China and one out of every three people in Europe, Central Asia, India and the Middle East. (If the Black Death hit the world today with the same ferocity, and we had no defences against it, it would claim two billion lives.) The Black Death was carried by the bacillus *Yersinia pestis*, which preyed on rats and other rodents (although this was not known until the twentieth century), and also spread by human contact with the bacteria. When environmental upheavals, such as floods, famines, war and earthquakes, hit, wild rats leave forests in search of food, which almost inevitably takes them to human communities. In fourteenth-century China, that meant communities where immune systems had been considerably weakened by starvation and stress, and where hygiene and sanitation (never good to begin with) were nonexistent. These were perfect conditions for *Yersinia pestis* to begin its journey through the human population, and the trade routes along the broad grassy steppes of Mongolia and Central Asia were the perfect highway.

In 1334, plague struck in the Chinese province of Hubei; by 1339, it had reached the shore of Lake Issyk Kul, in northwest China, a stopping point for travellers. The next major town where merchants met was Caffa, sixteen hundred kilometres to the southwest.

- -

BIOLOGICAL WARFARE THROUGH THE AGES

Long before contemporary uses of chemical weapons— of serin nerve gas in Japanese subways, of weapons- grade anthrax spread through the United States mail as a fine white powder—biological warfare was used to spread horror and death among enemies.

In the sixth century BC, for example, Assyrians poisoned the water supply of their enemies with rye ergot, a fungus that can produce LSD-like hallucinations. In 600 BC, Solon of Athens poisoned the water supply of the town of Krissa with the herb hellebore, a violent purgative in large doses.

In the twelfth century, the Holy Roman Emperor Frederick I polluted water wells in the rebellious city of Tortona, Italy, with human bodies. In 1495, the Spanish mixed the blood of leprosy patients with red wine and exported it to their enemies, the French. And in 1763, British soldiers deliberately gave smallpox-infested blankets to American Indians. More recently, during World War I, the Germans attempted to ship livestock infested with anthrax and glanders to the United States and France; they may also have attempted to spread bubonic plague in Russia.

This fourteenth-century illustration of a typical medieval siege shows a trebuchet, a catapult of the type that was used by the Mongols to hurl dead, plague-ridden bodies into the Genoese-ruled Black Sea city of Caffa.

BEGINNING WITH A BRAWL

It's ironic that one of history's most significant instances of large-scale biological warfare began with what was essentially a street fight. In 1343, Genoese from Caffa were trading in the town of Tana, on the Don River, just up the river from the Sea of Azov, which flows into the Black Sea. The local Muslims and Mongols traded with the Genoese, but didn't particularly like them. They thought them vain and egotistical, and crooked in their business

The route travelled by the plague, or Black Death, as it made its way from China through Central Asia to Caffa on the Black Sea, and from there to Italy, from where it spread quickly through mainland Europe.

dealings. For their part, the Genoese were suspicious of the foreign ways of the easterners. According to Gabriel de' Mussis, who was not there but heard the story from those who were, a Muslim merchant in Tana thought a Genoese was cheating him. Words were exchanged, a fight ensued and a Genoese pulled a knife and killed the merchant. The Muslim community appealed to the Mongol khan Janibeg, a Muslim himself and their protector, for help. Janibeg, always ready to beard a Christian or two, showed up with a large Tartar force and attacked. The outnumbered Genoese retreated to their boats, and set sail west for Caffa. They could see the Mongols riding their horses along the shoreline, trying to beat them there. The Genoese made it first, raised the alarm and closed the gates of their city. De' Mussis described it this way: 'See how the heathen Tartar races, pouring together from all sides, suddenly invest Caffa … The trapped Christians … hemmed in by an immense army, could hardly breathe'.

There then ensued a seesaw battle that lasted on and off for four years. The Mongols tried to starve the Christians out, but the Genoese had plenty of provisions and water. In February 1344, the siege was temporarily lifted when a Genoese relief force arrived and defeated

Janibeg's forces soundly, killing fifteen thousand Mongols. Janibeg, however, was not about to allow the Christians to escape unscathed. He came back in 1345, this time with a larger force and many more siege machines, ready to invest Caffa, destroy its walls and butcher all of its inhabitants. But, then, as de' Mussis recorded:

> Behold, the whole army was infected by a disease which overran the Tartars and killed thousands upon thousands every day. It was as though arrows were raining down from heaven to strike and crush the Tartar's arrogance. All medical advice and attention was useless; the Tartars died as soon as the signs of disease appeared on their bodies: swellings in the armpits or groin caused by coagulating humours, followed by a putrid fever.

This was obviously a Christian point of view—God smiting the heathens—but it's understandable that the Genoese in Caffa might have felt grim pleasure in seeing the suffering of their tormentors. During the four-year siege, trade had nearly come to a standstill and thousands had died. The accursed Mongols were feeling the wrath of Almighty God. It wouldn't be long now before they would have to turn tail and drag themselves back up the Don to where they came from—those who hadn't already been sent to *Tartarus,* that is, to Hell.

A HARD RAIN

People in medieval times had no real idea of the nature of infectious disease, but those who came in contact with this deadly plague certainly knew that it was transmitted from person to person, in some fashion. It may be that Janibeg knew this, and that it led him to implement his fiendish and devastating ploy. Of course, using the bodies as projectiles not only helped assuage Janibeg's thirst for revenge, but also solved his body-disposal problem. Whatever his reasons, Janibeg's strategy had a devastating effect, as de' Mussis recorded:

> [The Tartars], fatigued by such a plague and pestiferous disease, stupefied and amazed, observing themselves dying without hope of health, ordered cadavers placed on their hurling machines and thrown into the city of Caffa, so that by means of these intolerable passengers the defenders died widely ... What seemed like mountains of dead were thrown into the city, and the Christians could not hide or flee or escape from them, although they dumped as many bodies as they could into the sea. And soon the rotting corpses tainted the air and poisoned the water supply ... Moreover, one infected man could carry the poison to others, and infect people and places with the disease, by look alone.

The range of a medieval siege engine like a catapult or trebuchet was roughly two hundred metres—human bodies could possibly have been hurled further. It didn't much matter, though, because the Mongols could aim anywhere in Caffa: their target was an entire city.

It is hard to imagine what it would have been like to have been one of the seventy thousand inhabitants of Caffa at this time: looking up into the sky to see a tiny figure growing bigger and bigger until it is revealed as a twisting corpse, which then lands with a spray of body fluid on the street in front of your home. Thousands and thousands of corpses rained down on the city. Everywhere the inhabitants went, they would have had to keep their eyes to the sky, watching for falling bodies, and they would have heard continual heavy thuds as the bodies crashed to the ground.

And then the dying would have started. Professor Mark Wheelis, a microbiologist who has studied the siege of Caffa, thinks the disease would have spread quickly as city inhabitants, many of whom almost certainly would have had 'cut and abraded' hands, handled the torn-apart corpses, trying to drag them out of the way. As people in the town began to die, chaos would have set in. Judging by the later plague outbreaks, the infected would soon have been left dying in the streets, to be devoured by animals, who would then have passed the disease on to more humans. In the meantime, hordes would have swarmed to the waterfront, the only way out of the ghastly town of Caffa, to try to beg, bribe, or fight their way onto any seagoing transport available.

A DEADLY CARGO

By the spring of 1347, what was left of the Mongol forces abandoned Caffa and straggled back home. Any Genoese who could find a berth on a ship fled back to their home. It was a very long journey—more than 2,500 kilometres—first to Constantinople, then across the Mediterranean. No one knows how some of the infected travellers managed to survive that long—the only explanation is that some had hardier genes than others—but, in October of 1347, a fleet of ships carrying Genoese from Caffa reached Messina, in Sicily. Most of the crewmen were either dead or dying. Some ships washed ashore on the coast with no one on board left alive.

From Messina, the plague spread to Genoa and Venice, then to France, Spain, Portugal and Britain by 1349, before infecting Scandinavia, Germany and northwestern Russia. It burned through Europe for the next three years, killing one-third of the population. Then it was gone, although cycles of plague would return, again and again over the next few centuries.

Biological warfare has taken many forms over the years, but few instances before the twentieth century have been as horrible as the infected cadavers smashing down on the

This illustration from an illuminated manuscript depicts the burial of victims of the Black Death at Tournai, Belgium, in 1349. The plague reached Belgium in that year and devasted large areas of the country.

streets of Caffa. It is certain that the plague would have reached Europe another way had the siege of Caffa not occurred, but it struck faster and with greater impact because of a Mongol khan's decision to hurl his corpses—dead men on a mission of vengeance—into the shining city of his Christian enemies.

- -

STING LIKE A BEE

It is widely known that armies have long employed mammals to aid them in warfare—horses, elephants, camels, dogs, even dolphins—but far less well known is the military use of bees. The Romans used bees in battle, catapulting hives into enemy fortifications, and this was a practice that continued throughout the Middle Ages, in sieges and in ship-to-ship naval battles. In the nineteenth century, Nigerian warriors kept bees in powder horns full of poison, which they believed made their stings more potent, and then released them at their enemies (and then presumably ran like hell to get out of the way). In the Vietnam War, the Viet Cong even used beehives in booby traps, to sting unwary Americans.

THE TERRIBLE POWER OF PA: THE BATTLE OF OHAEAWAI, 1845

When we were within fifty paces of the stockade front we cheered and went at it with a rush … The whole front of the *pa* flashed fire and in a moment we were in a one-sided fight—gun flashes from the foot of the stockade and from loopholes higher up. [There were] yells and cheers and men falling all around. Not a single Maori could we see. They were all safely hidden in their trenches and pits, poking the muzzles of their guns under the foot of the outer palisade. What could we do? We tore at the fence, firing through it, thrusting our bayonets in, or trying to pull it down, but it was a hopeless business.

THE ABOVE SENTENCES FORM PART OF THE RECOLLECTIONS OF A YOUNG BRITISH corporal named William Free of an assault on a Maori fortification known as a *pa*. The words 'hopeless business' aptly describe the feelings of most nineteenth-century British soldiers when confronted with a *pa*. These complex fortifications—systems of interlocking trenches, bombproof bunkers, hidden firing ports and almost bulletproof palisades—have been likened to the elaborate trench fortifications of World War I. Certainly nothing like them had ever been built by an indigenous force fighting European colonists. At one particular *pa*, Ohaeawai Pa, the focus of this story, the Maori defenders themselves were so appalled at the British foolishness in continuing their attack that they pleaded with their enemies to abandon their effort. The pleas did little good.

LAND OF THE LONG WHITE CLOUD

Consisting of two large, mountainous islands (the North Island and South Island) and several smaller ones, New Zealand is one of the most isolated places on Earth—it lies almost two thousand kilometres from the nearest continental landmass, Australia—and as a result

The Warrior Chieftains of New Zealand, as painted by Joseph Jenner Merrett in 1846: Hone Heke, centre, and his wife Harriet, with Ngapuhi chief Kawiti, at right.

was one of the last to be settled by humans. Polynesian explorers, ancestors of the Maori, arrived some time after AD 800—the date is still debated—in giant canoes that have become part of Maori legend. Their descendants called New Zealand *Aotearoea*, or the Land of the Long White Cloud, for the clouds that hang over the mountains and can be seen from far across the ocean. Maori culture developed in isolation for perhaps eight hundred years; though the Maori did not have access to metal, they were extraordinarily innovative: in place of iron, they used whale bones, ivory teeth and dog and human bones to fashion weapons and tools of strength and beauty.

The word *Maori* means 'the local people', and *Pakeha* is the Maori word for non-Maori people, who first appeared when the Dutch trader Abel Tasman stopped briefly at the Land of the Long White Cloud in 1642. Captain James Cook's visit in 1769 was of much greater significance, as far as the Maori were concerned. He surveyed the country and reported back on its rocky bays and teeming sea life. Within thirty years sealers, whalers and traders arrived, both from Australia and Europe.

This first wave of Europeans had fairly peaceful relationships with the Maori, mainly because they were not interested in venturing far into Maori land. As of 1840, the settler population of New Zealand was still only about two thousand, while the Maori numbered perhaps ninety thousand. But things were changing rapidly. In 1839, a land company called the New Zealand Company had sent agents to acquire land in New Zealand, with the purpose of shipping more and more settlers to the country. (These settlers subsequently set up permanent villages with very British names like Wellington, Nelson, New

---

MAORI AND MOKO

One British soldier meeting the Maori for the first time during the fighting of 1843–48 remarked that, while the men fought nearly naked, 'the appearance of nakedness is completely taken away by the tattooing … Every man is without exception covered with tattooing from knees to waist; the face is also covered with dark spirals'.

Moko, as the Maori art of tattooing is known, was an ancient custom that started out when Maori warriors painted their faces with spiral lines of charcoal in preparation for battle. Gradually, these temporary marks were replaced by permanent ones, and the tattoos were applied to almost every area of the body, although only the most important of chiefs could be tattooed on the forehead, upper lip or chin. Male tattoos also had a practical purpose: since in their intertribal wars, the Maori had a habit of decapitating their enemies, tattoos could identify a headless body.

Maori women were also tattooed, at puberty, although their *moko* were confined to their chin and lips.

Plymouth and Canterbury.) The company's activities forced Great Britain, which had previously refused to annex New Zealand, to send Captain William Hobson to the country to establish British sovereignty.

Soon after his arrival in January 1840, Hobson decided that the only way to protect Maori land from the encroaching settlers was to sign a treaty guaranteeing them rights to the territories they currently owned, in return for their pledging allegiance to Queen Victoria. On 6 February 1840, such a treaty was signed at Waitangi, near the northern tip of the North Island. As with so many treaties signed with indigenous peoples in the nineteenth century, however, it was one fraught with misunderstanding and treachery. The forty Maori chieftains who signed that day (five hundred Maori ultimately signed) may have thought that their land and possessions would henceforth be protected against New Zealand Company encroachment, but it was not to be the case. The Maori were to be 'amalgamated' into the new settler communities, rather than the other way around. As one historian put it, New Zealand was no longer a Maori country, with space reserved for the *Pakeha*. Instead, it was *Pakeha* territory, with room now needing to be found for the Maori.

FIRST BLOOD

In 1839, on the Wairau Plain, near the present-day city of Blenheim in the South Island, a sea captain, John Blenkinsopp, offered a cannon to two Maori chiefs, Te Rauparaha and Te Rangihaeata, in return for timber. He got them to sign a document that they thought was a receipt, but which he later claimed assigned him much of the Wairau Plain. After his death, Blenkinsopp's widow sold the document to the New Zealand Company, which then started to survey and parcel out the land.

The Maori chiefs objected and took the dispute to the Government Land Commissioner, as per the Treaty of Waitangi, to have it resolved. But in the meantime, on 17 June 1843, a magistrate and a group of settlers marched from the settlement of Nelson to the Wairau Plain to 'arrest' Te Rauparaha for obstructing surveyors. A fierce battle ensued in which numerous Britons and Maori were killed, among them Te Rauparaha's daughter, and the Maori then took eleven settlers captive. The deaths were a slight on the tribe's *mana*, or prestige (which in Maori culture was vital to a people's well-being). For Te Rauparaha, the only way to remedy this was by *utu*, or revenge, so he had the prisoners executed.

In all, twenty-two settlers died at Wairau and it became a cause célèbre among the whites, who called it the 'Wairau Massacre'. Even the colonial government asserted that the settlers had caused the incident, but it was the Maori, according to the bloodthirsty cries, who were going to pay.

'THE WHITE MAN'S ANGER'

The ensuing wars between Maori and settlers would last on and off for twenty years and have been called by a number of names. These days they are known as the Anglo-Maori Wars or the New Zealand or Land Wars. The British, true to their habit of naming wars against indigenous peoples after the 'hostile' groups, initially referred to them as the Maori Wars and to the battles after Wairau, from 1845 to 1848, as the First Maori War. These first conflicts have often been dubbed the Northern War, since they took place mainly on the North Island. The Maori's name for the fighting was, perhaps predictably, at once more poetic and more accurate: *Te riri Pakeha*, 'the White Man's Anger'.

Another name for the early conflicts was the Flagstaff War, a name that derives from a famous incident that took place at the town of Kororareka, on the Bay of Islands in the North Island. Hone Heke, leader of the Ngapuhi *iwi*, or tribe, had been one of the original signatories of the Treaty of Waitangi but had grown increasingly dissatisfied. The British had unexpectedly shifted the country's capital from Kororareka to Auckland, which had caused a loss of important revenue to Heke; too, the flag fluttering in the stiff ocean breezes coming off the Bay of Islands was—according to the French and American seamen who had Heke's ear—a sign of British mastery of the Maori.

In June of 1844, Heke marched into Kororareka and cut down the flagstaff, the first of four different times he would do so. Each time the British erected a new staff, Heke cut it down. The British then sheathed the pole in iron. On 11 March 1845, Heke struck Kororareka with a war force of 450 Ngapuhi. Undeterred by the colonists' artillery and entrenchments, Heke divided his men into three different forces and stealthily entered the town in a three-pronged attack. The British fled to their ships, the flagstaff came down again and Kororareka was burned to the ground. Eighteen British soldiers and one sailor were killed, and twenty-seven wounded. The shooting war was on with a vengeance.

FORMIDABLE FORTIFICATIONS

Possibly as a result of the significance of concepts such as *mana* and *utu* in their culture, the Maori were prone to intertribal warfare long before Europeans arrived. As a result, they were highly skilled in the arts of war. Traditional arms included spears, axes and clubs, but by 1845 the Maori had also acquired muskets from the settlers. The Maori were extraordinarily brave and quite original in their tactics. In particular, they excelled at defensive strategies, most notably the construction of a type of fortification they called a *pa*.

A *pa* was normally a fort made of wood and earth, usually fifty to a hundred metres long and roughly twenty-five metres wide. The Maori refined the construction of *pas* until they

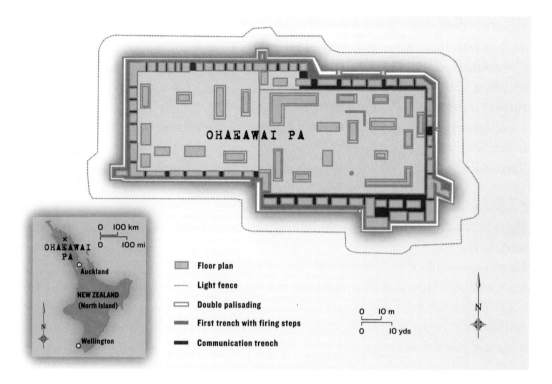

OHAEAWAI PA

Main map: A plan of Ohaeawai Pa, based on a drawing made by a British soldier who fought in the battle, showing the main palisades and trenches. **Inset:** The location of the *pa* in the northern North Island.

could assemble them remarkably quickly. One day there might be no *pa* in an area, then, literally the next day, the British would find one there. Historians estimate that eighty or so Maori could throw up a good-sized *pa* overnight.

Whenever possible, a *pa* was sited in an elevated position. Often, it was built against a swamp or river or some other barrier, so that it was difficult to surround completely. A *pa* was protected by palisades made of tree trunks roughly four and half metres in height and fifteen centimetres in diameter. Critically, the Maori learned to caulk the cracks between the tree trunks with green flax leaves—tough, stringy plants which, the Maori had discovered, were almost bulletproof, or at least musket-ball-proof. Most palisades were raised up a little, so that defenders in trenches could fire from underneath the palisades, up at their attackers. Inside, the Maori constructed interconnecting trenches and, eventually, deep bunkers in which they could shelter during artillery bombardments.

The Maori developed a range of tactics for use in the defence of their fortifications, which often turned the tables on attackers. For example, in a tactic reminiscent of the Mongols, they would make one side of a *pa* more inviting to attack, sometimes even by breaking down a wall, so that the enemy would charge in and could then be ambushed by warriors concealed in camouflage pits in front of the *pa*. The fortifications themselves were often expendable—the Maori set them up in order to draw the British to attack, inflicted damage on their enemy and then destroyed the fortifications and withdrew.

The British had never seen anything like these defences before, not in fighting the Indians in America nor the Sikhs in India, which may have been what moved a later British commander, Sir John Fortescue, to call the Maori: 'the grandest native enemy'.

PIÈCE DE RESISTANCE

After the attack on Kororareka, the British sent a task force under Colonel William Hulme to retake the town—by this time the Maori had fled—and punish Heke for his actions. In this, they were joined by a Maori tribe led by a chieftain named Waka Nene, who was a sworn enemy of Heke and his people, and who helped the British locate them.

The British and their allies fought their first pitched battle against Heke, who was joined by a legendary Ngapuhi chief named Kawiti, at Puketutu Pa, four days march from the Bay of Islands. The *pa* was not quite finished, so the two chiefs decided to ambush the soldiers. As the British attacked the *pa*, Kawiti attacked them from the rear. A fierce battle ensued, involving hand-to-hand combat, until the British were able to drive off the Maori, but at the cost of fourteen killed and twenty-eight wounded.

In June, the British mounted a large expedition, hoping to capture Heke and destroy his forces. On 23 June, they arrived at Ohaeawai, near present-day Kaikohe, and found themselves facing a truly formidable *pa* for the first time.

You could say that Ohaeawai Pa was Heke's and Kawiti's masterpiece. After the battle at Puketutu Pa, the two Maori leaders had hastened to build a *pa* that would stand up to the punishment they knew the British would inflict. The perimeter of the new *pa* was double-palisaded, and there was a third, lighter, fence ten metres outside the other two, which was there to slow up the British and make them easier to kill. The main two perimeter palisades were extra-strong, being made of heavy logs sunk two metres into the ground, and their corners were pushed out at flanking angles—'zigzagged', in military parlance, meaning that those Maori manning the angles could catch their attackers in a crossfire.

Trenches up to two metres deep, with wooden firing steps (much like the trenches of World War I), were cut directly behind the palisade, so that the Maori could fire through loopholes. The trenches were built with great ingenuity: they were not continuous, but rather separated by walls, so that if an attacker chanced to leap into one, he could not traverse the

A contemporary illustration of the British encampment at Ohaeawai. In the background, smoke rises from British artillery fire. Despite a continued British bombardment over several days, the *pa* did not yield.

whole trench easily. And if a shell fell into one, only a few Maori might die, instead of many. The trenches also incorporated, for the first time, bomb shelters, with roofs of timber and earth. Heke had been forewarned that the British were bringing artillery. And they were.

A SUICIDAL CHARGE

On 23 June, the British force set up a four-gun battery and began pounding the *pa* from about five hundred metres away. They continued this all the next day, even moving the guns closer, to within two hundred metres, but still no breach appeared in the walls. This was partly because of the strength of the walls, but also because of poor firing on the part of the British, who would have done better to concentrate their fire on just one area of the palisades in order to break through.

On 1 July, the British commander, Colonel Despard, grew impatient and ordered a charge against the *pa*. Two hundred and fifty British troopers were told to ready their bayonets.

British officer Major Cyprian Bridge, who participated in the attack on Ohaeawai Pa, made this watercolour of the siege. Note the gaps at the bottom of the palisade, through which the Maori could fire up at attackers.

Hearing this, Waka Nene, the Maori chief loyal to the British, protested, telling them it was foolhardy, but he was ignored. As the British spread into formation, the Maori inside the fort could see them, and even they called for the troops not to charge.

Yet the British troops were ordered to advance. When they got within twenty-five metres of the *pa*, the Maori opened up with a concentrated volley and stopped the attackers dead in their tracks. Major Cyprian Bridge, an officer who took part in the charge, later wrote: 'It was a heart-rending sight to see the number of gallant fellows left dead upon the field and to hear the groans and cries of the wounded for us not to leave them behind'.

Leave them behind they did, however. Within the space of a few minutes, the British reeled back, having lost 110 men dead or wounded. One hundred defenders had defeated 250 British attackers.

Greatly frustrated, Colonel Despard ordered his artillery to continue to shell the *pa* for seven more days. But, on 8 July, much to the anger of Despard and his forces, it was discovered that Heke and his men had slipped away during the night.

MANA SATISTFIED

The prestige of Heke and Kawiti and their men increased greatly after their success at Ohaeawai Pa, and the victory inspired other Maori groups to defend themselves. Heke even built a scale model of the *pa* and sent it around the country, so that other Maori leaders could imitate its innovations. Several more battles were fought between the Maori and the British, with each one ending in the British being repelled or stalemated—not once did the British overcome a completed and defended *pa*.

In 1846, a new Governor of New Zealand, Sir George Grey, indicated a willingness to make peace; at the same time, Hone Heke offered the third combatant in the war, Waka Nene, a ceasefire. War was costly not just in human life, but also in time taken from the work of planting and hunting. With the two Maori tribes coming to terms, the British followed suit.

Despite cries for Hone Heke's head, he was not arrested; in fact, he was left at the head of a fighting force that was still very powerful. Any victory that the Maori won was ultimately a delaying action against the inevitable encroachment of European power. In the short term, however, quite significantly, *mana* was satisfied: the flagstaff at Kororareka was not re-erected.

THE BATTLE OF GATE PA

The battle of Gate Pa, during the second round of Maori-British hostilities in New Zealand, in the 1860s, displayed that Maori fortress as one of the most brilliant ever constructed. Scholars have calculated that the Maori within Gate Pa, exposed to a day-long British bombardment, received greater punishment per square metre than the Germans did in a week of shelling leading up to the first battle of the Somme.

Gate Pa was designed by the Maori chieftain Pene Taka and was about ninety metres long by thirty wide. Bunkers were built into it, larger even than the ones at Ohaeawai, connected by underground passageways. Another innovation was shallow covered mounds with loopholes in them, from which the warriors could fire.

On 28 April 1864, 1,700 British troops besieged Gate Pa, seven times the number of Maori defenders.

With artillery that included eight mortars, two howitzers and two naval cannon, they bombarded the *pa* for a full twenty-four hours. During this time, the Maori were careful not to fire back. At last, a breach opened in the wall and the British charged, believing their enemy incapacitated. The Maori let them mill about inside the *pa* for a few moments, thinking they had won. Then, at a signal, the warriors rose out of their covered trenches and hidden bunkers and let fire with their muskets. One hundred and twenty British were left dead and wounded, the most grievous British casualty count of the entire war.

The British retreated and the Maori abandoned their *pa*. Never again did the colonial forces make a frontal attack on a defended Maori position—they had learned that the cost was just too high.

'THAT HORRID PIT': THE BATTLE OF THE CRATER, 1864

IT WAS THE BIGGEST EXPLOSION EVER SET OFF ON THE FACE OF THE EARTH TO that date. Much later, when one Union soldier ventured to write about what had happened that last morning in June of 1864, you could still sense the awe in his words:

> First there came a deep shock and tremor of the Earth and a jar like an earthquake, then a heaving and a lifting … then a monstrous tongue of flame shot fully two hundred feet [sixty metres] in the air. [Then] a great spout or fountain of red earth rose to a great height, mingled with men and guns, timber and planks, and every other kind of debris, all ascending, spreading, whirling, scattering and falling with great concussion to the Earth once more.

The soldier describing this, Byron Cutcheon of the Twentieth Michigan, was a veteran of numerous bloody engagements in one of the bloodiest wars of all time, and yet the explosion that opened up the yawning crater haunted him for the rest of his life. The detonation of almost four thousand kilograms of gunpowder under the Confederate siegeworks outside Petersburg was only the beginning of the terror that day—and in a way least of it—for the Union soldiers who went down into what another soldier called 'that Horrid Pit' were soon to experience what was perhaps the most vicious and ultimately futile battle of the Civil War. It had all begun, however, with a brilliant idea.

THE ROAD TO RICHMOND

By the late spring of 1864, America's Civil War had been going on for four years. The previous summer, the Union Army of the Potomac had bested the Confederate Army of

Northern Virginia at the battle of Gettysburg, arresting the latter's progress north, but since then had been unable to defeat the hardened Rebels under the command of the brilliant Robert E. Lee. The Army of the Potomac was led by Major General George Meade, victor at Gettysburg, but was under the overall command of Lieutenant General Ulysses S. Grant, the hard-bitten, hard-drinking, cigar-smoking general in chief of all the Northern forces.

By mid-June, Grant and Meade and their army were arrayed outside Petersburg, Virginia, a railway and supply terminus just over thirty kilometres from Richmond, the Confederate capital city. Richmond represented the Holy Grail of the Union cause: if Richmond fell, so then would the Confederacy. And the way into Richmond was through Petersburg. It had been a long spring for the Union, however. In three battles since the beginning of May—the Wilderness, Spotsylvania Court House and Cold Harbor—it had lost sixty-five thousand men, killed, wounded or missing. Now, the two adversaries sat staring at each other, like medieval armies, from elaborate trenches in places only one hundred metres apart.

THE BRILLIANT IDEA

The Union army had finally learned, from gore-soaked battles like Fredericksburg and Cold Harbor, that frontal attacks on an entrenched enemy were disastrous. Lee, with a manpower shortage, had perhaps fifty thousand men at Petersburg, half of Grant's total forces, but that was more than enough when they were protected by earthworks. However, Grant was a man of action; simply waiting Lee out in front of Petersburg did not appeal to him. The Southern air was blisteringly hot, it had not rained in a month and Grant's men seemed to be melting into the ground, deep into their dirt-and-log trenches. Lassitude was the order of the day.

To add to Grant's problems, Robert E. Lee had sent his crusty commander Jubal Early with an entire army corps on a diversionary expedition north into the Shenandoah Valley— in fact, as far as Washington D.C., where he sowed panic among the civilian population. The Confederates were finally turned back outside of Washington, but political pressure mounted on Grant to break the Petersburg siege and destroy Lee.

As Grant argued with Meade about what could be done, an idea was taking shape in the mind of a Union mining engineer named Henry Pleasants, as he stared across the lines at the Confederate forces. Pleasants was a lieutenant colonel and commander of the Forty-eighth Pennsylvania Infantry of Major General Ambrose E. Burnside's IX Corps. The part of the Union line where he was stationed was across from a small Confederate fort known as Elliot's Salient; the opposing forces were separated by only about one hundred and twenty metres. Burnside's IX Corps saw hard duty: with the enemy in such close proximity, sniper and artillery fire rang out constantly, which perhaps inspired Pleasants to come up with his plan.

In civilian life, Pleasants had been a mining engineer in Pennsylvania, a state with more than its share of coalmines. And he had within the ranks of his regiment numerous ex-miners. What if, he thought, he could build a tunnel that might travel below Union lines, across the short distance of no-man's-land, and end in a hollow right under the Confederate fort's gun emplacements? And what if he filled that hollow with thousands of kilograms of gunpowder and then lit them? If a hole could be punched in Confederate lines and massed Union troops made ready to charge through it, Petersburg—and Richmond—could be taken and the war ended.

'KEEP THE MEN OCCUPIED'

Pleasants duly reported his idea to his commander, Ambrose Burnside, who had once been a major player in the Union high command, but whose dismal performances at the battles of Fredericksburg and Spotsylvania Court House had caused him to be viewed with disfavour by his superiors. When Burnside took the idea to Meade and Grant, both men acceded reluctantly, as modern senior management might to a suggestion by a not terribly trustworthy junior executive. They gave the go-ahead not, as Grant later wrote, because they believed the idea would succeed, but as 'a mere way to keep the men occupied'.

Pleasants began tunnelling on 25 June, starting behind the Union lines, at the base of a hill that obstructed the Confederate view of the proceedings. Despite the fact that he was given almost no support at all by his superior officers, Pleasants—in his pictures a neat-looking man with a precise moustache and speculative eyes—worked wonders. The men he used in his digging were taken only from the Forty-eighth Regiment (four hundred soldiers were to work on the tunnel, each shift lasting about two and a half hours). Since he was not given the shorter mining pickaxes needed in confined spaces, Pleasants had his men cut the larger army pickaxes to size. No wheelbarrows were provided, so Pleasants attached handles to old hard-tack boxes. Wood for shoring up the tunnel was not available, so he and his men ripped off timber from an old bridge and fashioned it in local sawmills.

Despite this official indifference to his labours, Pleasants managed to finish the tunnel in one month, by 23 July. It was a marvel, given the arduous circumstances under which the Pennsylvania lieutenant colonel had laboured: 155 metres long, averaging 1.4 metres in height, elevated as it sloped towards Confederate lines so that moisture would not linger inside and ventilated by a fresh-air pump at the mouth of the tunnel so that ventilation shafts would not have to be dug and possibly give away its location.

The Confederates had heard rumours of a tunnel and dug counter-tunnels in their lines, but they never got close to discovering its location. When Pleasants finished, he was six metres

This 1864 photograph captures the boredom of Union soldiers on the Virginia front. It was partly to keep men like this busy that Union high command ordered its men to start the digging of the tunnel under Confederate lines.

under the Confederate gun emplacements at Elliot's Salient. He and his miners could hear the Confederates walking above them through the wooden planks set in their trenches. The mine ended in a T-shape, with each wing of the 'T' extending about eleven metres. Into these were placed the powder magazines that would literally blow the Confederates sky high.

A CONTROVERSIAL FORCE

Attitudes towards the tunnel in the Army of the Potomac high command had changed during the month that Pleasants had been digging. Partly this was because it was evident the mine was going to reach successful completion, and partly it was because of circumstance.

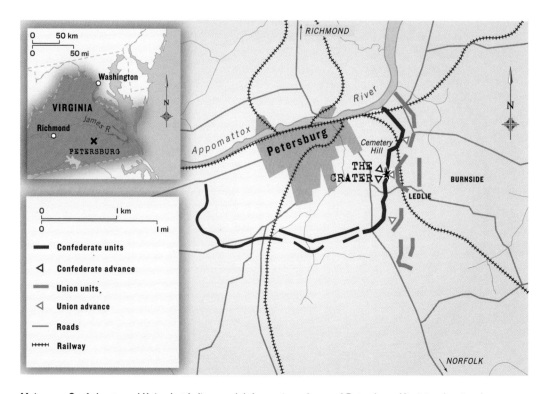

Main map: Confederate and Union battle lines and defences in and around Petersburg, Virginia, showing the location of the crater. Inset: The area of operations in Virginia, 1864.

Grant had sent an entire army corps on a 'demonstration'—a raid in force, involving an army corps and two divisions of cavalry, towards Lee's lines of communications with Richmond north of the James River—in order to see if he could get Lee to shift troops to meet it. Somewhat to Grant's surprise, Lee had taken the bait and moved a sizeable portion of his forces towards the Union threat, leaving only about twenty thousand men to hold the line at Petersburg. This was still an impregnable force behind battlements, but if the line could be breached by the explosion, the Union might be able to punch through.

Ambrose Burnside, seeing the seriousness with which the Union high command had begun to take the tunnel, decided to train a single division (about 4,500 men) of the United States Colored Troops (USCT) for the attack. The USCT was a controversial unit. Manned by freed blacks or runaway slaves and led by white officers, it would see fierce combat during the war (seventeen black soldiers would be awarded the Medal of Honor). But many white soldiers and their commanders saw black troops as a political response to Abraham Lincoln's Emancipation Proclamation, and consistently spread the rumour that such men could not fight. Whites serving with or near the black troops were also disturbed by the knowledge that Confederates routinely murdered black soldiers taken prisoner—and any whites caught with them.

Burnside was more practical: the division of USCT that he had available was fresh and competently led. Why not have it breach the fortifications after the mine explosion?

THE 'UNLUCKY VICTIM'

The date for blowing the mine was set for 30 July, at about three in the morning. Unfortunately, on 29 July, Meade countermanded Burnside's decision to have the USCT troops lead the assault. It was one of the worst decisions of the war, done with no military rationale at all. Meade, aside from having little faith in black troops, decided that their slaughter in what was sure to be a risky attack would be a poor political move. He convinced Grant, as Grant wrote later, that 'it would be said … that we were shoving these people [the USCT troops] ahead to get killed because we did not care anything about them. But that could not be said if we put white troops in front'.

Instead of arguing with Meade and Grant that his USCT troops were trained for such an attack and ready to fight, Burnside, knowing his superiors did not value him highly, acceded. And, in a fit of what we might today call passive-aggressiveness, he did not hand out the assignment to lead the attack to the unit he considered next-best qualified, but instead had three of his commanders draw straws for the job. The person who drew the short straw, Brigadier General James H. Ledlie, commander of the First Division, was perhaps the worst possible choice. One officer who had served under him called him 'a drunkard and an arrant coward'.

IT TAKES ONE TO KNOW ONE

General James Ledlie's alcoholism certainly had a major effect on the battle of the Crater, but he was just another hard-drinking general in an army whose commander in chief, General Ulysses S. Grant, was the biggest drunk of all.

Or was he? Grant had long had a reputation for hard drinking, even before the Civil War, when his career as a haberdasher in small-town Illinois had been marred by excessive consumption of whisky. Once in the army, however, it appears that Grant held his drinking down to

the occasional binge—during one of which, admittedly, he commandeered a Union steamboat and insisted it travel up the Yazoo River, straight at Confederate forces.

Unlike General Ledlie, however, Grant was a brilliant commander who knew how to stay sober long enough to get the job done. Without him, it's safe to say, it would have taken the Union a good deal longer to win the war, which is why Abraham Lincoln supposedly told an aide to find out which brand of whisky Grant was drinking—and send a case to each Union general.

Ledlie looked at the short straw, muttered that he was the 'unlucky victim', and went off, ostensibly to make preparations for the assault. In fact, he began drinking almost immediately and did little to prepare his division for its spearhead role.

LIGHTING THE FUSE

Pleasants had packed the 'T' under the Confederate works with three hundred and twenty kegs of gunpowder, totalling almost four thousand kilograms. Dirt was walled up on either side of the explosives to direct the charge upwards rather than outwards. Typical of his continual supply problem, Pleasants could not find a fuse long enough, so he spliced two together to make one thirty-metre line.

At 3.15 am on 30 July, Pleasants personally lit the fuse. The explosion was expected at 3.30—Grant and Meade and Burnside were all up and ready to watch the fireworks—but the gunpowder did not ignite. Finally, at 4.15, two extremely brave volunteers from the Forty-eighth Regiment went back down the tunnel and found that the flame had gone out at one of the splices. Relighting the fuse, they ran like mad, heading for the safety of a trench far in the rear.

At 4.45, the explosives blew. 'The earth seemed to tremble', one Rebel soldier wrote, 'and the next instant there was a report that seemed to deafen all of nature.' There were 300 South Carolinian soldiers manning Elliot's Salient, just above the mine; 278 of them died instantly, obliterated in a split second or tossed high into the air. A moment later, there fell to earth, remembered one nearby Confederate, 'showers of stones, broken timbers and blackened human limbs'.

For perhaps a minute, there was silence, both sides in shock at the enormity of what had been wrought. And then 160 Union cannons opened up, pouring fire upon Confederate lines on either side of what would forever be known as 'the Crater': a yawning chasm fifty metres wide, fifteen metres across and ten metres deep.

As the smoke cleared, Union observers could see in the pale light of the rising sun that the Jerusalem Plank Road lay just half a kilometre beyond the crater. Beyond that was Cemetery Hill, a high point that overlooked Petersburg. If Union soldiers could cross the road and gain that high ground, they would be able to bombard Petersburg at will, ending the siege. And right now, there was not a single Confederate in front of them.

'THE JUBILEE OF FIENDS'

Pleasants' brilliant idea had worked. Burnside had fifteen thousand men poised for the advance, and the plan was, in theory, almost perfect. General Ledlie's First Division were to

High embankments and deep trenches surrounded the Confederate positions at Petersburg. In places, they were rimmed with rows of sharpened sticks, known as *chevaux de frises* and traditionally used to block cavalry.

fan out on either side of the crater, move around its sides and then form a line before charging across the open space to the high ground of Cemetery Hill.

However, Ledlie's poorly trained division, instead of going around the crater, entered it, deciding it would make perfect cover from which to fire upon the Confederates. Had a commander been present to force the men onwards, this problem might have been resolved—but Ledlie remained in a bombproof bunker at a safe distance, to the rear of the battlefield, drinking rum. Whenever an impatient Meade sent him an urgent message, Ledlie would simply pass it on to a runner to send to a battlefield commander.

The result was chaos, with more and more Union soldiers simply entering the crater, rather than going around it. The huge hole was soon packed, literally shoulder to shoulder,

A group of well-dressed tourists, led by guides, inspects the infamous Crater in 1867, only two years after the war's end. Today covered with grass and partially filled in, the crater remains a popular tourist attraction.

with blue-coated soldiers. The Confederates had been slow to react—an hour or more passed before they were able to muster a counterattack—but when they did, their response was ferocious. Batteries of artillery rained fire down upon the Federals in the crater, causing mass carnage in their ranks.

When the Confederate artillery had done its job, the two brigades of infantry under General William Mahone—the Confederate hero of the day—moved from positions down the line, surrounded the crater and began firing volley after volley into it. It was like shooting ducks in a barrel. After the volleys, the Confederates charged.

'This day was the jubilee of fiends in human shapes and without souls', said one Southern soldier. The fighting in the crater, much of it hand-to-hand, went on for hours in the blazing heat. Thousands of Union soldiers lined up behind the crater, in a human traffic jam that caught rifle and artillery fire from the Confederates. To make matters worse, Burnside then decided that it was time to commit his USCT divisions, after all. Into the crater the black soldiers went, to be massacred. Word spread among the Confederate infantry, according to one

Georgia soldier's remembrance, that 'our comrades had been slaughtered in a most inhuman and brutal manner and slaves were trampling over their mangled and bleeding corpses'.

Black soldiers were shot and bayoneted after they surrendered. Some of the Union soldiers, fearing they, too, would be killed, bayoneted their own black comrades. Finally, after a fight that lasted all day, the two sides broke apart. Confederate officers restored order in their ranks and 500 prisoners were taken, including 180 black soldiers. Only seven of these would survive their imprisonment.

A WASTED OPPORTUNITY

After the fact, Grant wrote that the failed attack was 'the saddest affair I have witnessed in this war … such an opportunity for carrying fortifications I have never seen and do not expect again to have'. The Union lost nearly five thousand men killed, wounded or captured, the greatest number of these men from the USCT Fourth Division. Predictably, blame was apportioned. General Ledlie was relieved of duty and cashiered. Burnside went on voluntary leave and was not allowed to return.

Despite the Confederate victory at the battle of the Crater, the siege of Petersburg continued as it had until March 1865, when Lee, cut off on all sides, was forced to abandon Petersburg and Richmond. A month later, he surrendered to Ulysses S. Grant at Appomattox Courthouse, and the war was over.

The only man on the Union side to come out of the battle well was Henry Pleasants. After all, the only part of the battle that had worked was the explosion. As the war neared its end, Pleasants was promoted to brigadier general, specifically for his accomplishment. He then returned quietly to Pennsylvania and lived out the rest of his days as a mining engineer.

- -

THE BATTLE OF MESSINES RIDGE

The Crater explosion was the biggest manufactured explosion in history up to that point, but it was to be dwarfed by the enormous explosion set off under German lines before the battle of Messines Ridge, in France, in 1917.

The British laboured for a year, tunnelling under the German lines, to plant about four hundred tonnes of high explosives in twenty-one different mines. At 3 am on 31 July, they set the blasts off. Nineteen of the mines exploded, killing an estimated ten thousand German soldiers and making a noise said to have been heard as far away as Dublin. The shock registered as an earthquake in Switzerland. British and Commonwealth troops then went on to take their objective. One of the two unblown mines was ignited by a lightning strike in 1956, killing only a cow. The other remains undiscovered.

PART FOUR
SMOKE AND MIRRORS
intelligence, deception and subterfuge

'Now will I show myself
to have more of the
serpent than the dove.'

Christopher Marlowe,
The Jew of Malta, 1589

WHISPERS AND LIES: THEMISTOCLES AND THE BATTLE OF SALAMIS, 480 BC

EARLY IN THE MORNING OF 25 SEPTEMBER, 480 BC, SEVEN HUNDRED TRIREMES—the battleship of choice in the ancient world—belonging to the Persian Empire lay in wait on one side of a narrow strait of water that separates the Greek mainland from the island of Salamis. To hear a roll call of the nationalities of the oarsmen, archers, marines and sailors on the Persian war vessels—Cicilians, Thracians, Lydians, Mysians, Bactrians, Phoenicians—is to hear, afresh, the sound of a lost and ancient world.

On a throne high on a hill above his fleet, with Athens, the city he had just set on fire, smoking behind him, stood Xerxes, the Great King of Persia, son of Darius, grandson of Cyrus the Great—'king', so his inscriptions read, 'of every country and every language, the king of the entire earth'. It was Xerxes' intention to spend the day watching his armada win a fabulous victory for his empire, an empire that stretched to modern Pakistan in the east, through central and western Asia to Macedonia in the north, and across the Sinai Peninsula to Egypt in the south.

Victory against the Greek fleet, which awaited him on the other side of the strait, near Salamis, seemed assured. After all, the Greeks possessed at most 370 triremes. More significantly, the evening before, his opponent, a blunt Greek general named Themistocles, had sent word to Xerxes via a slave that he was ready to betray his own countrymen and everything they stood for, and had advised him to attack immediately before the Greek forces fled.

What Xerxes didn't realise was that Themistocles's apparent betrayal was a ruse. Indeed, in one of the greatest deceptions of all time, Themistocles was gambling everything—his life, the lives of his family, the lives of his countrymen—on convincing Xerxes of his disloyalty, on the whisper of a slave into the ear of the King of Kings.

AVENGING DEFEAT AT MARATHON

Like most wars, the Athens–Persian conflict of 480 BC had its origins in events that occurred much earlier. Xerxes' father, Darius I, had extended the Persian Empire all the way into Macedonia, northeast of Greece. But in 490 BC, he had been defeated at the famous battle of Marathon, on the Greek mainland, where a small force of Athenian infantrymen stopped his much larger army of Persians, forcing them to retreat back to Asia. Darius had died in 486 and his son Xerxes was hungry for revenge against the Greeks. He and his advisers planned their next campaign carefully. It was decided that the Persians would attack Athens both by land and by sea. They would come with over thirteen hundred triremes and over one hundred thousand combatants, which included large forces of elite cavalrymen and crack infantrymen. In May of 480, Xerxes set forth to march to Greece, travelling north and west from Iran through Assyria, Thrace and Macedonia, and then into northern Greece.

One of the Greek soldiers at the battle of Marathon—possibly a *strategos*, or commander—was an Athenian named Themistocles, who was known to be ill-educated and often ill-mannered (it is said that his father disowned him as a result), but also immensely crafty and ambitious. In 480 BC, he was probably about forty-five years old and may have been the *archon*, or chief magistrate, of Athens. At the very least, he was one of the city-state's most prominent military or political leaders. Unlike most of the Athenian leaders—and certainly unlike his opponent, the godlike Xerxes—he was not an aristocrat, but instead a blunt-spoken and pragmatic administrator.

Realising at least three years before the fact that the Persians were going to invade again, Themistocles had worked tirelessly to turn Athens into a first-class sea power, building a navy of over two hundred triremes

Themistocles, the Athenian general and statesman. His fellow Greeks were ambivalent about him, but he undoubtedly saved his country at Salamis.

DID THE TROJAN HORSE EXIST?

To the Greeks is attributed one of the greatest subterfuges of all time: the Trojan Horse. The story is chronicled in Homer's *Illiad* and *Odyssey*, and in Virgil's *Aeneid*, where it is recounted that the Greeks attacked and besieged the city of Troy, where Helen, the wife of Greek king Menelaus, was held captive. The siege went on for ten years. In the tenth year, the Greeks built a huge wooden horse, filled it with warriors and left it outside the city before sailing away. Not having learned to beware of Greeks bearing gifts, the Trojans brought the horse inside the city. That night, the concealed Greeks crept out of the horse and opened the gates of the city for their army, which had secretly returned, and Troy fell.

Did this really happen? Archaeologists believe that Troy existed, on the site of the ancient city of Hisarlik in northwest Turkey, and was probably attacked by Mycenaeans, ancestors of today's Greeks, sometime in the late Bronze Age (roughly 1200 BC). Who knows if a Helen was the *casus belli*—probably not—but there is evidence that the city was destroyed after a siege. It seems highly unlikely, though, that anyone would be stupid enough to tow a huge horse into a fortress town without checking it out first, so this is not a tale to be taken literally.

However, there is another theory. Archaeologists have recently discovered that a powerful earthquake occurred in ancient Troy around the time of attack by the Mycenaeans. Troy's walls came tumbling down, according to this hypothesis, because of the quake, and the Greeks saw it as a god-given opportunity. After they entered the city and defeated the Trojans, they built a huge horse and left it as an offering to Poseidon, the god of earthquakes, whose symbol is a horse.

manned by forty thousand sailors. In the spring of 480, he convinced the Hellenic League—the confederation of Greek city-states that had organised to oppose Persia—that he should become the chief strategist in the defence of Greece.

In August, the Spartan commander Leonidas was sent with eight thousand troops to defend the mountain pass at Thermopylae against the Persian land forces trying to enter from the north. For three days of brutal fighting, the Greeks, led by Leonidas's three hundred Spartans, held off a force twenty times their size, before being betrayed by one of their own and slaughtered to the last man. Having achieved victory at Thermopylae, Xerxes and his army headed for the plains of Attica, and Athens.

Expecting this, Themistocles had already moved to evacuate the region and the city. All told, approximately 150,000 people lived in Attica at this time, including the city of Athens. In what was one of the greatest evacuations of its time, Themistocles sent the women and children to several different locations and ordered any man who could fight to make his way to the island of Salamis, which lies almost two kilometres off the coast of Attica, just a few kilometres away from Athens.

When Xerxes' men entered Athens, they slaughtered the few citizens who had remained and set fire to the city. The Greeks waiting on Salamis could easily see the flames. They watched with horror and hatred in their hearts as their city burned to the ground.

AN EXTRAORDINARY GAMBLE

By this time, twenty-two city-states of the Hellenic League had gathered forces on Salamis. Each had its opinion on how best to deal with the situation. Late on the night of 23 September and early into the morning of 24 September, fevered arguments took place. Many of the commanders wanted to flee to protect their homelands, or to stage a tactical retreat to the Isthmus of Corinth, about forty kilometres away, where they could join up with Greek and Spartan infantry, who were preparing a last-ditch stand against the Persians. The arrival of the imposing Persian fleet, offering to do battle, on the afternoon of 24 September, lent weight to their arguments. When the Greek ships remained in their harbour, the Persians lingered almost tauntingly, and then slowly returned to their base at Phaleron, a small harbour to the southeast of Salamis.

Having learned through his extensive spy network that the Greeks on Salamis were squabbling among themselves, Xerxes sent columns of troops marching along the coast of Attica, heading to the Isthmus of Corinth. There were already plenty of Persian troops at Corinth, but Xerxes wanted the Greeks on Salamis to hear the thundering sound of, and see the dust rising from, their massed footsteps. The din went on into the night, and many

This somewhat romanticised rendering of the battle of Salamis nevertheless captures the tumult of the battle. Themistocles's subterfuge ensured that the Persians would struggle to operate efficiently in the narrow straits.

Greeks began to panic. Some fled to their boats and had to be restrained from setting sail then and there. The situation on Salamis was spiralling out of control.

Only Themistocles, it seemed, realised that there was an opportunity here: a chance to fight a decisive battle. He knew that the large Persian naval force could not operate well in the confines of Straits of Salamis, only a mile wide. The Persians' chief advantage—the ability to outflank their enemy using their numerical superiority—would be lost due to the narrowness of the waterway. The key to victory, he realised, was to incite Xerxes to do battle here—to make sure the Persian king committed his forces to this engagement and didn't choose one of the other options available to him, which included simply waiting the Greeks out until they starved or surrendered. But how could he achieve this?

Themistocles decided on an extraordinary gamble. Aware of the Persians' regular use of a spy network and intelligence from Greek traitors—one, Ephialtes, had helped secure victory for the Persians at Thermopylae by guiding them to a secret mountain pass from where they were able to outflank the Greeks—he decided to supply them with false intelligence, what would today be termed 'disinformation'. Not only that, he himself would supply this information, and send it directly to the Great King, Xerxes. And to make it all the more convincing, Themistocles would offer to be 'bought'.

The risks for Themistocles were enormous: he was literally staking everything on convincing Xerxes to attack. If Xerxes saw through his ruse, there were many things he might do—including inform Themistocles's fellow Greeks that their commander was a traitor. There would have been no way for Themistocles to defend himself against this charge, since it was essential for him to keep his plan to himself. Had the Greeks thought him a traitor, he would have been executed and his family completely disenfranchised and dishonoured.

While his nervous commanders bickered, Themistocles sent his personal slave, Sicinnus, alone on a small boat, on a nighttime mission to the Persian headquarters on the mainland. Sicinnus was a trusted retainer, the tutor of Themistocles's children, and he came from a small kingdom not far from Persia, so he might even have spoken some of that language. It is possible that Themistocles, expecting Sicinnus to be tortured, lied to his slave, making him believe that he really intended to defect. In any event, the slave was no doubt surrounded as soon as he came to shore—those first few minutes, with bristling Persian spears pointed at him, would have been perilous for Sicinnus. But somehow he was able to convince the Persian soldiers that he carried with him a message for Xerxes from Themistocles, and he was taken to the Great King.

The Greeks are getting ready to flee, Sicinnus told Xerxes, and Themistocles was ready to go over to the Persian side. On behalf of Themistocles, he strongly urged Xerxes to mobilise his forces now, at night, to bottle the Greeks up in the Straits of Salamis. When the dawn came, Xerxes could pick off the disorganised and panicky Greek triremes one by one.

It must have been with a sigh of relief that Themistocles heard, later that night, a report that the dark shapes of Persian triremes had been observed moving out on both sides of the straits and across from the Greeks, blocking their exit. Now there was nothing for the Greeks to do but fight.

THE BATTLE FOR GREECE

Shortly before 8 am on 25 September, as described by the Greek dramatist Aeschylus, who was present at Salamis, 'a song-like shout sounded triumphantly from the Greeks'. The waiting Persians heard it echo off the rocky confines of the strait. It was the paean, a huge cry uttered by thousands of Greek voices at once, both an invocation and a fearsome rebel yell. It told the Persians that the Greeks were not retreating this morning, but coming straight at them, ready to fight for their lives and liberty. For the crews of the Persian triremes, having rowed in place most of the night, this was not a welcome sound. Xerxes, watching high on his hill, could not have welcomed it either, but there was nothing he could do about it now. Themistocles had outwitted him and the battle would now be joined.

The battle of Salamis is one of those extraordinary moments that make lovers of history wish they could enter a time machine and dial 'Greece, 480 BC'. It would have been a spectacular scene, and the mind's eye fills to overflowing with images. Imagine a thousand brightly painted triremes, each with an eye of polished, painted marble on either side of the prow, being rowed furiously towards each other, three levels of oars striking the water, splashing up foam and spray. The Persian triremes, with their long, sleek rams, looked like swordfish; the Greek vessels, with their blunter, wider rams, resembled hammerhead sharks. Imagine the rowers below decks, wearing only loincloths, sweating profusely, able to see nothing, hearing only the shouted directions of their rowing master and the piper keeping time on a shrill pipe. Imagine the helmsman of the ship, steering with double rudders, one in each hand, while the captain—normally the owner of the ship and the wealthiest man on board—shouted directions. The triremes would have constantly been closing up gaps in their ranks, much like a modern fleet of bombers on a mission, to make sure that no enemy would intrude to strike and ram.

Themistocles was out on the water behind his triremes, sitting on a large chair at the back of his vessel, directing through signal flags or possibly trumpets. Xerxes, on shore, had his aides call out to him the names of individual vessels, so that he could tell which were doing well and which were panicked and retreating.

As soon as the ships got within a few hundred metres of each other, the archers on board rained down arrows, and then each captain chose targets and attempted to break through enemy ranks, either to ram, or, in another vital manoeuvre, to slash close to an enemy to break off his oars. (This would take split-second co-ordination, since rowers on the attacking vessel were trained to pull in their oars just at the last moment, to keep them from snapping off.)

As Themistocles had foreseen, because of the narrowness of the straits, the Persians were unable to bring their superior numbers to bear—many Persian triremes waited outside the

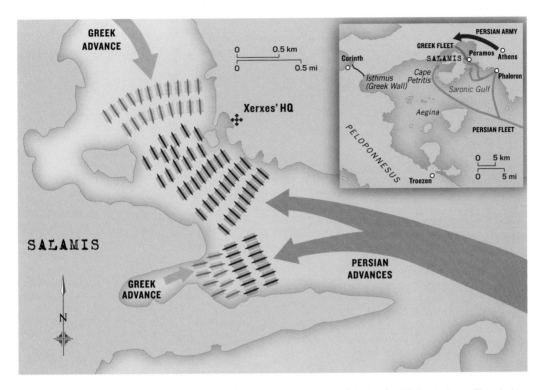

Main map: The positions of the Greek and Persian fleets at the beginning of the battle of Salamis. Inset: Though the Persian fleet had originally sailed from the Middle East, it had set up a base at Phaleron prior to the battle.

straits, jockeying for their turn to enter. The Persians were also exhausted after having rowed for up to twelve hours. Furthermore, the Athenians fought with the ferocity of those fighting to preserve their homeland. Soon, the tide began to turn in favour of the Greeks.

After four or five hours, the Persians broke. Most of their triremes fled to the southeast, back to Phaleron. The Greeks began hunting out individual Persian triremes and ramming them mercilessly: 'they boned them like tuna or some catch of fish', wrote Aeschylus, his tone catching the bloodthirsty nature of the final hours of the battle. For days afterwards, Persian corpses covered the waters of the strait, and washed ashore both on Salamis and on the beaches of Attica. It is estimated that twenty thousand Persians lost their lives at Salamis. The Greeks sank perhaps four hundred of their ships and lost only forty of their own.

After the battle, awards were given out to the bravest of the Greeks—those commanders whose ships had rammed and sunk the most Persian triremes, those warriors who had been the most daring in their hand-to-hand combat. Themistocles was honoured, Herodotus writes, as 'the smartest man in all Greece'.

Down through the centuries, Themistocles's victory at Salamis has been celebrated in art as the salvation of Western civilisation. This rendition of the battle was painted by the nineteenth-century German artist Wilhelm von Kaulbach.

DEMOCRACY IS BORN

On the day after the battle, Xerxes, who had lost a brother in the fighting, called a conference of all his commanders. He knew he had lost a great battle, but—since Persians did not measure themselves by ships at sea, but rather by the horses and men of their superb army—did not think he had lost the war. He ordered a general withdrawal, leaving behind his commander Mardonius with a portion of the army to keep a foothold on Greek territory until he could invade again. Mardonius camped out all winter, but, in the August of 479, he was killed and his army defeated by a united Greek army at Palatea. At around the same time, the Greek navy attacked what was left of the Persian naval force, near the island of Samos, and destroyed it.

Although a few final battles remained to be fought against Persian domination, the Greeks were now free. Having won their great victory, they set about attempting to make an even greater peace. In 477, the Athenians founded and led the Delian League, an alliance of 150 Greek city-states. Under this league, the Golden Age of Athens began, spawning dramatists such as Aeschylus, Aristophanes, Euripides and Sophocles, philosophers including Plato and Socrates, and historians like Thucydides and Herodotus.

Things did not turn out so well for Themistocles, however. The squabbling Athenians soon reverted to their distrust of this brave but not terribly political leader and he received no further honours. Worse was to come. In 464, the prime strategist of the battle of Salamis found himself meeting the Great King of the Persians in a royal palace in Susa, not far from Persepolis. The Great King was not Xerxes, who had been assassinated in a palace intrigue two years before, but his son Ataxerxes. Themistocles had come, with all his family, to go to work for his old enemy. Having been driven out of Athens by accusations that he took bribes and was a Persian agent (the former was probably true, but not the latter), he had landed here to spend his remaining years as governor of a Persian city.

THE TRIREME

The word 'trireme' comes from the Greek *trieres*, which means 'three-rower', for there were three levels of oars on each ship, worked by 170 oarsmen. These vessels usually had a crew of about two hundred and were roughly 40 metres long and 5.5 metres wide—so narrow for their length that they were not seaworthy in the open ocean and spent most of their time hugging the shoreline, putting in each night to camp on the shore.

Each trireme had marines and archers on board whose job it was to battle enemy vessels, but the chief weapon of these war vessels was its fearsome ram, which was encased in bronze, tipped with three cutting blades, and extended more than two metres out from the bow of the vessel at the waterline.

A battle between triremes normally involved attempting to penetrate the enemy's line of defences by ramming hard into opposing vessels—although not so hard that the attacking trireme would become stuck and helpless, a target for other rammers and for showering arrows. Indeed, ramming was more of an art than it would appear: just before impact, the captain would give the signal for the rowers to pull backwards with all their might, so that just as the collision occurred the attacking vessel was already moving to extricate itself.

In fact, due to its narrow width, it took great skill just to keep the trireme afloat and on course: in order to, literally, not rock the boat, soldiers learned to throw their spears from a sitting position. Despite this, the trireme was a formidable warship that could accelerate from a standing start to ten knots in under sixty seconds, and it remained the combat vessel of choice for the next two hundred years.

THE PERFECT TRAP: THE BATTLE OF THE TEUTOBURG FOREST, AD 9

ONE SEPTEMBER DAY IN THE YEAR AD 9, THE SOLDIERS OF LEGIONS XVII, XVIII and XIX of the great imperial power of Rome find themselves marching in a three-kilometre-long column through a dark forest which, these soldiers fear, is the home of savage creatures—the worst of which are not animal but human. For the men of Roman governor Publius Quinctilius Varus, marching four to six abreast through this wilderness east of the Rhine River, the experience is not a happy one. They are crowded onto a narrow path, which forces those on the outside of the column to continually push and jostle back in, lest they trip over roots or become stuck in mud.

The path begins to climb along the flank of a high hill on their left, perhaps one hundred metres tall, covered with tangled woods. To the right, the trees open out a little, but reveal only black marshes and bogs stretching to the horizon. All of this is a far cry from the sun-splashed streets of Rome, twelve hundred kilometres to the south. Perhaps some soldiers pray to their favourite gods to deliver them from this place, while others chide themselves for letting their childhood fears take over—most monsters, after all, turn out not to be real.

But in the shadows surrounding these twenty thousand legionaries, mere metres away from them, in fact, *are* the stuff of these nightmares: eighteen thousand German warriors, carrying lances and razor-sharp swords. If the Romans weren't making so much noise on their journey, they might be able to hear the Germans' rapid breathing or the creak of their feet as they shift themselves while crouched, their spears ready in their hands.

A large proportion of these Germans are concealed behind a 1.5-kilometre-long wall built, at great cost in time and human effort, to conceal them from their Roman enemies. The wall is chest-high, made out of sod, and camouflaged to fit in perfectly with the surrounding forest. It is the work of one Arminius, son of a chieftain of the Cherusci tribe.

The Romans believe him to be an ally. But the reality is that Arminius is about to spring a devastating ambush that will not only kill twenty thousand Romans on this day alone, but also, quite literally, stop an empire dead in its tracks.

UNRULY TRIBES OF THE NORTH

As part of Rome's rapid expansion in the first century BC, Julius Caesar led his legions into Gaul (modern-day France) and spent eight years conquering the tribes from the Pyrenees to the Rhine River. Eleven years after Caesar's murder in 44 BC, his great-nephew, adopted son and heir, Octavian, assumed control of Rome as its first emperor—taking the name Augustus, which means 'dignified' and 'sacred'.

Soon after, Augustus was forced to deal with numerous uprisings on the eastern borders of Gaul, as warlike tribes crossed the Rhine and skirmished with Roman forces. Deciding that his borders needed to be pushed outwards, to keep these tribes away, in about 12 BC he began what would become a twenty-year campaign against the Germanic tribes east of the Rhine.

Augustus had a far tougher time with these tribes than Caesar had had with the Gauls. Under threat, the Gauls tended to gather in the large, fortified, hilltop cities that were also their commercial centres, which the Romans found relatively easy to destroy. In contrast, the Germanic tribes east of the Rhine—the Canninefati, the Bructari, the Chatti, the Cherusci and others—would launch hit-and-run attacks on the Roman legions, then disappear into the forest, then reappear again in a different place. Pacifying 'Germania' was a difficult process. Like many a future imperial power with an 'indigenous problem', Rome tried resettling some of the troublesome tribes, in areas west of the Rhine where there was a stronger Roman presence. Others, like the Cherusci, they attempted to co-opt.

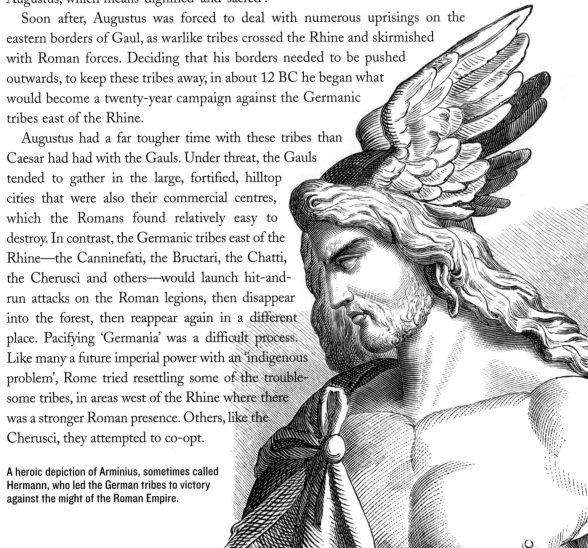

A heroic depiction of Arminius, sometimes called Hermann, who led the German tribes to victory against the might of the Roman Empire.

By AD 5, Rome had managed to fashion a friendly relationship with an elite faction of the Cherusci nobility. A member of that elite was Arminius (no one is quite sure where the name came from, and whether it is Germanic or Roman), who was probably about twenty-two or twenty-three years old. In AD 6, Arminius served as chief of the auxiliary troops who fought with the Romans to put down a rebellion among German tribes in Bohemia. So pleased were the Romans with Arminius's contribution that he was not only given Roman citizenship, but was also declared an equestrian, or knight.

VARUS RISES TO THE BAIT

Arminius returned home from Bohemia to a landscape that was rapidly changing as the Romans made more and more inroads into Cherusci land. A Roman governor, Publius Quinctilius Varus, had been appointed to the area east of the Rhine and was busy consolidating Roman control. Then in his mid-fifties, Varus was a former governor of Syria and husband of Emperor Augustus's great-niece, a bond that may have greatly advanced his career. Varus's duties may have been more those of a civilian governor than a military

THE PLACE IN THE FOREST

The story of Arminius's triumph was resurrected to the status of heroic myth following the rediscovery of the works of Tacitus and other Roman writers in the fourteenth and fifteenth centuries, and Arminius subsequently became a national hero in Germany. However, the site of the battle remained lost for almost two thousand years and its location became a focus of debate.

The distinguished nineteenth-century German historian Theodor Mommson suggested the battle site was near the town of Kalkriese, about 140 kilometres northeast of the Rhine, on the basis of topography and of numerous Roman coins found there. But he was in the minority, with most historians positing another site in a forest in Lower Saxony, which was then renamed the Teutoburg Forest (Teutoburger Wald in German).

In 1987, however, an amateur British archaeologist living in Germany, Tony Clunn, began wandering the fields near Kalkriese with a metal detector. Not only did he find more Roman coins from the period of the massacre, but he also came across lead weights used as ammunition for Roman slings. These signs of Roman military activity in an area where the Romans had ventured only once, to be slaughtered, could only mean that Clunn had found the site of the battle.

Subsequent archaeology has proved him right. Among the many recent finds at the site are arrowheads, spear points, parts of swords and daggers and iron nails from the legionaries' hobnailed sandals. But probably the most exciting discovery was the remnants of the wall built by Arminius—the first real evidence of his carefully prepared and lethal trap.

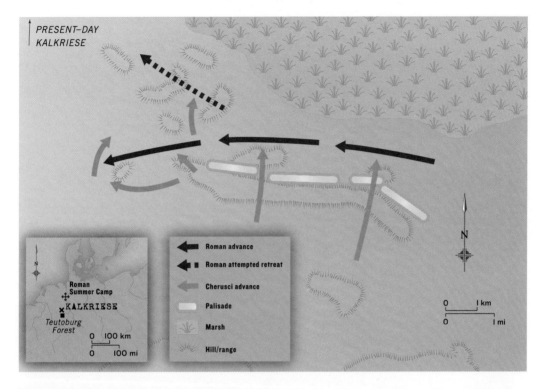

Main map: The Roman army's route through the forest and the site of Arminius's ambush. **Inset:** The so-called battle of Teutoburg Forest is now thought to have taken place near Kalkriese, over sixty kilometres northwest of Teutoburg.

leader, but he retained a strong military force: Roman Legions XVII, XVIII and XIX, which included some of the finest fighting men in the empire.

One day, probably in late August or early September of AD 9, Arminius went to see Varus, who was stationed with his legions at his summer headquarters near the Weser River in central Germany. He told him that a small tribe living two days' march to the west had decided to revolt against Roman rule and that he was willing to help Varus put the uprising down. Varus had no reason to distrust Arminius and putting down the rebellion seemed to be a small matter, since, conveniently, Varus was about to march east, back to his winter headquarters near the Rhine. He could make a detour with his legions—a show of force was probably all that was required—and then continue to his destination. Arminius thanked him and said he would ride ahead to organise the German tribes that would help put down the uprising. A Cherusci nobleman named Segestes warned Varus that Arminius was not to be trusted, that he was leading the army into an ambush. But Varus, confident that his legions could deal with any trouble from such 'savages', refused to listen, and set off.

In the nineteenth century, Arminius became a powerful symbol of German nationalism. This monument to the Cherusci warrior was built in the Teutoburg Forest and completed in 1875, four years after the unification of Germany.

AN ELABORATE TRAP

None of the available evidence indicates when or why Arminius decided to betray his Roman allies. The plan was daring and dangerous: if it went wrong, it would result in certain death for Arminius and his family and enslavement for his tribe. It may be that Arminius was, as later legend made him out to be, an early German nationalist, risking all to unite the region's tribes and repel the Roman invaders. But it is also conceivable—in fact, likely—that he was out for personal gain and glory, perhaps in conjunction with this larger goal. Whatever the reasons, the planning and preparation of his trap must have been long and complex, and have involved numerous co-conspirators.

Arminius decided to ambush the Roman legions in the vast, dense, primeval forest near the modern town of Kalkriese, about 140 kilometres northeast of the Rhine (though the site was long thought to be further south, in the Teutoburg Forest, hence the name of the battle). He selected the location for the attack with great care: a path flanked by a high, forested hill on one side and a wide marsh on the other. Here, the Romans would have no choice but to take the narrow path along the hillside. Just to make sure, Arminius and his men refashioned parts of the landscape. Where a fork in the path appeared, the plotters dug a deep hole and diverted water into it, making it look like a natural waterway and obscuring the alternative route.

Most extraordinary of all (and unknown until archaeologists discovered the battle site in 1987), Arminius built a hiding place for a large part of his army—a wall 1.5 kilometres long, made of sod and earth, which ran along the edge of the hill above the track the Romans would take. To construct the wall, the conspirators first marked off a 4.5-metre wide and 1.5-kilometre-long swath of land with wooden stakes or other markers. After that, hundreds of people—probably men, women and children—dug up chunks of turf with wooden spades, and packed them to form a foundation. They then used their bare hands and excavated dirt to build the wall up to a height of about 1.5 metres and camouflaged it with branches. The whole task took more than a month.

Then Arminius and his lieutenants rounded up warriors from far and wide and brought them to the ambush site. Historians speculate that maybe five thousand or so warriors were hidden behind the wall, and another five thousand in the woods behind them. Perhaps seven thousand or so concealed themselves among the trees by the path to the wall. About another thousand were hidden near the marsh, waiting to pick off those who fled once the battle began.

A FRENETIC ONSLAUGHT

The three-kilometre-long Roman column would have taken about an hour to pass any given point. Movement was slow because of the narrowness of the path and because the Romans often had to push fallen trees out of the way (possibly left their by the Germans to impede their progress) so that the baggage trains, bringing up the rear, could proceed. According to some ancient sources, women and children travelled with the baggage trains (archaeologists have found some women's jewellery at the battle site).

By most accounts, it was early afternoon. According to some sources, the sun was out; others have a storm beginning to pelt the woods with rain. But all sources agree on one

In this adaptation of an 1864 work by German artist Friedrich Gunkel, Cherusci warriors pour down the forest slopes behind Arminius on his white charger, cutting a swathe through the traumatised Roman ranks.

thing: the destruction of the Roman legions began with terrifying screams and shouts and a shower of iron spears. Modern estimates indicate that one warrior could throw a spear every four seconds; on that basis, twenty thousand spears may have rained down on the Romans in the first minute of the attack. Then thousands of Germanic warriors charged down the hill against the column, along its full length. The defenders, reeling from the surprise, tried to fight back, but they were unable to form the deep, cohesive ranks in which they had been trained to fight. Struggling to hold their lines and slipping over the dead and wounded, they were overwhelmed by the frenetic onslaught of the Germanic warriors.

Most ancient sources describe the battle as taking place over a three-day period, with all combat ceasing by the morning of the fourth day. In these accounts, the Romans broke up into small, desperate groups who built fortified night encampments in the woods, but who were all killed in a series of encounters. However, some historians believe the Romans could not have survived as long as this, and that the battle was over in a day, even hours. Almost all accounts have Varus and his lieutenants falling on their swords to escape capture.

However it happened, the carnage was terrible. Some legionaries tried to flee through the woods or bogs, but only one or two escaped, if any. When the massacre ended, the Germanic tribes took about 1,500 prisoners. They sacrificed five hundred of them to the gods to thank them for this victory, slashing their throats on makeshift altars, hanging them from tree limbs or gutting them and throwing their bodies into sacred ponds. The rest they kept as slaves.

'GIVE ME BACK MY LEGIONS!'

When Emperor Augustus found out about the annihilation of his men, according to his biographer Suetonius, he apparently cried 'Quintili Vare, legions redde!' ('Quintilius Varus, give me back my legions!'). Legions XVII, XVIII and XIX—three out of a total of twenty-eight Roman legions—were never reconstituted, however; the numbers simply disappeared from military annals.

Some historians believe that Augustus never recovered from this blow either. In AD 13, he gave power to his son Tiberius and retired from public view, dying the next year. Roman armies campaigned for a few more years in Germany, fighting Arminius in indecisive battles, but after the battle of the Teutoburg Forest (as it later came to be known), enthusiasm for northern conquest was lacking.

Arminius was murdered by rivals in his own tribe in AD 21. But his perfectly constructed trap in the forest ended up having a profound effect on the future of the world. It stopped the Romans from pushing their empire east of the Rhine, and laid the foundations of modern Germany and central Europe—in response to their calamitous defeat, the Romans built a series of heavily fortified military bases along the Rhine, which grew to become major German cities, including Bonn, Cologne and Strasbourg. It was the beginning of the beginning for Europe, and the beginning of the end for Rome.

OFFERED UP BY THE BLACK WATERS

The Germanic tribes who defeated Varus and his legions worshipped nature, which they believed contained spirits of both good and evil. Groves of oak trees were set apart for worship and for ritual sacrifice. It was thought that certain bogs contained evil spirits. Lakes and ponds, particularly those containing black water, were regarded as sacred. As an offering of thanks to the gods, victorious tribes would drop the weapons of their vanquished foes into bodies of water.

This has been a boon for archaeologists, who have found sizeable deposits of skulls and swords deep in lake water wherever the Romans campaigned and lost. In one lake in Jutland alone, hundreds of Roman lances, spears, swords and shields were found. The fact that many of these items were embossed with silver and gold and would have been highly prized indicates how important it was to the Germanic tribes to placate and thank the spirits of nature.

THE PRINCE OF DECEPTION: JOHN MAGRUDER AND THE PENINSULA CAMPAIGN, 1862

EVEN BY THE EXTREMELY COLOURFUL STANDARDS OF THE AMERICAN CIVIL WAR—a war that included fighting circus acrobats, insanely brave cavalry officers, balloon aerialists and genteel lady spies—Major General John Bankhead Magruder was a colourful figure. Over 190 centimetres tall, dressed always in the most ornate uniforms, born with the gift of the gab—'he can talk twenty-four hours incessantly', a fellow officer complained— although also possessing an extreme lisp much parodied by his contemporaries, Magruder cut an extraordinary swath across mid-nineteenth-century America. 'The Prince', as he was known from his days at West Point onwards, made acquaintances ranging from Edgar Allen Poe and Thomas Jefferson to Abraham Lincoln and Emperor Maximilian I of Mexico.

Unfortunately, Magruder was also an alcoholic who wasted much of his promise and intellectual powers and was to die alone in a hotel room. But for a brief shining moment in the spring of 1862, a moment towards which his whole life seemed to have been aimed, he was in control of the tiny Confederate Army of the Peninsula which, thanks to Magruder's ingrained powers of drama and self-aggrandisement, managed to halt the progress of a far superior Northern army and save the day for the South.

UNFULFILLED POTENTIAL

John Bankhead Magruder was born in Port Royal, in Virginia's Shenandoah Valley. Like many Virginians of the time, he grew up proud of the state's military tradition, which had provided numerous commanders in chief, as well as U.S. presidents. Magruder went to the University of Virginia, where one of his fellow students was Edgar Allen Poe and where he dined with the ageing Thomas Jefferson. After that, he applied for and won a place at West Point, from which he graduated in 1830, before taking up a commission as a second lieutenant

Major General John Bankhead Magruder. The twinkle in his eye and the upturned moustache hint at the dandyism and theatricality for which Magruder came to be recognised.

Some of the cannon batteries under Magruder's command in 1862. These, however, are real cannon, not the ingeniously fabricated 'Quaker guns' that Magruder would employ so effectively at the battle of Yorktown.

in the U.S. Army. Although he came only fifteenth out of forty-two cadets in his West Point class, he had a reputation second to none as a man-about-town, a hard drinker and a larger-than-life personality. This was enhanced, a year after graduation, when he married a Baltimore heiress named Henrietta van Kapff, described by a friend of Magruder's as 'a weak woman, but good', of whom Magruder was fond, but whose wealth was also a decided attraction for a man on a meagre army pay.

With his personal magnetism, intellectual powers and rich wife, Magruder could have gone far—as did fellow West Point classmates Robert E. Lee, Jefferson Davis and Joseph E. Johnston—but alcohol did him in. From the very beginning, he was a loud, dramatic drunk who would often black out in one city and find himself in another. So a career that might have been brilliant saw Magruder stay a second lieutenant for nearly thirty years, through postings to Florida, Maine, New York, Baton Rouge, San Diego and Mexico City.

Mexico was to save the Prince's career, for it was during the Mexican–American War in 1848, where he performed gallantly in action commanding a mounted light artillery unit, that he attained the rank of captain, and was even brevetted a lieutenant colonel (meaning that he was promoted temporarily for bravery, but without the pay commensurate with such a rank). It is typical of Magruder that he celebrated the army's victory and his personal achievement long and hard in Mexico City, forming something called the Aztec Club, a gaming and drinking group his fellow officers remembered fondly to the end of their days. It was also at the Aztec Club that Magruder got into a scrape with a fellow officer named Franklin Pierce, slapping him and sending his friend T.J. Jackson (later to be nicknamed 'Stonewall') to challenge Pierce to a duel. Fortunately Pierce—four years later to become President of the United States—did not accept.

A SOUTHERN GENTLEMAN GOES TO WAR

By 1861, Magruder (his rank had reverted to captain) had knocked around more army posts and finally become commander of the garrison protecting Washington D.C. His wife Henrietta, unable to stand his drinking and carousing, had taken their three children and moved to Europe. With the Civil War about to break out, Magruder met personally with Abraham Lincoln and explained that, as a Virginian patriot, he was obliged to fight for the Rebel cause. (According to Magruder's somewhat suspect remembrance of the occasion, Lincoln accepted the loss with equanimity, complimenting Magruder for being 'a Southern gentleman'.) Then Magruder took a cab across a guarded bridge into Virginia and accepted a commission from his old classmate Jefferson Davis, now president of the Confederate States of America, as a major general in the Confederate Army. Fellow generals included Robert E. Lee and Joseph Johnston, his old West Point mates.

The war went badly for the Confederates at first, with the Union triumphing at Nashville and New Orleans. By late 1861, the high command at the Confederate capital of Richmond, Virginia, was aware that the Federals' next step would be an attempt to capture Richmond. And they knew where the invasion would come from: right up the historic peninsula of Virginia, formed by the York River on the north and the James River on the south.

With little in the way of options, Jefferson Davis stationed Robert E. Lee to defend the city of Richmond, Joseph Johnston to guard the western approaches of the state and Prince John Bankhead Magruder to command the thirteen-thousand strong Army of the Peninsula.

THE BEGINNING OF THE CHARADE

The new Union commander, General George B. McClellan, did exactly as the Confederates expected. But slowly. Despite his youth, the thirty-five-year-old was a plodding soldier who hated to move until he thought everything was in his favour. He spent the whole of the winter and early spring of 1862 gathering his forces at Fort Monroe, at the tip of the peninsula. Opposing him, John Magruder placed his thirteen thousand men in two lines across the peninsula. The first was a thin line about twenty kilometres from Fort Monroe, a line that was intended only to briefly halt the Yankees. The second was anchored at Yorktown in the north and the James River in the south, and ran along the line of the twisting Warwick River.

Because he had nowhere near enough men or materiel to populate the line, Magruder had to improvise. In this, he was in his element. While stationed in Corpus Christi, Texas, before the Mexican War, he had built an eight-hundred seat theatre, created scenery and directed plays performed by the soldiers under his command, so he knew a little something about the magic of performance. He dammed the Warwick to create flooded areas in front of his defensive lines, cut down huge trees and had them sanded down, painted black and assembled as 'Quaker guns'—logs posing as cannon. He also instructed his officers on the art of 'diversion by marching'. Any large army, naturally, creates a great deal of noise and movement, since in the natural course of business, men, horses and materiel shift from one place to another on a regular basis. So Magruder told his officers to keep his men marching back and forth, constantly, often dragging covered supply wagons (filled with wood or rocks). Some of his men didn't understand what he was up to—'Gen. Magruder is always drunk and giving foolish and absurd orders', wrote one soldier in his diary—but there was method in his madness.

On Friday 4 April, General George McClellan finally moved his sixty-five thousand men towards Yorktown. As it marched west from Fort Monroe, the army divided into two columns, the northern column, on the right, heading for Yorktown, the southern column, on the left, aiming to sweep past and come up on Yorktown's flank. That first day, things went better than even McClellan could have hoped. The line of Confederates in front of him (Magruder's first line of defence) simply vanished before the onslaught of Union forces.

The next day, however, was a bit different. Not only did it begin to rain, revealing to Union forces that the previously firm-seeming roads of the peninsula were covered with thin layers of topsoil that quickly turned to knee-deep mud, but, to McClellan's astonishment, he encountered a second line of defence that ran, not just around Yorktown, which was to be expected, but all across the waist of the peninsula. As one startled Union soldier later wrote, 'We saw across an open space a long line of rebel earthworks with a stream in front; the rebel flag was flying and we could see secesh [secessionist] officers riding along their lines inside the works'. The 'stream' was the Warwick River. McClellan had thought it would be a mere trickle, but now, somehow, it presented a formidable obstacle. Not only was it swollen from the rain, but also the Union commander began to receive reports from up and down his line that part of the river was comprised of large ponds—the result of Magruder's damming.

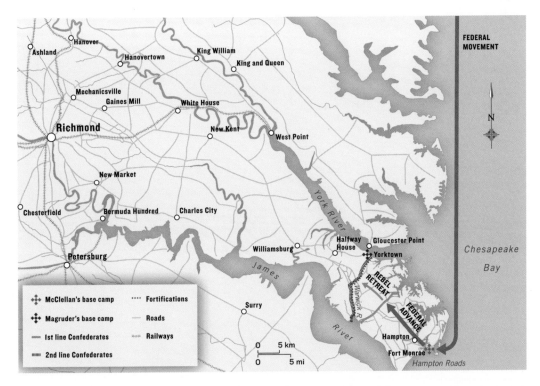

Union and Confederate troop positions during the Peninsula Campaign of 1862. Union commander Magruder formed an effective blockade across the entire peninsula, following the line of the Warwick River.

On 5 April, as his soldiers stared from their earthworks at the massive enemy force five times the size of theirs, Magruder gave a ringing speech of encouragement to his troops and then telegraphed Robert E. Lee in Richmond that the enemy was on the march. He told Lee the truth: 'I have made my arrangements to fight with my small force, but without the slightest hope of success'. There was nothing for Magruder to do now but set his grand deception in motion.

CONJURING UP AN ARMY

While the Yankee officers and men were watching his line, Magruder took a force of perhaps six thousand troops, split them in half and sent them marching up and down behind his lines in two groups. The Yankees could just see them moving through gaps in the woods behind the Confederate works. Occasionally, one column or the other would flock to a point on the defences, as if to man it. Once concealed behind the battlements, most of them would sneak back along trenches, hidden from the enemy, into the trees, and then resume their marching up and down within sight of the Yankees. One Alabama trooper wrote: 'We have been

Under the guidance of pioneer balloonist Thaddeus S.C. Lowe, the Union side made effective use of hot-air balloons for reconnaissance. Here, soon after the evacuation of Yorktown, Lowe sets off to observe the battle of Fair Oaks.

travelling most of the day, seemingly with no other view than to show ourselves to the enemy at as many different points … as possible'. By repeating the operation over and over, Magruder created the impression that a sizeable force was concealed in the woods.

Whenever the Yankees ventured close to the Confederate lines, the Southerners responded with ferocious fire that not only kept them away, but also convinced the Yankees that there were a good many aggressive enemy soldiers manning the works. While all this was going on, Confederate soldiers hidden in the woods produced sounds that also enhanced the impression of a massive military force: yelling (of the infamous Rebel yell), shouting of orders, playing of bugles, pounding of drums, firing of muskets. And Magruder's infamous

'Quaker guns' poked their wooden snouts out amid the real artillery, greatly amplifying Union fears of a slaughter if they decided to make a frontal assault.

Magruder's deception successfully brought the Federal forces to a halt, but life during the ensuing month-long stalemate was not easy for anyone. Torrential rains turned trenches into mud pits. Rations were short on the Confederate side, where the men existed on flour and beef jerky. The Union army employed a contingent of sharpshooters who fired at anything that moved, even African-American slaves delivering ammunition to Rebel trenches. At the same time, artillery shells burst repeatedly on both sides, taking a daily toll.

Meanwhile, in one of the first instances of balloons being used for observation in the Civil War, McClellan began sending 'Professor' Thaddeus S.C. Lowe, Chief Aeronaut of the Balloon Corps, aloft to observe the Confederate lines. Whenever this happened, Magruder kept his troops constantly on the move, and directed his artillerists to fire at the balloon, forcing Lowe to remain at a distance and thus rendering his observations inaccurate.

FULL OF HOT AIR? NO, HYDROGEN

Observation balloons were first used in warfare by French forces at the battle of Fleurus in the Netherlands in 1794, and the Union side made early use of them during the Civil War. The prime mover in this was 'Professor' Thaddeus S.C. Lowe, a character almost as colourful in his own way as John Magruder. Lowe, born in 1832, was not actually a professor but enjoyed being addressed by that title. Not that his accomplishments weren't truly amazing. A self-educated New Hampshire boy, he had become fascinated with French ballooning and begun building his own balloons. He then perfected a portable hydrogen-gas generator that allowed the balloon to be filled in the field. So impressed was President Abraham Lincoln that he created the Union Army Balloon Corps and awarded Lowe the grand title of Chief Aeronaut.

In September of 1861, Lowe ascended more than three hundred metres above Arlington, Virginia, to report on Confederate lines over five kilometres away, in Fall Church. Using a series of prearranged semaphore signals, he disclosed the enemy location and directed a devastating artillery fire against them—the first time in the history of warfare that gunners were able to fire accurately at the enemy without actually seeing them.

Lowe went on to create a fleet of seven balloons, which were used during the siege of Yorktown and in other battles. He also invented the world's first aircraft carrier, the *George Washington Parke Custis*, a modified coal barge with a flight deck superstructure that towed balloons into place for launching.

Balloons never completely proved their mettle in the Civil War, and the Balloon Corps was disbanded in 1863. However, Lowe lived to the ripe old age of eighty-one and became a millionaire by inventing and patenting a hydrogen-based refrigeration process that revolutionised the cold-storage industry.

As time passed, reinforcements, sent by Joseph Johnston, gradually poured in. By early May, Magruder's army numbered thirty-three thousand, a respectable force, although still nowhere near McClellan's numbers. In a move to unify his command, President Jefferson Davis combined Magruder's Army of the Peninsula with Johnston's command. The joined troops became known as the Army of Northern Virginia, with Johnston as overall commander. Magruder was far too junior in rank to expect to be given this command, but he may have been disappointed by Davis's actions, and his drinking increased. Despite this, he was the hero of the moment for the South. 'It was a wonderful thing, how he played his ten thousand before McClellan like fireflies and utterly deluded him', wrote Mary Chestnut, the Richmond diarist.

A BRILLIANT SUCCESS?

After a month, McClellan finally brought up his huge siege guns from Fort Monroe and all was made ready for a grand offensive that was to begin on 5 May. On the night of 3 May, however, the Confederate lines opened up with a huge artillery barrage, using all of their heavy guns. The surprised Yankees kept their heads down, which was just what the Confederates wanted. When Professor Lowe went up again in his balloon on the morning of 4 May, he discovered that the Confederate works were empty. The entire Confederate army had retreated.

'Our success is brilliant', McClellan wrote, sure that his actions had caused the enemy to 'run away'. Others in the Union high command, including President Lincoln himself, were not so sure. McClellan had had the Confederates within his grasp and had taken a month to even begin a serious attack on them. And it wasn't as if Joe Johnston was defeated—he had simply withdrawn his army to more defensible positions surrounding Richmond.

The retreat, however, was the beginning of the end of the glory days for John Magruder. During the subsequent weeks of fighting—which saw Robert E. Lee take over command of the Army of Northern Virginia after Joe Johnston proved too defence-minded—Magruder began taking morphine in addition to alcohol, possibly as a buffer against some of the dreadful sights he was seeing, for the fighting was the fiercest of the war to date. At the battles of White Oak Swamp and Malvern Hill, he seemed confused; at the latter battle, he ordering a futile attack after reading an outdated order from General Lee. This was not entirely his fault, but common sense and a clear head might have stopped an unnecessary loss of Confederate life.

Magruder was not a coward, as some charged. But his intake of alcohol and drugs, combined with stress and lack of sleep, caused him to make poor decisions. Even in a war that boasted heavy drinking on both sides, his 'purplish, swollen veins' (as his aide described them) and air of being continually drunk or suffering from the effects of alcohol did not go unnoticed. In late 1862, after Robert E. Lee had defeated McClellan on the peninsula,

Magruder was relieved of his command and sent to fight in the more remote western theatre of the war. There he partially redeemed his reputation by capturing the port city of Galveston, Texas, from the Yankees.

THE LAST DAYS OF MAGRUDER

After the Confederate surrender in the spring of 1865, Magruder fled to Mexico, where he was hired by Emperor Maximilian I as a major general in the Imperial Mexican Army (numerous ex-Confederates took this route, forming a kind of expatriate colony). But after the forces of the Austrian-born emperor were defeated in May of 1867 and Maximilian executed, Magruder returned to the United States, where he was forced to take an oath of allegiance to the Union and was then pardoned.

He was sixty years old, without family and nearly penniless, yet, with typical aplomb, he managed to make a life for himself travelling and giving lectures, not on his peninsula display, but on Mexico and Emperor Maximilian. By 1870, because of his advanced alcoholism, this means of employment had ended. Magruder was forced to move to Houston, where he was supported by a former aide de camp, who provided him with a stipend and a room in a hotel. It was in that hotel that John Magruder died alone, on 19 February 1871.

By no means was John Bankhead Magruder the most distinguished general the South ever produced, and it is true that his charade at Yorktown was aided by the excessive caution of George McClellan (indeed, Joe Johnston gruffly remarked, upon viewing Magruder's embattlements, 'no one but McClellan could have hesitated to attack'.) But the Prince's extraordinary deception in defence of his beloved Virginia is one of the most fascinating episodes in the annals of the American Civil War.

MYSTERIOUS MAGRUDER

Long after his death, Magruder keeps playing tricks on people. Not John Magruder himself, but the town named after him. Built on the Yorktown Peninsula after the Civil War, Magruder was appropriated by the U.S. Navy during World War II as a top-secret prisoner of war camp for German POWs captured from subs and surface vessels, forcing all of its small population to evacuate. After the war, the town, by then known as Camp Peary, was taken over by the CIA, which closed the area to the public and established—although the American government has never publicly admitted it—the infamous facility called 'The Farm', where CIA agents are trained in the black arts of their tradecraft. Rumour has it that the original buildings and roads of Magruder are still there, in use and intact. A historical treasure trove then, though seeing it might cost you your life.

GETTING HIGH ON SUBTERFUGE: RICHARD MEINERTZHAGEN AND THE THIRD BATTLE OF GAZA, 1917

WHEN PEOPLE THINK OF WORLD WAR I, THE IMAGE THAT COMES TO MIND IS usually that of its western front—long trenches zigzagging across desolate landscapes so torn apart by shellfire that they resemble lunar wastes. But there were other and very different conflicts going on at the same time—among them, the bloody fight over the Middle East. Far from being a sideshow, this theatre pitted hundreds of thousands of British, Australian and New Zealand troops against an equal number of Ottoman Turks and Germans.

The Ottomans had made a secret pact with the Germans and Italians in 1914, in the hope that joining forces with the Central Powers would help them regain the territories in the Caucasus that they had lost to Russia in the Russo–Turkish War of 1878. For the British, the entry of the Turks on the side of the Central Powers was a worst-case scenario in the Middle East. Certain to be chief among the Ottoman targets was the British-controlled Suez Canal, through which shipping flowed from the Mediterranean to the Red Sea, from Europe to Asia. Oil supplies were also likely to come under threat. The First Lord of the Admiralty, Winston Churchill, had taken what even he called 'a great gamble' when he converted the British fleet from Welsh coal to oil in 1912. For the fleet to keep sailing, for the increasingly mechanised British forces to keep moving, now and in the future, the oil of the Middle East, as yet barely tapped, was essential.

ORNITHOLOGIST ... AND KILLER

Although the war in the Middle East had global implications, it was a decidedly different kind of war from the conflict on the western front. It was often fought with sweeping mounted infantry and cavalry actions—including, as we shall see, the last successful cavalry charge in history—in a brutal environment where sunstroke was almost as much of a danger as artillery

Richard Meinertzhagen in England, 1922. According to his comrade T.E. Lawrence, Meinertzhagen 'knew no half measures'.

Turkish soldiers marching through Jerusalem's Jaffa Gate in 1915. The city became the Turks' and Germans' Middle East headquarters. On December 11, 1917, General Allenby would lead Allied troops into the city via this same gate.

fire. Unlike the war in France, the Middle East front was rarely in stasis, regularly moving back and forth following sudden shifts and developments. The war was planned in exotic locales— the British headquarters was in Cairo, that of the Turks and Germans in Jerusalem—which were riddled with double agents. Deception was highly prized by both sides.

The war in the desert was dangerous, but liberating: the most successful soldiers were those of an independent and unorthodox turn of mind. T.E. Lawrence, the famed 'Lawrence of Arabia', was one such warrior, a British liaison officer who 'went native' and helped Husayn ibn Ali lead an Arab revolt against Ottoman rule in 1916, and whose guerilla actions against the Turks were effective and damaging in the extreme. Another such soldier, a friend and contemporary of Lawrence, was Colonel Richard 'Dick' Meinertzhagen.

If anything, Meinertzhagen was an even stranger and more enigmatic man than Lawrence. He was born in Britain in 1878 to a wealthy family, and grew up on the family estate in Hampshire, 110 kilometres southwest of London. Although he liked to pretend later in life that he was of Viking stock, his family origins could be traced to fourteenth-century Germany. Early in his life, he became a passionate ornithologist. When he was twenty-four, he joined the King's African Rifles as a lieutenant and was shipped off to British East Africa, where he cultivated another passion: killing.

Meinertzhagen, it turned out, was extremely good at killing. T.E. Lawrence described him as 'a student of bird migration who drifted into soldiering … His instincts were abetted by an immensely powerful body and a savage brain, which chose the best way to its purpose, unhampered by doubt or habit'. In suppressing a rebellion of the East African Nandi tribe, Meinertzhagen and his native soldiers killed the men and women of an entire village. 'As soon as we could see to shoot, we closed in', he wrote in his journal. 'Every soul was either shot or bayonetted.' It was Meinertzhagen's habit to steal out at night on long, solo scouting expeditions, during which he would crawl up on his Nandi enemies and kill them with knife or bayonet. When World War I started, Meinertzhagen and his trained force of scouts attacked an enemy encampment in German East Africa on Christmas Day, slaughtering its inhabitants. Dick personally shot a German officer—a count, as it turned out—pushed the corpse aside and sat down to eat the meal the man had been about to consume. 'One of the best though most gruesome meals I ever had', he wrote.

Meinertzhagen was a man of contradictions: a racist who would become a passionate Zionist; a hunter who loved animals so much that he beat an Indian orderly to death with a polo mallet for mistreating a horse; a respected ornithologist who was later discovered to have stolen specimens from museums, relabelled them as his own finds and submitted them to other museums. Which brings us to another of Meinertzhagen's great passions: deception.

ASSIGNMENT TO CAIRO

In the early stages of the war in East Africa, Meinertzhagen was assigned as an intelligence officer to the British high command, where he took an unorthodox approach to spying. He set up a network of informants that consisted mainly of African or Arab orderlies in the employ of the Germans. When one man told him that, because of a shortage of toilet paper, the Germans were using documents and personal letters, he ordered that these be retrieved from the latrines and washed. This 'DPM' or 'Dirty Paper Method', as he called it, resulted in numerous German codes being broken. On another occasion, Meinertzhagen had his men scatter dead birds around water holes to give the Germans the idea that the creatures had died from poisoned water. As a result, the Germans, with no other water sources in the dry African bush, retreated from several strategically important positions.

In May of 1917, Meinertzhagen was assigned to Cairo as chief intelligence officer under General Edmund Allenby, the new commander in chief of the Egyptian Expeditionary Force. The British had not fared well in their fight against the Turks, mainly because of poor leadership and a lack of good intelligence. In 1915, the Turks, at the instigation of the Germans, and after their failed attack on Russia, turned westwards, as expected, to advance on the Suez Canal. In February of that year, and again in August of 1916, Ottoman forces led by the brilliant German Colonel Kress von Kressenstein, made two attempts to seize control of the canal from the British. The attacks were repelled, but von Kressenstein and the Turks stayed in the Sinai Peninsula to harry and harass their enemy.

British commander in chief Archibald Murray and his field commander, Lieutenant General Sir Charles Dobell, decided that they needed to push the Turks further away from the canal. Moving a large force across the barren desert was a huge challenge, given that food and water were nowhere available. Murray and Dobell came up with some ingenious solutions. In late 1916, thousands of local labourers working for the British advanced through the trackless Sinai Desert, building a standard-gauge railway along the route. Parallel to the railway, a freshwater pipeline linked to a portable reservoir held nearly two million litres of water. The pipeline and railway would supply advancing troops; men further forwards would be supported by the Camel Transport Corp. It was a superb feat of engineering and logistics. As a result, more than twenty thousand British and Allied troops stood ready to attack the Turks, who had retreated to a line that stretched from the fort of Gaza, on the Mediterranean coast, to the town of Beersheba, fifty kilometres inland to the southeast.

The first British attack on Gaza took place on 25 March, 1917. Dobell sent sixteen thousand infantry and six thousand mounted infantry and cavalry on a sharp, pre-dawn punch

---

LOST ORDERS

Few intelligence services have matched Meinertzhagen's opium cigarette drop, although it's known that the CIA experimented in the 1950s with the idea of poisoning an enemy's water supply with LSD. The 'fake war plans' trick has, however, been used more than once, although seldom so successfully.

In September 1918, the U.S. Army under General John Pershing was planning an offensive at St-Mihiel, near the Meuse River in France. They knew that servants at local hotels were in the employ of the Germans. So a member of Pershing's staff checked into a hotel and typed up a fake battle plan, then dropped the carbon paper into the wastebasket. He left the room; when he returned a few hours later, the carbon paper was gone. It was apparent as the battle opened that the Germans were convinced the attack was going to come from elsewhere.

But sometimes 'lost' orders really are lost. In 1862, in Virginia, in the United States, a Union soldier found a copy of General Robert E. Lee's Special Order Number 191 lying under a tree, wrapped—à la Meinertzhagen—around a few cigars. The order described the movements of Lee's troops over the next few days in detail. It was, in fact, genuine. But Union commander General George B. McClellan decided it was a trap and ignored it, thus missing a huge opportunity to defeat the Confederates.

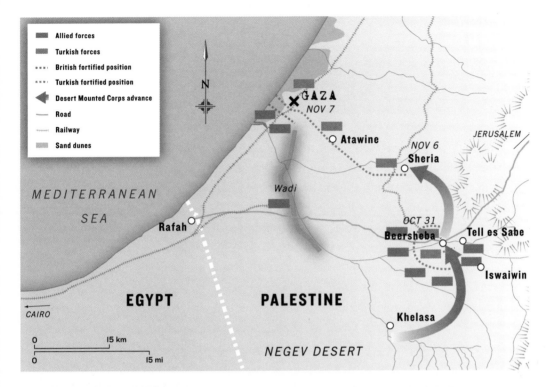

The Third Battle of Gaza. While the Turks strengthened their defences around Gaza as a result of Meinertzhagen's deceptions, the Allies' Desert Mounted Corps moved furtively across the desert then swept into Beersheba.

against the Turkish defenders holding the town. But faulty intelligence resulted in a debacle. The British infantry overestimated the size of the opposing force—there were only four thousand defenders—and delayed their advance. This allowed the Turks to regroup. When the British eventually moved forwards across a wide plain, they were cut down by machine-gun and artillery fire. Then, just as the British were making headway, and to the soldiers' astonishment, the generals ordered a retreat. They had fallen prey to a false rumour that massive Turkish reinforcements were on the way. The British withdrew, having suffered 400 killed and 2,900 wounded, and having gained nothing.

A second attack on Gaza took place in April, the month before Meinertzhagen arrived. Seeking to guarantee success, the British employed tanks, and shells full of poison gas, both for the first time in the Middle East. They also increased their forces by twenty thousand men and attacked all along the Gaza–Beersheba line. But it proved to be a disastrous western front-style assault against fixed positions. The Turks were unaffected by the gas, the tanks never got close—in fact, they became convenient targets for the Turkish artillery—and after a day-long battle the British were repulsed. Generals Murray and Dobell had made no progress and suffered 5,900 casualties. They were immediately relieved of duty. The new commander in chief was the experienced and imaginative General Allenby.

JERUSALEM BY CHRISTMAS

Allenby's directive was to break through the Gaza–Beersheba line and capture Jerusalem by Christmas, and this was the first thing he told Meinertzhagen when they met in May of 1917 at the Savoy Hotel in Cairo. Allenby, however, did not want another frontal assault; his plan was to capture Gaza from the rear, with a massive cavalry sweep through the Negev Desert.

This would work only if the Turks at Gaza were looking the other way, so Allenby instructed Meinertzhagen to make sure they were. Meinertzhagen set to work immediately. The first task he applied himself to was counterintelligence. Knowing that Cairo was rife with secret agents working for the Central Powers, Meinertzhagen found out that an Arab stationed in Beersheba was 'running' these spies. He therefore sent a flowery letter of thanks to the Arab, enclosing a large sum of money, intimating that the Arab was really working for him. He entrusted the letter to a dull-witted agent of his, whom he knew would be captured by the Turks. On discovering the agent, the Turks immediately executed the Arab spymaster for being a counteragent—thereby cutting off their own supply of intelligence—along with Meinertzhagen's own agent, which Meinertzhagen viewed as a necessary sacrifice of war.

Once he had blinded the opposition, Meinertzhagen turned to the task of sowing disinformation. Starting in September, he had 'secret' British radio messages suggest that although a mounted reconnaissance force would approach Beersheba, the main British thrust would be a massive frontal assault on Gaza. At the same time, Meinertzhagen heard that the Turks were desperate for tobacco. So he bought thousands of packets of cigarettes on the black market and wrapped them in propaganda leaflets that urged Turkish soldiers to 'Have a Smoke—and Surrender!' Then, on numerous occasions, he had himself piloted over the Turkish lines and rained the cigarettes down on the trenches. On his first outing, his pilot was injured and Meinertzhagen, who had had only two flying lessons, was forced to crawl into the front seat of the open biplane. Sitting on top of the unconscious pilot, he flew back to the British base, dropped a note explaining the situation and then received instructions on how to land via pieces of calico cloth laid on the runway, which spelled out helpful phrases such as 'Land at 80 [miles per hour—130 kilometres per hour]'. He managed to land safely, although, in an uncharacteristic statement of nerves, he wrote that night in his journal: 'I was very frightened and cannot work this evening'.

The next thing Meinertzhagen did was to prepare a dispatch case to be 'lost' near Turkish lines. The case belonged to a fictitious British staff officer. In it were some personal items— a letter from the officer's wife, actually written by Meinertzhagen's sister; photos of children; a twenty pound note—and a private letter from another fictitious officer criticising Allenby's plan to feint at Beersheba while attacking Gaza. In a moment that has become legend—in fact, it inspired a scene in the movie *The Young Indiana Jones*—Meinertzhagen rode out towards the Turkish lines, where he was shot at. Pretending to be wounded—he dropped a rifle smeared with horse's blood—he abandoned the dispatch case and sped away on his horse, with bullets whizzing around him.

Meinertzhagen's deception was masterful. The Turks fell for it, hook, line and sinker. They began extending and strengthening their trench lines in front of Gaza, while pulling forces away from Beersheba. On 31 October, Allenby opened up on Gaza with a furiously heavy bombardment, followed by a two-infantry-division attack. Turkish attention was completely focused on Gaza.

Then, suddenly and with no advance bombardment, the Desert Mounted Corps, made up of the Australian and the ANZAC (Australian and New Zealand Army Corps) mounted divisions, moved south of Beersheba, wheeled and rode towards the rear of the Turkish army. The ANZAC mounted infantry was led by Lieutenant General Harry Chauvel, an Australian who would come out of the war with a reputation as the greatest leader of mounted troops in his era. Chauvel had examined reconnaissance photos before the battle, which showed that the southeastern approach to Beersheba was guarded only by two lines of trenches—manned, to be sure, by Turkish infantrymen, but with no tangles of barbed wire to stop a cavalry charge. He now ordered two regiments of the Australian Light Horse—the Fourth (Victoria) and Twelfth (New South Wales)—to assault the Turkish lines.

The advance started slowly, through rolling countryside, with lone riders out front, checking for steep wadis, or ravines, that might be hidden from view. The pace picked up to a trot about a kilometre from the Turkish lines, then to a canter. With two hundred metres to go, eight hundred horses broke into a furious gallop, charging directly at the

General Edmund Allenby in 1916. Allenby's experience as a cavalry commander on the western front was to serve him well in the Middle East.

The Charge of the Australian Light Horse at Beersheba, 1917, George Lambert's 1920 painting of the 'last great cavalry charge in history', depicts the moment when the Australian mounted forces stormed the Turkish trenches.

Turkish trenches. It was an awe-inspiring sight and those who saw it never forgot it. One trooper wrote: 'The men were knee-to-knee, horse-to-horse—the sun glinting on their bayonet points. Machine-gun and rifle fire rattled, but the Fourth Brigade galloped on. We saw shellbursts among them and horses crashed … but suddenly men ceased to fall'.

The Turks thrust bayonet points up at the horses' bellies. The men of the Fourth, the first to reach the lines, dismounted and engaged the enemy hand to hand in their trenches, while the other regiments leaped over the Turkish lines and galloped, shooting wildly, into Beersheba. As a result of what is now considered the last successful massed cavalry charge in history, Beersheba fell.

SMOKE, ANYONE?

Soon the Turks were retreating to the east as fast as they could. But Meinertzhagen had one more trick up his sleeve. Remember the cigarettes he had dropped over Turkish lines? Well, his intelligence reports told him that although the Turks laughed at his surrender requests, they greatly enjoyed the good British tobacco. On 5 November, the Turks were attempting to make a stand at Sheria, about fifteen kilometres southeast of Gaza. The British were hammering them, but they showed no signs of surrender. So Meinertzhagen went up in his plane and dropped thousands of packets of cigarettes once again. The Turks didn't even bother to take a shot at him, so grateful were they for a smoke.

The difference this time was that Meinertzhagen had laced the butts with opium, also bought from his black market contacts. When the British attacked the next day, they found the Turks in an incoherent state, barely able to defend themselves. General Allenby wrote after the war that 'a high percentage' of Turkish troops were unable to do combat because they were incapacitated by the drug.

From then on, thanks to Meinertzhagen's brilliant campaign of deception, it was plain sailing for the British and their allies, who captured Jerusalem on 9 December, two weeks ahead of schedule. An interesting footnote is that Allenby actually vetoed the opium cigarette plan, saying it was a waste of time, but Meinertzhagen, in typical fashion, went ahead anyway. And he pilfered a few of the cigarettes for his own use, finding the effect, as he wrote, 'quite sublime'.

A STRANGE AND REMARKABLE LIFE

After the Gaza campaign, Dick Meinertzhagen was stationed in the British War Office but found himself unable to stand the bureaucracy. After the war, he managed to get himself appointed to General Allenby's staff as Palestine's chief political officer. He used his position to lobby for Zionist interests in the Middle East. Meinertzhagen had become a passionate supporter of the Jewish cause in 1910, during a brief visit to Odessa, Russia, where he had witnessed a pogrom in progess. 'I am deeply moved by these terrible deeds', he wrote in his journal, 'and have resolved that whenever and where I can help the Jews, I shall do so to the best of my ability.'

Death followed him. His wife, the noted ornithologist Annie Constance Jackson, died in a shooting accident in 1928. She shot herself in the head, so her death was thought by many to be suicide, although others felt that Meinertzhagen might have killed her. There was, however, no proof of this and he was so distraught that he had a nervous breakdown.

Meinertzhagen's first-born son, Daniel, was killed in combat in World War II. By then, Meinertzhagen had been working for British intelligence for some time. In the 1930s, he had actually brought a pistol with him to a meeting with Adolf Hitler, but decided not to pull the trigger, because Hitler had bodyguards stationed just outside the room they were in and he knew he would be killed.

In 1954, thirteen years before his death, Meinertzhagen published a book called *The Birds of Arabia*. In the 1990s, around the same time that his bird specimen thefts were uncovered, it was revealed that he almost certainly based this work on the unpublished manuscript of another naturalist.

'THIS MOST SUCCESSFUL THREAT': OPERATION FORTITUDE, 1944

THE MARTIAL PHILOSOPHER SUN TZU ONCE SAID, 'ALL WARFARE IS BASED ON deception'. Nothing could be truer. Little kids playing soldier instinctively learn to sneak up on their 'enemy', to lie motionless and 'play dead', to camouflage their faces, to feint left and go right. Big kids involved in world-spanning wars do the same thing, but on an unimaginably massive scale. Operation Fortitude, the Allied plan to convince the Germans that the 1944 invasion of France would strike anywhere but where it actually did, in Normandy, is the most extraordinary example of deception in war in history. An entire department of the Supreme Headquarters Allied Expeditionary Force (SHAEF), the innocuously named London Controlling Section, spent the better part of a year convincing the German High Command that the D-Day invasion would strike the Pas de Calais region, east of the Seine River, rather than the Cotentin Peninsula and Normandy, to the west. Aiding in this crucial charade were numerous German agents who were actually Allied agents (or simply didn't exist at all) and thousands of Allied troops, as well as dummy ships, tanks and airplanes. As a result, an entire German army—the German Fifteenth Army—which could have driven the Normandy invaders back into the sea, was held, frozen in place east of the Seine, and untold thousands of lives were saved.

NEED FOR A DIVERSION

At the Casablanca Conference, held in January 1943, British Prime Minister Winston Churchill, American President Franklin Delano Roosevelt and Charles de Gaulle, leader of the Free French forces then fighting the Germans, made aggressive plans for the future of the war in Europe. Sicily would be invaded in June of that year, Italy in September. And by the spring of 1944, there would be a cross-Channel invasion of France.

The problem here was that the German high command (OKW) knew they were coming. The entire coast of Fortress Europe (as Hitler called it)—from Holland all the way down to Spain—had been heavily fortified with mines, beach obstacles and seawalls, pillboxes and artillery emplacements. The Germans had also created mobile reserve forces of tanks and infantry located further back from the beaches at strategic locations. Their job was to respond quickly to the particular point where the invasion would take place.

Any trained military planner on either side, looking at a map of France and England, would pick one obvious point for the invasion: Pas de Calais. Not only was this area the closest to England—on a clear day you could look across the Channel from here to the White Cliffs of Dover—but it contained numerous port cities, whose harbours and facilities would be desperately needed by any invading force. From here, the Allies could move in a direct line towards Paris and, ultimately, Berlin.

Allied planners, however, had different ideas. Their invasion scheme, dubbed Operation Overlord and submitted for approval in the summer of 1943, was ingenious and audacious. Instead of taking the shortest route across the English Channel, at the Straits of Dover, SHAEF planners instead recommended an invasion of Normandy, specifically the Cotentin Peninsula. There were no sizeable natural harbours here, but so what? SHAEF intended to build its own, with shiploads of materials and concrete docks floated over from England. It also planned to lay an underwater fuel pipeline across the ocean floor from the Isle of Wight.

These were ingenious ideas, but the only way the invasion would work would be if the Allied forces had the element of surprise. If the Germans suspected for one moment that this was the main invasion force, then the Fifteenth Army panzer divisions further north and east would be quickly shifted to Normandy and the American, Canadian and British forces pounded into the sand of their beachheads, before any artificial harbour could be built or pipeline laid.

'A BODYGUARD OF LIES'

In 1943, Winston Churchill commented, 'In wartime, truth is so precious that she should always be accompanied by a bodyguard of lies'. His comment provided a name, Operation Bodyguard, for the overall Allied plan that was needed, as SHAEF put it, 'to deceive the enemy as to the strength, objective and timing of Overlord'. It was decided that the tactical plan of deception itself would be called Operation Fortitude and it would have three main objectives: to convince the Germans that the main attack would take place in Pas de Calais, around 15 July 1944; to convince the Germans that any Normandy invasion was a diversionary attack, not the real thing—and to keep them thinking this for at least two weeks after the actual attack; and to convince the Germans that another attack might come as far north as Norway.

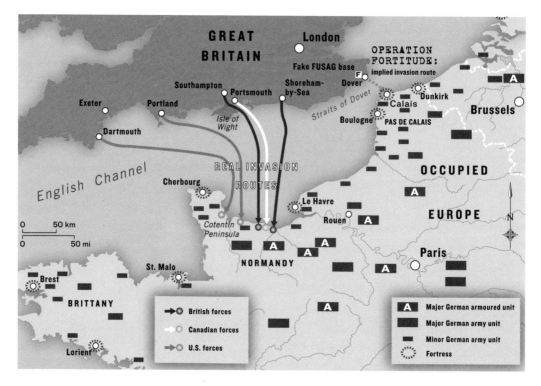

Operation Fortitude South fooled the Germans into thinking that the Allied invasion of Europe would target the Pas de Calais region. In the event, the Allies landed in Normandy, in five main landings, as shown here.

There would be two Fortitudes, then: Fortitude North would help create the impression that a flanking invasion was about to take place in Norway, while Fortitude South would aim to convince the Germans that the main invasion would come across the Straits of Dover.

The assignment to oversee and implement these highly detailed deceptions—where one wrong note might spell death for soldiers of the invading forces, fell to the London Controlling Section, newly created for just this task, whose bland, bureaucratic-sounding name belied the top-secret nature of its task. It consisted of a small group of officers led by Colonel John Bevan, but the man now almost universally acknowledged as the prime mover behind Operation Fortitude was the operations manager, lawyer Roger Hesketh. Hesketh was a member of Britain's upper class whose home, Meols Hall in Lancashire, had been in his family for eight centuries, and who had been educated at Eton and Oxford. He had joined the army at the outbreak of the war and had risen through the ranks of British intelligence.

Hesketh and his colleagues had one great advantage over the Germans: Ultra. This was the code-name for intelligence obtained by decoding German wireless transmissions, in particular the messages encrypted by a highly complex machine called Enigma. With the help of Polish scientists, the British had been able to reconstruct the German machine and, by studying it, a team led by scientists including Alan Turing had managed to crack its supposedly unbreakable code as early as 1940. As a result, Hesketh and others working on Fortitude were able to tell almost immediately if the ruses they were using were having any effect.

FICTITIOUS ARMIES

To help convince the Germans that the attack was going to target Pas de Calais, Fortitude South created the impression of a build-up of troops in the southeast through the construction of physical decoys. Dummy airbases and infantry camps, even fake tanks and landing craft, were built by special British and American camouflage units. From the ground, these sheds, tanks and boats, mainly constructed of wood and canvas, looked decidedly fake. However, from a distance, or from a wandering German reconnaissance plane, they seemed like the real deal. (In aerial photographs taken by the British of dummy landing craft in Dover harbour, the fakes can't be told apart from the real thing.)

One of the major achievements of this strategy was to create the belief in the minds of the German high command—and Adolf Hitler—that the First U.S. Army Group (FUSAG), commanded by General George Patton, was in place in southeastern England, opposite Calais. Fake FUSAG camps and bases were placed around possible embarkation points on the coast there, and an enormous amount of fake radio traffic regarding its presence was engendered. Furthermore, Patton, who was of course quite real, was often seen visiting these locations.

This success aside, however, the physical decoy strategy was found to have limited effect. Ironically, Allied air superiority was so complete over Britain, and German reconnaissance so poor, that the Germans seldom noticed the dummy bases. Something further was needed, and for this, Hesketh relied on spies—German spies.

IMAGINARY SPIES

In early 1944, the Abwehr, the German intelligence service, had fifty agents operating inside Britain. Unbeknownst to them, MI5, the British intelligence service, controlled every single one of them. The prime example of this was the agent code-named Garbo by the Allies and Arabel by the Abwehr. His real name, which he agreed to reveal only in the 1980s, was Juan Pujol. Pujol was born in Spain in 1912 and took a strong dislike to the Nazis during the Spanish Civil War. MI5 brought Pujol to England, gave him a cover story and a case officer, and, most astonishingly, helped him create a system of twenty-four 'subagents'—all of whom were entirely imaginary.

The Supreme Commander of the Allied Expeditionary Force, General Dwight D. Eisenhower, centre, with other Allied commanders just before the D-Day invasion. These men were counting on Operation Fortitude to deceive the enemy.

In the run-up to the D-Day invasion in the winter and spring of 1944, these imaginary agents were put to good use. The subagent known as Seven, for instance, was an ex-seaman whom Pujol described to his Abwehr handler in Madrid as 'a thoroughly undesirable character' who worked solely for money. But he lived in southeast England and was able to observe the build-up of forces there, presumably for the invasion of Pas de Calais. There were other such 'agents' stationed, supposedly, throughout the country. As Pujol later stated, if one of these agents reported something the Abwehr knew to be false, Pujol could simply blame the imaginary agent for the mistake and 'liquidate' him.

Hesketh never had agents like Garbo merely feed the Germans false documents or information. It was of the utmost importance, when it came to Fortitude, that the Germans decide for themselves, by piecing together reports from numerous sources, where the invasion was likely to come from. Thus, although Garbo's subagent Seven might report a build-up of men and material in southeastern England, Hesketh knew there really had to *be* troops there, in case someone, somehow, checked.

SCHEMING ON TWO FRONTS

Although Fortitude North was secondary to its southern counterpart, it was also an extraordinary undertaking. A fictitious British 'Fourth Army' was created and 'placed' in Scotland, Ireland and Iceland. Only a few visual dummy props were used, due in part to a lack of resources and the fact that there was little German air reconnaissance in these places. Instead, simulated wireless communications were sent out to make the Germans believe that the Fourth Army was there. This was no easy feat, as such communications were studied very closely by Abwehr operatives experienced in unit-to-unit radio contact, and quite aware that such radio chatter could be manufactured as a ruse.

Adding to the verisimilitude was a move to open diplomatic relations with neutral Sweden, with an eye towards having that country give the Allies the right to land and conduct reconnaissance missions from Swedish territory. Hesketh and the Allies knew that Sweden was unlikely to grant them these rights—it would then have to grant Germany the same—but they wanted word of the initiative to reach German ears, so that the OKW might deduce that the Allies were preparing an invasion of Norway.

No one quite knows if the deception of Fortitude North worked as well as the Allies hoped—although for whatever reason, German divisions in Norway *were* reinforced. All told, some 280,000 German troops were stationed in Norway. Had the Germans divined the

- -

OPERATION MINCEMEAT

No recounting of World War II deceptions by the Allies is complete without the story of Operation Mincemeat, the classic though ghoulish story of a dead man disguised by British intelligence to fool the Germans into thinking the invasion of Sicily would in fact be an attack on Greece.

Later made into a movie called *The Man Who Never Was* (1956), Operation Mincemeat began when two bright young British intelligence operatives got the idea to take a corpse from a London morgue, dress him in the uniform of a Royal Marines Major and eject his body from a submarine just off the coast of Spain, on 30 April 1943, near where a Nazi agent was known to be operating. The body was given the identity of 'Major William Martin,

R.M.' Attached to his wrist by a chain was an attaché case containing forged documents suggesting that Greece would be the location for an upcoming Allied attack in the spring. The plan worked to perfection, so much so that even after the invasion of Sicily, many in the German high command believed that Greece was still the real target.

The true identity of 'William Martin' has been much speculated upon. He is believed by many to have been a destitute alcoholic who committed suicide by taking rat poison. In any event, 'William Martin' was buried in a little cemetery in Huelva, Spain. His tombstone has become something of a tourist attraction.

After the success of the initial landings in Normandy on D-Day, June 6 1944, British troops take command of the shoreline, erecting the White Ensign flag of the Royal Navy and bringing military vehicles ashore.

real intentions of the Allies, they would almost certainly have rushed some of these troops to the south. Fortitude South, however, was, unmistakably, an immense success. The entire German Fifteenth Army—twenty-two divisions, totalling one hundred thousand men— would be held in place in Pas de Calais as late as two weeks after the Normandy invasion because, as German dispatches said, 'the main [Allied force] has not yet landed'.

AT LAST, A REAL INVASION

On 6 June 1944, after all the deception, the real attack on the European continent began in Normandy. Allied parachutists were dropped behind German lines during the night. At first light, Germans manning the pillboxes on the Normandy bluffs saw an astonishing sight: 6,500 ships, carrying 150,000 men, supported by 11,000 aircraft. The fighting was fierce— there were 9,000 Allied casualties—but by the end of the day the American, British and Canadian forces were moving inland. By summer's end, they were in Paris. The Germans had been taken completely by surprise.

As per the original plan, Fortitude South continued to operate after the landing. On 9 June, Garbo sent an urgent message to his Madrid handler saying that FUSAG was still held in place in southeastern England—meaning that this nonexistent army group was still poised in readiness to attack Pas de Calais. Because of this, Hitler himself issued orders that the Fifteenth not be shifted to aid in the defence of Normandy, much to the despair of Field Marshall Erwin Rommel, who was in charge of the Atlantic defences and knew he needed these men and tanks to beat back the Allied invasion.

After D-Day, General Dwight Eisenhower, Supreme Commander of the Allied forces, wrote that: 'Lack of infantry was the most important cause of the enemy's defeat in Normandy, and his failure to remedy this weakness was due primarily to the success of Allied threats levelled against the Pas de Calais … I cannot overemphasise the decisive value of this most successful threat'.

Astonishingly, the Allies weren't the only ones to congratulate Fortitude operatives. On 29 July 1944, Garbo's German handlers in Madrid advised him in a secret communication that Hitler had awarded him the Iron Cross. Even though the Pas de Calais invasion had not occurred, the Germans believed it was simply because the Normandy invasion had been so successful that FUSAG wasn't needed. And so they rewarded Pujol—who also received an MBE from the grateful British—as the good and faithful servant they assumed him to be.

Now, *that's* deception!

- -

CON ARTISTS

Few people in the American army knew it at the time, but within their ranks was a special unit made up of about eleven hundred men whose job it was not to fight the enemy on the field of battle, but to fool it. This unit was known as the Twenty-third Headquarters Special Troops and its ranks were full of artists, designers, actors and sound experts.

Specially trained for a year before the D-Day invasion, the Twenty-third went into action after the landing. They carried fake uniforms, inflatable tanks, jeeps and pup tents, to fool the Germans into thinking that entire units were encamped where there were none. One trick was to inflate a battery of heavy black rubber cannons; these had special igniters which touched off pans of black powder. Accompanied by quite realistic sound-effects of banging artillery, the guns flashed most of the night, often calling down a German artillery barrage—which was then answered in kind by real American artillery.

One particular incident showed just how convincing the Twenty-third could be. During heavy fighting in Brittany, a real American tank unit moved up to attack a German division just as the Twenty-third was setting up dummy tanks in a grove of trees a kilometre or so away. The Americans were beaten back by the Germans and reeled back through the grove of trees. Assuming the dummy tanks were real, one of the battered tank squad shouted: 'If you had been with us, we wouldn't have had to retreat. You let us down!'

THE TUNNEL BENEATH BERLIN: OPERATION STOPWATCH/GOLD, 1954-56

THE COLD WAR WAS AS DEADLY SERIOUS AS ANY FIERY HOT CONFLICT IN HISTORY, but the battles which took place between Russia and the United States and Great Britain after the end of World War II were largely unseen by the general public. These were mainly battles for information and hence leverage; the classic Cold Warrior was not an infantryman, but a spy, and nowhere did spies operate in greater numbers than in the ruined and divided city of Berlin, before the building of the Berlin Wall.

In 1954, British and American espionage agents moved with stunning audacity to tunnel half a kilometre under the Russian sector and tap into a bundle of telephone and telegraph cables lying only fifty centimetres beneath a busy intersection. Through these cables poured top-secret military messages from the Soviet military command in East Berlin to its head-quarters in Moscow. The tunnel was used for eleven months, producing huge volumes of information that were recorded on six hundred tape recorders—in fact, so many of these machines were used that some in the British and American intelligence community thought the sudden spike in demand for recording tape might give the strategy away.

In the end, the tunnel *was* betrayed to the Soviets—in fact, in the beginning, even before the first spade full of dirt was dug out of the ground in a quiet West Berlin suburb. So the question still debated to this day becomes: was the information flowing into those ticking and whirring tape recorders worth anything at all?

A HIGH PRICE ON INTELLIGENCE

Wars, cold and hot, are fought with information. When any commander knows the intentions of his enemy, he can more easily thwart it and develop his own plans. Since armies began taking advantage of telegraph, telephone and wireless (and now digital) communications, other armies have devoted untold hours to intercepting these messages. World War II was the era, at least for the Allies, of massively successful code-breaking. The British were able to read German intentions throughout much of the war as a result of their success in cracking the Enigma code. Americans knew much about what was happening in the Japanese military because a cryptanalyst named Frank Rowlett had led a team that broke the Japanese code. This led Allied leaders of the Cold War to expect an equal amount of similar high-level information on Soviet plans. In particular, they were depending on intelligence to alert them to a Soviet attack, which they felt could come at any moment. Even a few days notice of such an attack could be invaluable.

Following the collapse of the Nazi regime in 1945, Germany was divided into four different occupation zones, run by the British, American, French and Russian victors. Berlin itself, while isolated inside the Russian sector, was also divided into four sections controlled by these countries. By 1948, Britain, America and France had decided to merge their German sectors, effectively creating what would soon be known as West Germany. In response, Stalin ordered a blockade of Berlin in 1948, attempting to cut off the Allies from their sectors, but airlifts of food and necessary supplies for eleven tense months rendered this ineffective.

In 1954, Berlin was still a city marred by vast tracts of rubble from buildings destroyed by Allied bombing. Housing was at a premium, electricity a rare commodity and refugees by the thousands still lived in temporary camps. The Berlin Wall was not built until 1961; in the meantime, Berliners continued to move from West to East and vice-versa, but border crossings were manned and civilians subjected to rigid identity checks.

Perhaps the only human beings in town who truly thrived were those in the intelligence agencies. Primary among them were the British SIS (Secret Intelligence Service), the American CIA (Central Intelligence Agency), the Soviet KGB and the East German Stasi. Intelligence came to these agencies in all kinds of ways. Refugees were a prime source, and the intelligence agencies were quick to question and recruit those who came from enemy territory. Another prime source of information was moles, or double agents—men and women placed deep within the intelligence service of another country who fed streams of information to their true masters. Here the KGB bested the Allies. The British SIS (commonly known as MI6) was heavily infiltrated by the Russians, with such famous spies as Guy Burgess, Donald Maclean and Kim Philby, among others, continually feeding highly sensitive information to Moscow. (Burgess and Maclean defected to Russia in 1951; Philby fled in 1963.) But it was a Soviet mole among the Americans who was to cause the upheaval that ended in the fateful decision to dig the Berlin tunnel.

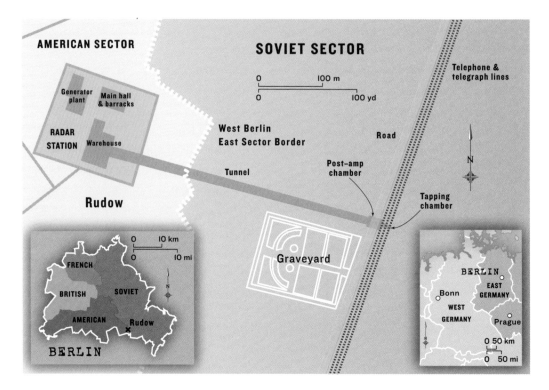

Main map: The secret CIA–MI6 tunnel extended from within a phony radar facility deep into the East German sector of Berlin. Left inset: How the occupying powers divided up Berlin. Right inset: Germany in 1954.

RESPONDING TO BLACK FRIDAY

Immediately after the war, American and British code-breakers scored a startling success with the Venona Project. This involved intercepting and decoding communications between the KGB and American spies, and led to the arrest and execution of spies Julius and Ethel Rosenberg in 1953. The Americans were also able to read some of the ciphers used by the Soviet Army in Berlin; these provided a valuable, if incomplete, picture of what Soviet divisions were doing. But, unbeknownst to the Americans, they had a Soviet mole in their midst, a man named William Weisband, a son of Russian immigrants to America, who worked for an American code-breaking division in the National Security Administration (NSA) as a linguist.

On Friday 29 October 1948, later known as 'Black Friday', Soviet cipher systems went 'dark'—that is, they were taken off the air. When they came back on, many had been changed to a nearly unbreakable code. Not only that, but, a few months later, the Russians changed their means of communication, from wireless communications to landlines, which were considered more secure. The NSA still calls this 'the most significant intelligence loss in U.S. history'.

For years afterwards, Americans sought a different way to divine Soviet military intentions in Berlin. Finally, around 1952, two fabled U.S. intelligence community operatives put their heads together. One was the legendary William 'Bill' Harvey, a counterintelligence expert who would eventually became CIA station chief in Berlin. The other American was the brilliant code-breaker Frank Rowlett, the man responsible for breaking the Japanese code during World War II. Together they decided that, if Harvey's CIA men could find and tap important Soviet army landlines, Rowlett's code-breakers might have a good shot at deciphering these communications. The two of them sold CIA top brass on the idea and a study was commissioned to find the location of crucial Red Army landlines; in the meantime, Rowlett moved over to the CIA, where he and Harvey shared oversight of the project.

DIGGING FOR GOLD

The CIA was not the only group interested in listening to the Soviets. The SIS wanted a piece of the action and had, in fact, already dug a successful listening tunnel—in Vienna, in 1949. Run by a brilliant head of station named Peter Lunn, this tunnel (or tunnels, for there were at least three) ran for twenty metres and tapped Soviet military phone calls successfully, until a streetcar passing overhead accidentally caused the main British listening post to collapse.

In February of 1954, the SIS and CIA came together at a meeting in London to discuss the planned Berlin tunnel. Present were Harvey, Rowlett, Lunn and a young SIS operative named George Blake, who took the minutes. It was decided that the CIA would find the site of the tunnel, dig it to a point beneath the cables and then be responsible for recording all the signals received. The British would be in charge of driving the vertical shaft up to the cable bundle and performing the all-important tapping procedure.

The CIA code-named the tunnel project (rather too openly for some tastes) Operation Gold. The British more circumspectly dubbed it Operation Stopwatch. Since Bill Harvey, by then station chief in Berlin, would be the man on the ground in charge of operations, the tunnel was more colloquially known as 'Harvey's Hole'.

The CIA study had narrowed in on an isolated part of southern Berlin known as Rudow. On the Western side it was an area of crumbling warehouses, deserted fields, a cemetery and a refugee shantytown. The frontier was marked by white posts and patrolling Eastern border guards. A few hundred metres beyond the frontier, on the Eastern side, was a highway running towards Schoenefeld Airport. Half a metre underneath this highway was a bundle of cables that the CIA had ascertained was a sort of crossroads of Russian military information, from both telegraphs and telephones. The trick was to dig a tunnel to that point, undetected, and bug these cables, right beneath the feet of the East Germans.

Even in 1954, Berlin had yet to recover from the trauma and devastation of World War II. Food and basic services remained in short supply, and tensions between the Soviet and Western occupying powers were escalating.

In order to do this, the British and Americans decided on a clever ruse. Knowing that *any* activity they engaged in on a large scale less than half a kilometre from the border would be seen as suspicious, they decided to actually do something suspicious. So they built a large warehouse in Rudow, ostentatiously put antennas on the roof, surrounded it with U.S. military personnel, and let it be leaked that they had installed a radar operation in order to keep track of the traffic at Schoenefeld Airport. In reality, that warehouse provided a great cover for the vast amounts of dirt that needed to be excavated (three thousand tonnes in all).

Beginning in September of 1954, U.S. Army engineers dug a six-metre vertical shaft beneath the floor of the warehouse. Immediately, they ran into problems: they hit an unexpected water table that did not show up on their charts. Their only option if they were to continue was to dig shallower, less than three metres below ground. This greatly increased the chances of discovery, but there was no help for it.

The digging was hard work. Sandbags lined the tunnel to deaden the noise, and portable air conditioners were brought in to keep the workers cool as well as to make sure that the cables being laid were kept dry and in good condition. As the tunnel progressed, two-metre-long circular steel sections were put in place, one after the other, forming a long, snaking sheath, stealthily heading in the direction of the Russians. Digging was dirty work, but in this regard Bill Harvey—who visited the site regularly, but only at night—turned out to be quite thoughtful. He had a washer and dryer installed to launder the workers' filthy uniforms.

AN INFORMATION BONANZA

In the spring of 1955, the half-kilometre tunnel was completed and the SIS was called in to place the tap. This was a highly delicate moment, one on which the whole operation rode. To place the tap, the British brought in a man named John Wyke, who had been their Vienna expert. The 'tap chamber', as it was called, was dug out right underneath the cable bundle. Late one night, when the chances of someone listening would be smaller, Wyke and his assistants entered the chamber and stripped the Russian cables of their covering. On 11 May, Wyke inserted a small wire in each of three cables to draw off signals. The signals were amplified and then sent through heavy cable lines to the warehouse, where they were recorded.

From that moment on, information from the Red Army began to pour in. The three cables carried 149 communication channels (28 telegraphic, 121 telephonic), which were recorded on tape recorders that eventually used 50,000 reels of tape weighing 23 tonnes. Hundreds of people in Washington and London were employed to transcribe the material. Much of it was in 'clear' or uncoded language; ciphered messages were passed on to the NSA in Washington for decoding.

Through the spy tunnel, America and Great Britain learned that the Russians were probably not going to make a surprise attack on Europe—America's nuclear deterrent was too great. They also learned that the relationship between the Russians and East Germans was fraught with mistrust on both sides. There was much else that Stopwatch/Gold brought out, including the addresses and names of important Soviet atomic scientists (immediately targeted by the CIA as possible defectors); information about flaws in Russia's new T-52 tanks; the identities of hundreds of Soviet army intelligence officers in East Germany; and

- -

DIGGING IN THEIR OWN BACK YARD

It was revealed in 2001 that the tunnel under Berlin was not the only American attempt to dig into a goldmine of Soviet information. The United States had also dug a tunnel right under the Russian embassy in Washington D.C. It was apparently built at the behest of the FBI and the NSA sometime in the 1980s, not long after the Russians were discovered tunnelling under the U.S. embassy in Moscow. Its goal was much the same as its Berlin counterpart: to tap Soviet communication lines.

As with the Berlin tunnel, the existence of the tunnel was revealed to the Russians by a defector, in this case an American FBI agent named Robert Hanssen. Government officials denied the existence of the tunnel, but there is little doubt that it was real—and filled with millions of dollars of sophisticated listening equipment.

It's heartening to know that a good tunnel really never goes out of style.

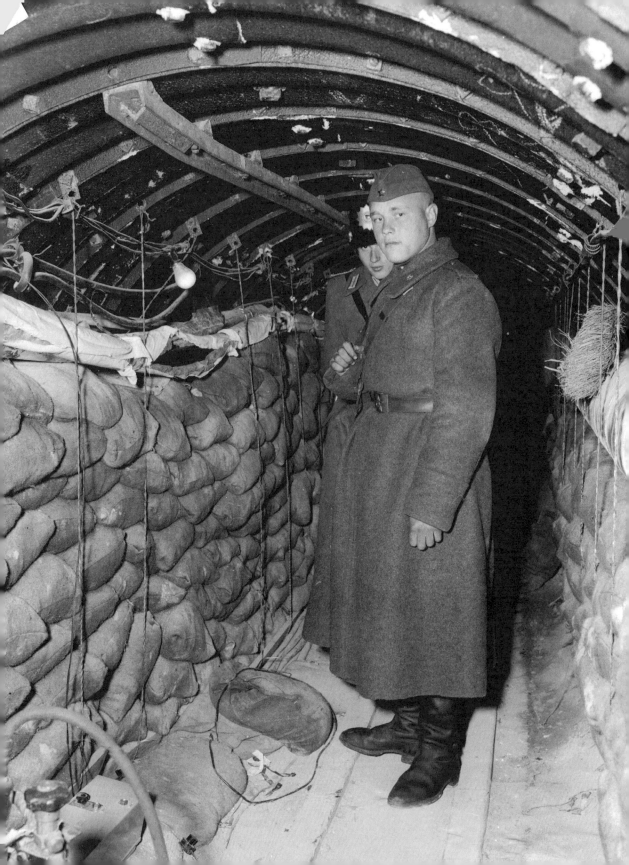

some details on the agents they were running. This information usually did not come from a single communication, but was pieced together from snippets of conversations, military orders and seemingly innocuous records such as leave dates and transfers.

A LUCKY STRIKE?

Professional intelligence operatives knew that no operation as risky as the tunnel could go on forever and, indeed, at one o'clock on the morning of Sunday 22 April 1956, CIA operatives using infrared binoculars watched from the 'radar' warehouse as forty men carrying picks and shovels gathered on the East German side of the border, right at the spot where the cable bundle was located, and began to tear up the pavement. Bill Harvey was awakened and immediately raced to the facility. He listened intently to tape recordings of the digging, hoping to hear, via casual conversations, whether the tunnel had been betrayed or randomly discovered. At last, after ten hours of digging, the Russians broke through and discovered the tap chamber. Moving further into the tunnel, they were amazed at the array of amplification equipment, the air conditioning, the state-of-the-art wiring.

In the meantime, Bill Harvey asked the American military commander in Berlin for permission to blow the explosives that lined the tunnel for just such an eventuality. But the commander refused when it was pointed out that the Russians entering the tunnel would almost certainly be killed, possibly setting off the hostilities everyone wanted to avoid. So Harvey set up an empty .50-calibre machine gun on a tripod halfway down the tunnel, on the Western side of the border, and crouched behind it. As he heard footsteps approaching him around a blind dip in the tunnel, he pointedly ratcheted back the slide of the gun. The footsteps retreated. Shortly thereafter, the Russians cut the taps from the cables and Operation Stopwatch/Gold was over, eleven months after it began.

Instead of keeping quiet about the tunnel, the Soviets attempted to use it for propaganda purposes, giving guided tours of it to the press and various Eastern bloc dignitaries, and protesting CIA perfidy. Allen Dulles, head of the CIA, refused to confirm or deny American involvement, but most in the CIA were pleasantly relieved when the American press trumpeted the tunnel as a victory for democracy.

The CIA and SIS came to the conclusion that the tunnel's discovery had been a lucky strike during routine searches for the sources of cable line cave-ins after heavy spring rains. But Bill Harvey's instincts told him that Stopwatch/Gold had been betrayed. And he was right. The

Opposite: Eighteen months after Operation Stopwatch/Gold commenced, the Soviet army found the tunnel under Berlin. It immediately brought reporters onto the scene to try to reap the propaganda benefits of the discovery.

KGB had known about the operation from the very beginning—thanks to the young man named George Blake who had taken minutes at the first operation meeting in London. For, in reality, George Blake was a Soviet mole who had gone over to the Russians while imprisoned in Korea. His betrayal was profound—as he himself said in his confession, following his eventual arrest in 1961 after a tip-off from a Russian defector, 'I must admit there is not an official document on any matter to which I had access that was not passed on to my Soviet contact'.

THE LAST LAUGH

After Blake's treachery was unmasked, almost every intelligence agent involved with Operation Stopwatch/Gold assumed that the KGB had used the tunnel to feed disinformation to the Americans. But this may not have been so. For in 1999, there was a meeting of the old enemies—an unlikely conference of ex-CIA and ex-KGB agents of the Cold War era. It took place, naturally, in Berlin. And here it was revealed that, in fact, the KGB had kept the discovery of the tunnel secret, deciding not to tell the Red Army that its communications were being tapped. The reason for this? To protect George Blake's cover. As one of

---

CON ARTISTS

George Blake a spy? Most people in SIS at the time gasped in astonishment when they heard the news. Blake was a well-liked man, a World War II hero who had conducted himself courageously as a POW in Manchuria—almost cheerfully enduring beatings from guards and doing a lot to bolster the spirits of other prisoners. He was married to the daughter of a respected British Foreign Service officer, had two children and was, as one colleague put it, 'a splendid chap'.

He was also a splendid spy and, despite being investigated after the collapse of Operation Stopwatch/Gold, not revealed as such until 1961. Soon after, he was sentenced to forty-two years in prison for treason, a crime, the judge said, that 'had rendered much of this country's efforts completely useless'. Blake's only excuse for his actions was that his experience in Korea, particularly the sight of American planes bombing civilians, had made him feel he 'was on the wrong side ... [and] that it would be better for humanity if the Communist system prevailed'.

Blake was sent to Wormwood Scrubs prison, where observers expected him to spend the rest of his life. Once again, he surprised them. In October of 1966, he escaped by kicking out a bar in a window, sliding down a roof and then climbing over a wall on a five-metre-long rope ladder. He may have been helped by Irish Republican Army agents hired by the KGB.

Evading a massive, nationwide manhunt, Blake turned up in Russia about a year later, to honours that included the Order of Lenin. He still lives there, though at the time of writing he is seriously ill.

Double-agent George Blake, as depicted in the photograph issued by Scotland Yard after his dramatic escape from Wormwood Scrubs prison in October 1966. A year later, Blake turned up in Moscow, where he has lived ever since.

the few Allied intelligence officers who knew of the operation, he would almost certainly become a focus of suspicion if the existence of the tunnel were revealed. The KGB did go so far as to warn the Red Army that, in general, they should increase the level of their communications security, but that was all. And, in fact, the tunnel *had* been uncovered accidentally. But, fortunately for the Allies, not before it provided some of the most valuable intelligence information ever received by the West during the Cold War.

BIBLIOGRAPHY

Babits, Lawrence E. *A Devil of a Whipping: The Battle of Cowpens.* Chapel Hill: The University of North Carolina Press, 1998.

Boot, Max. *War Made New: Technology, Warfare, and the Course of History, 1500 to Today.* New York: Gotham Books, 2006.

Cannan, John. *The Crater: Burnside's Assault on the Confederate Trenches.* New York: Da Capo Press, 2002.

Cantor, Norman F. *Alexander the Great: Journey to the End of the Earth.* New York: HarperCollins, 2005.

Casdorph, Paul D. *Prince John Magruder: His Life and Campaigns.* Hoboken, New Jersey: John Wiley & Sons, 1996.

Catton, Bruce. *Grant Takes Command.* Boston: Little, Brown & Co, 1968.

Chambers, James. *The Devil's Horsemen: The Mongol Invasion of Europe.* New York: Atheneum, 1979.

Contenau, Georges. *Everyday Life in Babylonia and Assyria.* London: Edward Arnold Publishers, 1954.

Daly, Gregory. *Cannae: The Experience of Battle in the Second Punic War.* London, New York: Routledge, 2002.

Dando-Collins, Steven. *Caesar's Legion: The Epic Saga of Julius Casear's Elite Tenth Legion and the Armies of Rome.* Hoboken: John Wiley & Sons Inc., 2002.

Devries, Kevin, Martin Dougherty, Ian Dickie, Phyllis G. Jestice and Christer Jorgensen. *Battles of the Medieval World, 1000–1500.* New York: Barnes & Noble, 2006.

Dunnigan, James F. and Albert A. Nofi. *Victory and Deceit: Dirty Tricks at War.* New York: William Morrow & Co., 1995.

Garfield, Brian. *The Thousand-mile War: World War II in Alaska and the Aleutians.* Fairbanks: University of Alaska Press, 1996.

Giddings, Robert. *Imperial Echoes: Eye-witness Accounts of Victoria's Little Wars.* London: Leo Cooper, 1996.

Greaves, Adrian. *Crossing the Buffalo: The Zulu War of 1879.* London: Cassell, 2006.

Green, Peter. *Alexander of Macedon, 356–323: A Historical Biography.* Berkeley: The University of California Press, 1991.

Groom, Winston. *A Storm in Flanders: The Ypres Salient, 1914–1918: Tragedy and Triumph on the Western Front.* New York: Atlantic Monthly Press, 2002.

Holland, Tom. *Persian Fire: The First World Empire and the Battle for the West.* New York: Doubleday, 2005.

Holmes, T. Rice. *Caesar's Conquest of Gaul.* London: Oxford University Press, 1931.

Keegan, John. *The First World War*. New York: Alfred A. Knopf, 1999.

———. *A History of Warfare*. New York: Alfred A. Knopf, 1994.

Kelly, John. *The Great Mortality: An Intimate History of the Black Death, the Most Devastating Plague of All Time*. New York: HarperCollins, 2005.

Lamb, Harold. *Cyrus the Great*. Garden City, New York: Doubleday & Co., 1960.

———. *Hannibal: One Man Against Rome*. Garden City, New York: Doubleday & Co., 1958.

Lyon, David. *Sea Battles in Close-up: The Age of Nelson*. Annapolis, Maryland: The Naval Institute Press, 1996.

McLynn, Frank. *1759: The Year Britain Became Master of the World*. New York: Grove Press, 2004.

Mann, Charles C. *1491: New Revelations of the Americas before Columbus*. New York: Alfred A. Knopf, 2005.

Marozzi, Justin. *Tamerlane: Sword of Islam, Conquerer of the World*. New York: Da Capo Press, 2004.

Morgan, David. *The Mongols*. Oxford, England: Basil Blackwell Ltd., 1986.

Morison, Samuel Eliot. *Samuel de Champlain: Father of New France*. Boston, New York: Atlantic Monthly Press, 1972.

Morris, Donald R. *The Washing of the Spears: The Rise and Fall of the Zulu Nation*. New York: Simon & Schuster, 1965.

Murphy, David E., George Bailey and Sergei E. Kondrashev. *Battleground Berlin: CIA vs KGB in the Cold War*. New Haven: Yale University Press, 1999.

Parkman, Francis. *Pioneers of France in the New World*. New York: The Library of America, 1983.

Perras, Galen Roger. *Stepping Stones to Nowhere: The Aleutian Islands, Alaska, and American Military Strategy, 1867–1945*. Annapolis: Navy Institute Press, 2003.

Prawdin, Michael. *The Mongol Empire: Its Rise and Legacy*. London: George Allen & Unwin Ltd., 1961.

Stafford, David. *Spies Beneath Berlin*. Woodstock and New York: The Overlook Press, 2002.

Steevens, G.W. *With Kitchener to Khartoum*. New York: Dodd, Mead & Company, 1911.

Strauss, Barry. *The Battle of Salamis: The Naval Encounter That Saved Greece—and Western Civilization*. New York: Simon & Schuster, 2004.

Thomas, Hugh. *Conquest: Montezuma, Cortez, and the Fall of Old Mexico*. New York: Simon & Schuster, 1993.

Wells, Peter S. *The Battle That Stopped Rome: Emperor Augustus, Arminius, and the Slaughter of the Legions in the Teutoburg Forest*. New York: W. W. Norton, 2003.

ACKNOWLEDGEMENTS

I'd like to thank everyone who did such good duty on this book, including Will Kiester, with whom I first brainstormed the idea; Scott Forbes, whose uncanny accuracy in editing makes all the difference; researcher Mark Cummins, who ferreted out unusual turns of military history; and the good people at Murdoch Books, especially Colette Vella and Desney Shoemark. Thanks, too, to Peter Long for his elegant design, to Ian Faulkner for his handsome maps, and to Amanda McKittrick for tracking down the images.

PICTURE CREDITS

INDEX

Midway, battle of 62–3
Mikasa (battleship) 109
Minden, battle of 88
Moghulistan 33
Mohi, battle of 28, 29
moko (tattooing) 172
von Moltke, Helmuth
(Field Marshal) 115,
116
Mommson, Theodor 204
Mongol army 20, 22, 23–5,
27, 28, 29
Mongol Empire 21, 22, 37,
163
Mongolian thumb lock 23
Montezuma II 72
Morgan, Daniel (Brigadier
General) 40, 42–8
Morris, Edmund 105
Mpande (Zulu King) 55–6
Murray, Archibald 224, 226
muskets 45, 91
de Mussis, Gabriel 163,
166, 167
muttonbirds 67

Nabonidus (King of
Babylonia) 126
Nandi (mother of Shaka)
50, 52–3
Nandi tribe 223
Napoleon 132
Napoleonic Wars 106
National Security
Administration (NSA)
240, 243
naval arsenals 91
naval engagements, of
twentieth century 104
Near East 124–5
Nebuchadnezzar II (King
of Babylonia) 126,
136
Negev Desert 226
Nelson, Lord (Admiral)
105, 106, 111
New France 80, 84, 88, 91
New Zealand 170–1
New Zealand Company
172–3
Newfoundland 81
Ngapuhi iwi 174
Nieuwport 119, 120, 121
Nimitz, Chester (Admiral)
62

Normandy 152, 154, 155,
230, 231, 236
North Carolina 41, 42
Nubian Desert 99, 100–1

Oak Swamp, battle of 218
observation balloons 216,
217, 218
Octavian *see* Augustus
Odyssey 194
Ögödei (son of Genghis
Khan) 22, 28, 29, 163
Ohaeawai Pa, battle of 170,
175, 176–9
oil, importance of 220
Old Testament 124
Olympias 132
Omdurman, battle of 96,
100, 101–3
Operation Bodyguard
231
Operation Fortitude 230,
231, 233, 235
Operation Fortitude North
232, 234, 237
Operation Fortitude South
232, 233
Operation Gold 241, 243,
245–6
Operation Mincemeat
235
Operation Overlord 231
Operation Stopwatch 241,
243, 245–6
opium 229
Oslyabya (ship) 110
Ottoman Empire 33, 221,
222
Owen, Wilfred 120

pa fortifications 170,
174–6, 179
paean 198
Pakeha 172, 173
Parkman, Francis 80
Parsuans 125
Pavia, battle of 85
Pearl Harbor 62
Pene Taka (Maori chief)
179
Pershing, John (General)
224
Persian army 127, 129–30
Persian Empire 33, 124,
134, 192, 193

Petersburg (Virginia), siege
of 181, 182, 184, 187,
189
phalangites 134
Philby, Kim 239
Philip II (King of France)
152, 154–5, 158–9, 161
Philip (King of Macedonia)
132, 134, 135
physical decoys 233
Pierce, Franklin 213
Pips, battle of the 67
Pizarro, Francisco 70–1, 73,
75–9
Plato 201
Pleasants, Henry 181–3,
186, 189
Poe, Edgar Allen 210
poison gas 225
Poland
attack by Mongol army
22, 26–7, 29
and battle of Liegnitz
20, 25, 26, 27–9
Port Arthur, Manchuria
106, 107
Port Natal 55
Porus, battle of 135
Poseidon 194
Pujol, Juan 233, 234,
237
Puketutu Pa 176
Pulleine, Henry (Lt.
Colonel) 56–7

Qosqo 73–5
'Quaker guns' 212, 214,
217
Quebec 81, 84, 88, 91
Du Quesne, Fritz Joubert
101
Quiberon Bay, battle of 88,
92–5

railway building 224
Ralph the Snubnose 154,
160, 161
recruitment campaigns 96,
97, 146
Red Army 241, 243, 246,
247
Remembrance Day 120
repeating rifles 102,
103
Resolution (ship) 94

retreat
as a tactic in War of
American Independence
44–5, 47, 48
by Mongols 23–5
use by Japanese 60,
65–7
Richard I (King of
England) 152–7
Richard the Lionheart *see*
Richard I (King of
England)
Richmond, Virginia 213
rifles 45
'Roaring Camels of Fire'
32, 37, 38
Roman army 146
Roman Empire 151, 203,
209
Romanoff dynasty 104
Roosevelt, Franklin D. 230
Rorke's Drift 59
Rosenberg, Ethel 240
Rosenberg, Julius 240
Rowlett, Frank 239, 241
Rozhestvensky, Zinovy
Petrovich (Admiral)
107, 108, 110
Russia
during Cold War
239–47
fear of Mongol attack
22
Russian Baltic Fleet 104,
107
Russian Pacific Fleet 106,
107
Russo–Japanese War 105–6
Russo–Turkish War 220

Saguenay, Kingdom of 81
St Lawrence River 81, 84
Saladin 152, 156
Salamis, battle of 192,
195–201
Salisbury, Lord 97–8, 99
Samarkand 32, 35, 37, 39
samose incendiary shells
110
Sandomierz 26
Saratoga 40, 43
Sargon II (King of Assyria)
125
sarissa (spear) 134
Sassoon, Siegfried 120

First published in 2007 by Pier 9, an imprint of Murdoch Books Pty Limited

Murdoch Books Australia
Pier 8/9
23 Hickson Road
Millers Point NSW 2000
Phone: +61 (0) 2 8220 2000
Fax: +61 (0) 2 8220 2558
www.murdochbooks.com.au

Murdoch Books UK Limited
Erico House, 6th Floor
93–99 Upper Richmond Road
Putney, London SW15 2TG
Phone: +44 (0) 20 8785 5995
Fax: +44 (0) 20 8785 5985
www.murdochbooks.co.uk

Chief Executive: Juliet Rogers
Publishing Director: Kay Scarlett

Commissioning editor: William Kiester
Concept and design: Peter Long
Project manager and editor: Scott Forbes
Production: Kita George

National Library of Australia Cataloguing-in-Publication Data

Cummins, Joseph.
Turn around and run like hell : amazing stories of
unconventional military strategies that worked.

Bibliography.
Includes index.
ISBN 9781921208645 (pbk.).

1. Strategy. 2. Tactics. 3. Ambushes and surprises. I.
Title.

355.02

A catalogue record for this book is available from the British Library.

Printed by 1010 Printing International Limited in 2007. PRINTED IN CHINA.